The Sum of Our Past

The Sum of Our Past

Revisiting Pioneer Women

BY

JUDY BUSK

Signature Books ✿ Salt Lake City ✿ 2004

Throughout this book, quotations from diaries, autobiographies, and letters have been italicized, rather than enclosed in quotation marks, to highlight the personal voices of individual writers and to distinguish them from commentaries by researchers and historians. Original spelling and punctuation have been retained.

Cover design by Ron Stucki

Cover photograph Getty Images

Frontispiece: In this typical photograph for the period, notice the four types of frontier women portrayed here: the stern, full-breasted lady in the Mother Hubbard dress, frying pan in hand; the innocent young woman in the white blouse and black skirt; the unsmiling woman in the loose-fitting jacket, seated and looking bored; and the slender, graceful woman in white, her attitude dreamy and pensive. It begs the question: How does one distinguish between pose and authenticity—between image and reality? *Photograph by C. L. Joy (kneeling front right, his wife, Nellie, behind him) in Utah's American Fork Canyon, ca. 1900; courtesy of Utah State Historical Society*

Signature Books is a registered trademark of Signature Books Publishing, LLC
www.signaturebooks.com

The Sum of Our Past: Revisiting Pioneer Women was printed on acid-free paper and was composed, printed, and bound in the United States of America
09 08 07 06 05 04   6 5 4 3 2 1

LIBRARY OF CONGRESS CATALOGING-IN-PUBLICATION DATA
Busk, Judy
   The sum of our past : revisiting pioneer women / by Judy Busk.
     p. cm.
   Includes index.
   ISBN 1-56085-184-8
    1. Women pioneers—Oregon Trail. 2. Women pioneers—Mormon Trail.
3. Oregon Trail—Description and travel. 4. Mormon Trail—Description and travel.
5. Busk, Judy, 1940—Travel—Oregon Trail. 6. Busk, Judy, 1940—Travel—Mormon
Trail. I. Title.

F597.B9725 2004
979.501—dc22

2004059126

for my mother and father,
Etheleen and Kenneth Shell,
who engendered the past,

for my husband, Neal,
who shared the journey,

and
for my daughters and sons,
Kerri, Michael, Kirsten,
Chris, Jeremy, and Noelle,
who engender the future

Contents

There is no such thing as was. To me, no man is himself, he is the sum of his past. There is no such thing really as was, because the past is. It is a part of every man, every woman, and every moment. All of his and her ancestry, background is all a part of himself and herself at any moment.

—William Faulkner

Introduction

Charting the Course

Stopping at the Des Moines River near Bonaparte in Iowa and having read Eliza R. Snow's diary entry written there, I imagined this Mormon woman—called by some *poetess, prophetess, priestess, and presidentess*—leaning over the edge of her ox cart, her cup on a string, dipping a drink from the river.[1] On the plains I remembered Edith Kohl proclaiming, "There was a pleasant flow of possession in knowing that the land beneath our feet was ours."[2] Facing a bitter wind at Devil's Gate and familiar with Patience Loader's ordeal here, I could feel her desperation in 1856 at being stranded with the Martin handcart company.[3] Standing on the edge of the Platte River, I visualized women counting the pioneer graves that lined its banks. And observing the wheel ruts in Wyoming, cut deep into the sandstone, I envisioned the wagons as they engraved their marks and the people within the wagons who longed for a new life in the West. Examining pioneer women's public personas and private lives as revealed in their diaries, letters, and reminiscences had opened my vision to a host of different types of frontier women. My research included a determination to retrace the immigrant trails; what was to be a physical trip became a metaphor for my own life journey. As I

Unidentified women, Oregon Territory, ca. 1858. As historian William Mulder has written: "In the unpretentious subliterature of ... journals, we ... find something of the daily living and dying of ... both [the] weak and valiant. Their story is not epic except as life and many days together give it sweep—it is the sweep of daily existence, the great movement that is the result of countless little movements, each life a tiny capillary, a vein, an artery contributing to the strong heartbeat of their collective existence." *Photograph courtesy of Lane County Historical Museum* traveled into the lives of pioneer women of the past, I traveled deep into my own life, my past and my present.

Willa Cather wrote, "The history of every country begins in the heart of a man or a woman."[4] Historian Wallace Stegner concurred: "A place is not a place until people have been born in it, have grown up in it, lived in it, known it, died in it—have both experienced and shaped it as individuals, families, ... communities, ... until things that have happened in it are remembered in history, ballads, yarns, legends, or monuments."[5] For me, the West became more real as I assimilated the experiences of those who had gone before, lending to my consciousness a more powerful sense of place.

A major discovery for me was the importance that women placed on their relationships to each other. As the need arose, they helped each other with childbirth. They talked as they walked beside the wagons. How much that must have shortened the long days! They shared recipes and cures. By spreading wide their full skirts to shield other women, they provided privacy for toileting on the empty prairies. In addition, I learned the power of women to keep family together and to preserve tradition. Many had the strength to do men's work, yet mothers worried that their daughters would lose their femininity, sacrificed

in the demanding physical world they inhabited.

I unexpectedly developed an appreciation for the rugged beauty of the West, which I had often taken for granted. During a simulated pioneer trip to the Tetons with my teenage daughter, she traveled by horseback and I rode a sure-footed mule along the cliff edges, through streams, and across meadows. I watched from a covered wagon as horses reared and raced downhill, finally stopping when one horse fell. I camped in a snowstorm. Through all of this, I absorbed the beauty: horses of all colors—ebony, roan, gray—and the clink of hobbles echoing in the clear mountain air; the calls of birds answering from the trees; mist circling through the tall grasses. Along with the beauty, I felt the grime of the trail and wondered what it would have been like to trudge through such dust week after week.

My book is framed on another trip, one my husband and I took in September 1993 along the Mormon and Oregon Trails. Neal was my driver, place-finder, and sounding board (or *sounding bored*, as the case would have it), as well as a foil for my attempts at humor. The material I had read about the trail, commentaries by historians, diaries of pioneers, and actual things seen on the trip, provided impetus for questions about the meaning of the pioneer experience and events in my life which have made me feel close to the trail blazers. Much of the content of this book is serious, but some is humorous. Laughter is sometimes an appropriate response to ironic situations, or even to tragic turns of event, and a response that was shared by pioneer women who sometimes found it to be the best way to cope with defeating circumstances. In addition to writing about the pioneer trails and my observations of them, I contemplate some aspects of my own personal journey from childhood to adulthood from the 1940s to the present. This journey of change is important to the book because my developing perspectives color how I view pioneer women's lives, as well as how I continue to view my own life.

Structuring the book as a combination of historical research and personal memoir was natural for me because I have always responded to other people's experiences by comparison to my own. I feel a kinship with women and, in writing this book, wished to solidify that bond by exploring common experiences. I hope that the reception will be one of appreciation and of mutual respect; I am nonetheless aware of the diversity that exists within the range of female experience, historically and contemporaneously. In fact, I have also felt that if modern women knew about the

broad spectrum of role models from the historical past, they could rid themselves of many of the unnecessarily narrow choices they feel are available to them for their own futures. In this regard, the ability to put oneself into the place of another person is of necessity a part of building a community. The separation of public image from private attitudes has been problematic for women who view the outside appearance of public figures and compare these images to their own inner attitudes, frequently finding themselves wanting.

In order to make sense of our lives, we have to connect in various ways to the lives of other people; otherwise, we would live in isolation and in confusion about what constitutes normal. In Mormon society, we have idealized pioneer women and can drown in guilt when we feel we don't measure up. With truer pictures of past women's experiences, as well as of contemporary women's struggles and triumphs, we can compare ourselves more realistically and with more gentleness.

I draw a considerable amount of strength from the various roles I have filled throughout my life as the daughter of a traditional mother and blue-collar father, wife of a businessman and community figure, mother of six children, a social worker in Los Angeles for a time, a teacher here and abroad, a local journalist, and as a "mature" graduate student. The variety of profiles one assumes in a lifetime allows connection with a wider range of women despite differing ages, nationalities, faiths, social and ethnic groups, life styles, and family backgrounds. I find a strong thread of commonality in women's experiences despite the diversity in heritage and lifestyle.

For instance, I have included in this book some material about my husband's colorful grandmother, Dorothy Delilah Hickman Pectol. She represents the pioneer woman in an isolated locale, in this case in Caineville, Utah, one who felt especially vulnerable when her husband was away from 1907 to 1909 in New Zealand. Her story is an often untold part of Western history: the woman left behind in otherwise stirring tales of Mormon missionary adventures. Exploring "Dot" Pectol's dependence and independence is a way of exploring my own dependence/independence, which frankly has been the source of some misunderstanding and tension in my marriage and family.

One important reason for writing this book was to convey my thoughts to my daughters. Certainly, over the years, I have shared similar thoughts with them and listened to their ideas, but I wanted something permanent for them to read when I am no longer

here. I want them to value their heritage and see their personal expressions of individuality, so different from one another, as a positive force in broadening how the world defines women. I also want them to know the feelings that pioneer women had in embracing—at times confronting—life as a woman so that their own encounters with society will be more contextualized and less threatening. In writing for my daughters, I discovered that I was also writing for my sons, who might better understand the women in their lives through this. In addition, I am writing for my husband so that he can better understand me. I hope this will be equally helpful to other women and the men in their lives.

Of course, my husband and children know me well beyond what I write and will see me differently than those who encounter me only through this narrative. As I have tried to write an honest confessional—connecting what I find in the writings of real pioneer women, separate from their more staid public images—there may be some surprises in store for my family. But I have not attempted to pen a personal, family history—only in the sense of "cannibalizing [my] life for [its useful] parts,"[6] as Annie Dillard has described the process of writing a meaningful memoir.

One realization along the way was the discovery

that there are many women whose experiences are so much like my own, we could be sisters. I was an only child, and I can't say that I missed having sisters; but I think I miss them now. I have enjoyed the sister-like feelings that come through associations with like-minded people including classmates, professors, and mentors, whose interests and experiences are so similar to mine, and the connection I have come to feel with pioneer women themselves.

Other major revelations resulted from the intellectual stimulation of going back to school after having spent a life as a teacher. It was delightful to be on the other side of the desk for a change. In a creative writing class, I learned to be more honest in my writing, to avoid the image-building clichés that come far too easily and conceal what one really feels. A frequent comment in the margins of my papers was "Who is your audience?" Initially I assumed an audience of middle-aged women, feeling that I could speak to those who had been where I had been. Over time, I dropped this mental image and decided that I could also address younger people who would be going where I had been and could benefit from my experience. I began to see men as part of the audience as well. Being questioned repeatedly by readers, "What exactly do you mean?" taught me to refine my ideas.

In trying to better communicate, I had to probe deeper inside and then search outside myself for other words and methods to communicate ideas I hoped would be evocative to others.

Women in the past fifty years have experienced alterations in their role definitions. For many women, this has produced a "future shock" as the world they anticipated gave way to an uncharted path and unpredictable future. Exploring changes in women's lives through history and literature, and considering the personal impact of former encounters with modernity, helped me see where women are now and where they may be headed. It helped me understand, as I compared my perceptions with those of other women, that differences of age, ethnicity, religion, socio-economic level, educational background, and marital status must not be barriers to understanding.

Recent historical research has focused attention on a broader body of women's literature including private writings which were once considered of little literary merit. The recovery of these narratives has become a way of validating female experiences and telling "the other half of the story," while also individualizing women and helping them emerge from the oblivion of stereotype.

In the seventeenth century, Margaret Cavendish,

Duchess of Newcastle, appended her autobiography to her husband's longer one. In justification for this, she posed a rhetorical question: "Why hath this lady writ her own life?" She answered, "Lest after-ages should mistake in not knowing I was the daughter to one Master Lucas of St. Johns, near Colchester, in Essex, second wife to the Lord Marquis of Newcastle; for my Lord having had two wives, I might easily have been mistaken, especially if I should die and my Lord marry again."[7]

Historian Maureen Beecher thinks that "Margaret was right. Historically she had no identity separate from that of her father and her husband; the existence of other daughters and other wives might obliterate from memory her very existence. 'Ultimately,' writes critic Sidonie Smith, 'the issue is one of identity versus anonymity. Cavendish is writing for her very life.'"[8]

Preserving diaries and personal writings has saved thousands of women from oblivion, no less the women of Utah, many of whom would have disappeared altogether. Looking at the broader field of pioneer women in general, I might be still wandering the musty archives of various libraries and trying to detect meaning from yellowed scraps of pioneer memoirs without the published works of such scholars as

Glenda Riley, Elizabeth Hampsten, Joanna L. Stratton, and Lillian Schlissel, to name a few.

In a sense, I have written for the "very life" of the women I discuss and my own "very life"—defining, assessing, shaping, sharing, and knowingly living it. To borrow Beecher's metaphor, I have been piecing together scraps from my life and the lives of others to present a collective work—a quilt, so to speak—depicting a unity of shared experiences. This process both creates and preserves identity.

Psychologist Bradley L. Edgington has found in south central Utah, where I live, a persistent identity crisis that fosters discontent: women who marry in their teens or early twenties just wanting "to be loved and cared for by their husbands," only to express profound dissatisfaction with the limitations of this "loving and caring" five, ten, or twenty years later. This change of heart is frustrating to their bewildered spouses, who cannot understand why their wives would suddenly want lives of their own.[9] In an interview, Dr. Edgington observed that although he repeatedly sees this problem elsewhere, he encounters it more frequently in small communities. Perhaps it is necessary to first define one's own life before sharing it with someone else as a wife or mother. My book explores such issues.

Much of the problem in female identity has to do with the undervaluation of the domestic sphere, which is so central to women's lives. Laurel Thatcher Ulrich's meticulous analysis in her book, *A Midwife's Tale,* was the catalyst for broader discussion of the importance of women's influence through their home life. As a woman, Ulrich was able to enter Martha Ballard's "woman's world" and, in a sense, live her subject's life—one that male scholars had previously found domestic and trivial.[10] I found Ulrich's approach an excellent model for understanding pioneer women. I had to step into their lives before I could understand them as people, just as other women scholars had entered the lives of their prominent and not-so prominent female subjects.

I think it is legitimate to lend a sympathetic but subjective ear to historical voices, knowing that it may not always be possible to know what a diarist or other writer meant. I have tried to listen more closely, not only to what is written, but to what remains unsaid between the lines, as Professor Beecher has noted: "Silences, the unwritten spaces of women's life writings, are as significant as the written lines themselves."[11] The voices and silences of historical women are like the threads flung out by Walt Whitman's noiseless patient spider, "Surrounded, detached in mea-sureless oceans of space / Ceaselessly musing, venturing, throwing ..." Retrieving fragile threads of meaning in order to see an entire web of experience takes patience as well.

One thread of meaning I detected was the connection of women to their mothers. Sections of my book discuss my relationship with my own mother and the comfort she has always been to me. In childhood, I remember her holding me close in the middle of a room while a wild electrical storm raged outside. Reading between the lines and finding the "silences" Maureen Beecher suggests, I realize now that when I married, I wanted a husband to take my mother's place, someone who would calm my adult fears rather than allow me to face them alone or expect me to calm his fears. A source of some tension between my husband and me has been the attention I give instinctually to my children, yet assume my husband can fend for himself in an emotional sense. In other words, we have difficulty defining the kinds of support we are willing to give each other.

I write about my mother ironing my cotton dresses and making sure that every ruffle stood out, starched and creaseless, also applying this same care to my father's heavy work clothes. What I don't say is that the reason this seems so remarkable to me is because

I hate ironing. I resented the imposition of my children's choice of cotton clothes after I was liberated by polyester. I made them iron their own clothes. I ironed my clothes or my husband's as little as possible because of the resentment that welled up in me when I became hot and bored and angry at wrinkles that wouldn't come out, as I longed for polyester. For years I felt guilty because my mother ironed so well and willingly. To be a good woman, I should do the same, I thought. After much effort, I finally voiced my frustration about what I thought to be a senseless, time-wasting activity; in finding a sympathetic ear in my husband, I freed my self-image from the ironing board. Now my husband, although somewhat less than graciously, refuses to let me iron his clothes.

I write about my mother turning the jump rope for my friends and me as if nothing else in the world were more important to her. Between the lines is a hidden message about my mother finding nothing more important than supporting me. In fact, I was her only child. She chose not to pursue a college education or career. In a sense, I was her education and career. She turned the jump rope for one period in her lifetime, while I did it again and again as I reared one child after another. I spent years pushing children on swings, reading stories to them, and turning jump ropes, mostly in joy but sometimes in boredom. For me, there were other alternatives. I wanted a teaching certificate, to be an educator, to write a newspaper column, to do oral history projects, to get my master's degree, and I had to fight the guilt that in doing so, I was spending less time with my children. Now at age eighty-seven, my mother openly wonders if she should have pursued other options in her life. Was it enough for her to be the supportive audience to the "others" in the family? I am just beginning to read between the lines of my mother's life in conversation with her, seeking to hear some whispers of aspirations and, by contrast, of things she found satisfying and would have done exactly the same if she had it to do again.

In doing the research for this book, I have read the words and read the silences of women of many different voices. I am now ready to send both my own words and my own silences out to other women (and men), who may find some comfort in my candid perspective and will hopefully find at least, within this book, grist for further conversations.

Judy Shell Busk
Richfield, Utah
September 2003

1.

Eastward Ho!

*I*n September 1993 my husband and I loaded our Ford van with books on pioneer women, copies of diaries, journals, letters, and photographs. Leaving our home in Richfield, Utah, we were ready to retrace the Mormon and Oregon Trails as a part of my study of pioneer women. Our suitcases and ice chest were safely stowed beneath the makeshift bed we had constructed in the back of the van. Our mattress consisted of two futons, placed side by side, certainly more comfortable than the straw ticks my pioneer ancestors slept on. As I covered the futons with sheets and placed a comforter on top, something seemed wrong. I ran into the house, climbed the stairs to the attic, and opened an old storage trunk, pulling out a wedding gift quilt I had suddenly recalled. The top was pieced together by Granny Pectol, my husband's grandmother, and the quilting was done by his mother,

Golda. As I replaced the comforter, smoothing the quilt over the sheets, the pieces of fabric in their multi-colored patterns reflected what I thought might have been a similar brightness in a pioneer wagon.

My husband, Neal, laughed when I called our van "our covered wagon." Having read numerous pioneer women's diaries, I supported my choice of metaphor. "The van is about the same length and a foot wider than a covered wagon." Despite the similarity in size, what a difference our van was in comfort and convenience. Still, the desire for privacy existed for us as well as for pioneers. We attached makeshift cotton curtains to Velcro bits above our windows so we could change clothes or sleep. Pioneers hung blankets over their wagon openings and concealed themselves in the relative privacy of tents. For bathroom needs, we would have the convenience of enclosed stalls in pub-

THE SATURDAY EVENING POST

Vol. 194, No. 40. Published Weekly at
Philadelphia. Entered as Second-
Class Matter, November 19, 1879, at
the Post Office at Philadelphia. Under
the Act of March 3, 1879.

APRIL 1, '22

5c. THE COPY
10c IN CANADA

Beginning **THE COVERED WAGON**—By Emerson Hough

lic restrooms. Women on pioneer treks, if fortunate, had brush or trees. Otherwise, the wide-spread skirts of companions veiled them, which was one good reason to cultivate female companionship along the trek.

Each night, Neal and I would be able to sleep comfortably in our "bed" in the back of the van. The pioneers had simple straw or feather ticks. How much more comfortably they would have slept if they could have substituted mattress for tick. The ticks were often placed on top of supplies, which usually more than filled the wagon beds: 1,000 pounds of flour, 100 pounds of sugar, 10 pounds of rice, 10 pounds of dried apples, 1 bushel of beans, 5 pounds of dried peaches, 20 pounds dried pumpkin, 1 pound tea, 5 pounds coffee, and a few pounds of dried beef or bacon. This is a partial list of the items suggested for a typical Mormon family of five "leaving this government next spring," as reported in the October 29, 1845, edition of the *Nauvoo Neighbor* under the heading "Bill of Particulars."[12] Modern-day Mormons who are familiar with the Word of Wisdom's prohibition against use of tea

---

W. H. D. Koerner's *Madonna of the Prairie* on the cover of *The Saturday Evening Post*, April 1, 1922. The painting portrays an idealized frontier woman. *Courtesy of Buffalo Bill Historical Center located in Cody, Wyoming; gift of the artist's heirs, W. H. D. Koerner III and Ruth Koerner Oliver; SEP.V194.90.1922.*

and coffee might be surprised that they were included in this list, but Mormons of that day were not as strictly compliant as they are today. Pioneer diaries often mention the enjoyment of tea and coffee.

In contrast to gathering extensive supplies like those packed by pioneers, how much easier it was for us to fill one storage box and an ice chest which could easily be refilled every few days. For lunch, I had planned bread with homemade raspberry jam. Pioneer women had homemade jam, but theirs was prepared on wood-burning stoves, bottled in the humid Midwest heat of late summer, rather than in an air-conditioned house as my jam had been. My bread would be picked up at convenience stores along the way. Pioneer women would have kneaded their bread while traveling, setting it to rise and ready to be baked during an evening stop. The mid-day stop, called *noonin'* in the diaries, was too short for baking. Cold food was the order there.

I wondered if women sometimes read books during these stops or even tried to read as the wagons bumped along, the letters jumping about on the pages. I had my store of books and typescripts on pioneer life packed between the front seats of our van for easy access. It was my "library," as Neal called it.

As we pulled out of our familiar driveway and waved

good-bye to the children, old enough to care for themselves for two weeks, I wondered what similarities and what differences I would discover as I tried to follow in the steps of pioneer women. I also wondered about what problems we might encounter. The answer was not long in coming. The first morning after spending the night in Lyman, Colorado, we awoke to find our car battery dead. A crisis, although a minor one. We had battery cables, and a neighboring camper was willing to help jump-start the car. I told my husband, "It's better than the oxen dying." He grinned weakly.

Being steeped in tales of pioneer miracles, I suggested my husband lay hands on the battery and give it a blessing to start. "I'll lay hands on the battery, all right!" he mumbled.

Fortunately, a few blocks away, we found George's Repair Shop and an auto parts store. We stopped to get an expert diagnosis, resulting in a new battery being installed while my husband and I stopped at a local café and ordered a breakfast of ham and eggs.

As we waited for our food, I said, "You know, I would be completely panicked if you weren't here. I'd be worried that a repairman would tell me I needed a whole new engine. How did the pioneers find skilled people, ones they could trust? I wonder how they felt when they had problems and needed help."

"Probably a lot more worried than us," Neal said as the waitress placed our plates on the table. "If a family were in desperate need, I wonder how many people would take advantage of them?"

"I sometimes think about what happened when someone else's oxen died. What if you were obligated to squeeze another family into your wagon? Would you resent it? Would you expect compensation of some kind? What if they couldn't contribute to the cost of supplies? Would you refuse to help them?"

The shrug of my husband's shoulders told me that these were questions he was glad he did not have to consider. Not being pioneers, we had credit cards. We could help others at minimal threat to our own survival.

We finished our meal and paid for the repairs at George's garage. Secure with a new battery, we got in the van and headed eastward toward Nauvoo, Illinois, where our westward trek would commence, as it had for many of our ancestors. I wondered what new definitions of womanhood I would discover on this journey. Would it metaphorically become my path of connection to pioneer women, to origins, to self-definition, and maybe even to future possibilities?

As we drove, I thought about the nature of faith in the 1800s on the prairies and plains. This was not a

Sunday school faith expressed theoretically in classes once a week, but a faith tested and tried in the mundane *ifs* of each day—finding enough buffalo chips to build a fire, being able to cure illness far from a doctor's help, putting one foot in front of another despite the force of winds, the scorch of sun, or the pelt of rain, and starting a journey when a child would be born on the trail. Having borne six children myself, I identified with the women who underwent pregnancy and childbirth on the westward trek like those historian Lillian Schlissel describes:

> Such women would have a need to believe in God. Each release from death was a miraculous chance to seize another year in which to encircle oneself again with the comforting rituals of daily routine. Perhaps the detailed pattern-making, the recounting of trivial daily tasks that one finds in the women's diaries was the necessary counterbalance in a life pitted against catastrophe.[13]

One of the books that expanded my vision of pioneer women was *Women's Diaries of the Westward Journey.* Reared on Mormon folktales of determined, sunbonneted women, I saw the westering woman as an ideal rather than a reality. This view is summed up nicely in this exaggerated description of the folklore that surrounds the pioneer woman:

She trod westward with grimfaced determination, clad in gingham or linsey-woolsey, her face wreathed in a sunbonnet, baby at breast, rifle at the ready, bravely awaited unknown dangers, and dedicated herself to removing wilderness from both man and land and restoring civilization as rapidly as possible. ... She was a woman of some culture and refinement, "domestic, submissive but sturdy, moral," the guardian of all that was fine and decent. ... The sturdy helpmate could fight Indians, kill the bear in the barn, make two pots of lye soap, and do a week's wash before dinnertime and still have the cabin neat, the children clean, and a good meal on the table when her husband came in from the fields—all without a word of complaint or even a hint of an ache or a pain. She was the Madonna of the Prairies, the Brave Pioneer Mother, the Gentle Tamer so familiar in western literature.[14]

A friend, reading this description, suggested that the woman's name must have been Paula Bunyan. I responded that I could more easily laugh at exaggerated descriptions of pioneer women if so many of them weren't believed, with modern women feeling inadequate by comparison.

Wanting to understand the roles and character of real female pioneers, I had read historians' descriptions of women in the context of the Western saga and had been long perplexed by the contradictions. Some historians feel that women had a limited place and interpret the westering movement in masculine terms because, after all, women "did not lead expeditions, command troops, build railroads, drive cattle, ride Pony Express, find gold, amass great wealth, get elected to high public office, rob stages, or lead lynch mobs."[15]

Other historians, unhappy with this male-oriented vision, point out that "women were generally reluctant to go West ... [and] their life there, whether on an isolated farm or in a frontier community, was one of unending toil and unnatural labor ... Suicides and insanity were common, ... their trail journals with their relentless record-keeping of the graves passed were ultimately indictments of men."[16] A common assessment in nineteenth-century accounts by both men and women was that "Western women were ... coarse, crude, unlettered drudges who were both slovenly and unfeminine."[17] Some writers exploited the soiled dove image of women like Belle Starr or the Calamity Jane who "drank, smoked, and cursed and was handy with a poker deck, a six-gun, and a horse."[18]

John Faragher concluded that the western experience did not provide women freedom, new opportunities, or more equal status but left them "confined to the domestic space, left without social power, ... dependent for status upon their relationship with their husbands."[19] In contrast, Julie Roy Jeffrey characterized pioneer women as courageous and successful in meeting the challenges of frontier life, "not weak but strong; ... not passive but active. They ... triumphed over frontier conditions heroically."[20]

When I initially confronted these varying historical views, I was bothered by the contrasts. However, in the process of studying diaries and memoirs, I realized that in reality, many types of pioneer women existed. I discovered that the women were from a wide range of social classes, had different educational backgrounds, and represented dissimilar racial and ethnic origins; their marital status and religious backgrounds were varied as well. Within each broad group, women were individuals who reacted differently to similar environments and challenges. Each woman's perception of the West was shaped by complex factors that colored her responses. I thought of the difficulty in defining modern American women or modern Mormon women—any individual woman within any group, for that matter. I was intrigued by the difficulty. Free of constricting definitions, would modern women feel better able to make choices based on what they perceived to be authentic in themselves and based less on unrealistic models? Could my lifelong struggle to define myself be considered a strength rather than a weakness? Could similar struggles strengthen other women?

2.

Across the Wide Missouri

We drove long hours, hurrying to cross the flat terrain of Kansas, then across the James Street Bridge into Kansas City, Missouri. We were only a half day from our planned destination in Nauvoo, so we decided to take a short detour and stop at Adam-ondi-Ahman before continuing on farther east.

Adam-ondi-Ahman is a lush valley that gained significance for early Mormons when they were told by their prophet Joseph Smith that it was "the place where Adam shall come to visit his people, or the Ancient of Days shall sit, as spoken of by Daniel the prophet."[21] This place was immortalized in song by Mormon writer and editor William W. Phelps and was included in the first LDS hymn book, compiled in 1835 by Joseph Smith's wife Emma:

> *This earth was once a garden place,*
> *With all her glories common,*
> *And men did live a holy race,*
> *And worship Jesus face to face,*
> *In Adam-ondi-Ahman.*
>
> *We read that Enoch walked with God,*
> *Above the pow'r of mammon,*
> *While Zion spread herself abroad,*
> *And Saints and angels sang aloud,*
> *In Adam-ondi-Ahman.*

> *Her land was good and greatly blest,*
> *Beyond all Israel's Canaan;*
> *Her fame was known from east to west,*
> *Her peace was great, and pure the rest*
> *Of Adam-ondi-Ahman.*
>
> *Hosanna to such days to come,*
> *The Savior's second coming,*
> *When all the earth in glorious bloom*
> *Affords the Saints a holy home,*
> *Like Adam-ondi-Ahman.*

When my husband and I visited Adam-ondi-Ahman in September, crickets swarmed around us, chirping a steady hum. Walking the path to the valley lookout point, we brushed the crickets off our clothing and risked crushing them under our feet. I wondered if they had been here in equal abundance in pioneer times, a menace to crops, or just an irritation to fastidious housewives.

We surveyed the wide valley, reconstructing the location of various buildings with help from our guidebook. My husband said, "How would it be to have such a vision, one that could make you so devoted?" I thought of the faith of early converts; the Mormon church was organized in 1830 with just six members, but by 1840 they numbered 30,000.[22] The missionary zeal caused people to share their faith with others, often at great personal sacrifice. Their dedication was fueled by a strong belief that together they would create a new Zion which, as the song says, would be "a holy home" where men would "live a holy race."

After crossing a bridge at Keokuk, Iowa, and winding along the Mississippi, we stopped near Nauvoo just as the sky was turning crimson. I thought about Mormon pioneer women and found myself both admiring and wondering at the nature of their devotion. They, like me, must have watched such sunsets, perhaps satisfied to add another day of building Zion or sometimes relieved to end another day of drudgery. Some of them must have welcomed the cool and restful night ahead. Some must have dreaded a fretful night of weighing conscience, evaluating self against strict gospel principles. For many women, nights demanded the tending of malarial children, husbands, and neighbors. For others, nights meant nursing babies.

In winter, women looking out across the Mississippi must have remembered the Missouri exodus of 1838-39, prompted by persecution and conflict that included the infamous order of Governor Boggs: "The Mormons must be treated as enemies, and must be exterminated or driven from the state if necessary."[23] Conditions existing at the time are best described by someone who lived the events—Elizabeth Haven Barlow. She wrote to her cousin, Elizabeth Howe

Louisa Barnes Pratt spoke of a blessing from Brigham Young given May 1850: "He said I was called, set apart and ordained to go to the Islands of the sea to aid my husband in teaching the people. That I should be honored by those with whom I traveled, that all my wants should be supplied, that ... I should have power to rebuke the destroyer from my house, that he should not have power to remove any of my family, that I should do a good work and return in peace." *Photo courtesy of LDS Archives*

Bullard, living in Holliston, Massachusetts, the place of Elizabeth's conversion to Mormonism and baptism a year and a half previous.

Quincy Feb. 24th, 1839

Dear Elizabeth

   ... O! how Zion mourns, her sons have fallen in the streets by the cruel hand of the enemy, and her daughters weep in silence. It is impossible for my pen to tell you of our situation, only those who feel it, know. Between five and seven thousand men, women, and children [have been] driven from the places of gathering out of the state from houses and lands, in poverty, to seek for habitations where they can find them. The Saints are coming as fast as possible; they have only to the 8th of March to leave the state. The Prophet has sent word to have them make speed, haste out of the state. About twelve families cross the river into Quincy [Illinois] every day, and about thirty are constantly on the other side waiting to cross. It is slow and grimy; there is only one ferry boat to cross in. ...The Stakes of Zion will soon be bereft of all her children. By the river of Babylon we can sit down, yes, dear E, we weep when we remember Zion.[24]

Forced from their homes in Far West, Missouri, their possessions robbed, their leaders arrested, how could they continue to trust in a new Zion? How could they renew faith in God's love for them? Perhaps their ability to praise God in their success and to believe he

was chastening and refining them in their failures sustained belief.

The town of Commerce, Illinois, was the site chosen for the next gathering place where church leaders began purchasing thousands of acres of land. In the summer of 1839, the town was renamed Nauvoo, with Joseph Smith's explanation that this Hebraic name signified a beautiful resting place.[25] In the beginning, Nauvoo was not a restful place; it was a swampy lowland near the Mississippi River and plagued by outbreaks of malaria every August and September. In these early days of clearing land and living in wagons and tents until cabins could be built, women, watching the river's smooth flow, must have wished for that same tranquility in their lives, wanting sickness, persecution, and poverty to fade away like the ripples on the river. Some must have longed to board a steamer, to see Nauvoo disappear in the boat's wake, to regain the security of prosperous farms and respected town life left behind when they converted and heeded the call to gather.

Others must have seen the river's power and pulled it to themselves, a channel to direct their faith. Husbands, brothers, and sons leaving on riverboats for church missions were common occurrences, and parting was painful. Bathsheba Smith wrote to her missionary husband, George A. Smith, on July 16, 1843, telling her feelings at his departure:

> *O my Dear it is nothing to cry when one feeles as I did when I saw the boat going down. I was pleased to think you would not have to wait any longer, but then how could I bare to have it carry you off so rapidly from me. I watched it until I could not see it any longer then I held my head for it aked [ached].*[26]

This trip was her husband's fifth departure in a series of missions.

Dedication to missionary work became a casting of bread on water, resulting in thousands of converts. Between 1837 and 1846, Mormon missionaries in England baptized almost 28,000 English citizens. Of these converts, nearly 5,000 immigrated to Nauvoo and its environs in the early 1840s.[27] Settling on the banks of the Mississippi, these immigrants who called each other "brother" and "sister" and "the Saints" built a city that justifiably could be called "Nauvoo the Beautiful," a city of about ten thousand—the largest in Illinois at that time next to Chicago.[28]

Early on, church leaders envisioned sending missionaries to the entire world, not only to Great Britain and Europe, but even to the Pacific islands. In 1843, Addison Pratt was sent from Nauvoo to Tahiti, known at the time as the Society Islands. He left his wife Louisa and four children behind to basically fend for themselves. Louisa records that:

> *The parting scene came. The two eldest daughters wept very sorely. We walked with [their father] to the steamboat landing: he carried the youngest child in his arms. ... He would be absent three years. ... It was unfortunate at the last[,] as he stept on to the steamboat[, that] the children saw him take his handkerchief from his eyes[;] they knew he was wiping away his tears [and] it was too much for them. They commenced weeping; the second daughter was inconsolable, the more we tried to sooth[e] her, the more piteous were her complaints; she was sure her father would never return.*[29]

When the settlers abandoned Nauvoo in 1845, Louisa Pratt took her children to Winter Quarters, Nebraska, more-or-less as a single parent. She continued on to Great Salt Lake City in 1848, where she was finally reunited with her husband who had returned from the Society Islands. Shortly thereafter, Addison was recalled to the mission. This time Louisa decided she would not be content to stay behind and insisted on following her husband, accompanied by their four daughters and Louisa's sister and brother-in-law. Louisa received the personal blessing of Brigham Young, and they left Salt Lake on May 7, 1850. As Louisa recorded in her diary that day:

He [Brigham Young] said I was called, set apart and ordained to go to the Islands of the sea to aid my husband in teaching the people. That I should be honored by those with whom I traveled, that all my wants should be supplied, that no evil should befall me on the journey, that I should lack nothing, I should have power to rebuke the destroyer from my house, that he should not have power to remove any of my family, that I should do a good work and return in peace; many things all of which he sealed upon my head in the name of the Lord.[30]

Louisa traveled to Sacramento and on to San Francisco by wagon, from there traveling by ship to the South Seas. For two years, she taught school to island children.

I am personally amazed at the faith of these early missionaries—people such as Addison and Louisa Pratt. I was born in America because missionaries came to Denmark in the 1850s. My great-great-grand-father, Niels Peter Domgaard, and wife, Else Kirstine Nielsen, were part of the harvest of conversion the missionaries experienced on Jutland peninsula. Niels Peter explained his religious seeking in a brief autobiography dictated in Danish and translated into English by one of his acquaintances:[31]

At the age of twenty I was sent to learn the blacksmith trade. I was apprenticed three years, after which I traveled about seeking work. As I suffered much through fatigue and became tired of my situation, I began to think of the Lord God and to call on him in prayer, reading good books and seeking to be led by him. After a space of two years, I became acquainted with some called Baptists, which was newly begun in Denmark; and I joined the society.

At the age of thirty-two, I got married to Else Kirstine Nielsen on the 12th of October, 1845. I lived in the town of Hals and was happy and doing well. In the year 1850, I heard of Mormonism having come to Denmark. I read a pamphlet treating on revelation being given to Joseph Smith on the restoration of the church of God in the last days which rejoiced my soul, and I went about twenty miles to Aalborg to have an interview with G. P. Dykes, who had been sent there to proclaim the Gospel. He taught me the first principles of Mormonism and I invited him to pay me a visit at my home. He accordingly did so and conversed with a great many. I believed the Gospel and was baptized on January 1, 1851, in Aalborg and was confirmed the same evening. My mother and my brother also were baptized at the same time.

He goes on to tell of being ordained to preside over a congregation of fifteen members and the hostility of his neighbors:

... persecution then began to rage against us and [some] threatened to kill Brother Dykes who had meetings at my home. A mob gathered around; but as they could not find him, they pelted the house and broke the windows and lamps to pieces. This was in January, and in the fall following I sold my house and moved to Noree Sunby, where

I took charge of an iron foundry. Then I was called to preside over the Aalborg Branch which was just across the firth.

In the fall, Niels Peter was counseled to gather to Zion, and he and his family became part of the first major Danish immigration to Utah, leaving Denmark in 1852 under the direction of John Forsgren:

> *I then prepared myself in temporal things and visited my relations and friends, testified unto them the restoration of the Gospel and the dispensation of gathering for the children of God in the last days. I then took my departure with my wife and family, my wife having borne me two children, viz, Caroline, born August 29, 1846, and Laurice Elias, born July 4, 1851.*
>
> *We started from Copenhagen on the 2nd of December, 1852, on the steamship called Ocobrit [Obotrit] which carried us to Kiel [Germany] and from there proceeded on our journey to Zion.*

The phrase that Niels Peter utilizes here, "proceeded on our journey to Zion," is too brief to describe the months of travel and effort expended before the Domgaards finally arrived in Utah Territory. Since they did not keep journals, I have looked for further details of their trip in the writings of the other emigrants and of later historians of the period.

The Danish converts of the Forsgren company consisted of 195 adults and 95 children under twelve years of age. They embarked from Copenhagen, disembarked from the *Obotrit* at Kiel on December 22, took a train to the North Sea port of Hamburg, and on December 24 boarded the English ship *Lion*. They celebrated Christmas Eve on board, although the ship did not weigh anchor until the next day. Even then, strong headwinds kept them from reaching the open sea until midnight. On the next day:

> a heavy gale blew up from the south-west which increased in violence until the next day when it assumed the character of a regular hurricane, the like of which old sailors declared they had never before experienced on the North Sea. The ship's bridge and part of the gunwale was destroyed and some goods standing on the deck were broken to pieces and washed overboard; otherwise neither the ship nor the emigrants were injured.[32]

The passengers felt grateful to arrive safely at Hull on the east coast of England on December 28, especially since 150 ships were said to have been lost due to the storm. From Hull, the immigrants crossed England to Liverpool, where they stayed in a hotel until they boarded the *Forest Monarch* on December 31. Then they were obliged to wait on board for seventeen days for favorable winds.[33] Personal tragedy came to the Domgaard family between the time that they boarded and set sail, as indicated by a fellow traveler's journal entry for Wednesday, January 12, 1853:

> *4 p.m. A son of N. P. Domgaard passed away. He was taken ashore and buried at Liverpool Jan. 12, 1853.*[34]

The entry is far too limited to chronicle what must have been utterly heart-wrenching to my ancestors. I wish I had something directly from Niels Peter and Else about the death of their only son at the tender age of one-and-a-half years. What were their feelings when that small body was taken ashore in Liverpool and buried in a grave they could never visit? Did they wish he could have been buried on Danish soil? Were they grateful not to have to stand at the rail of a ship and watch his weighted body buried at sea? Did they see their conversion and decision to emigrate as a contributing cause of his death? Did they question how God could allow their only son to die when they were bending their lives to His gospel? Another journal entry records that N. P. Domgaard spoke on January 31 in meeting, his topic "the gathering of Israel."[35] I would like to know what he said at that time, how he reconciled personal loss with loyalty to his religious convictions.

Five weeks after that sermon on the morning of March 7, 1853, the *Forest Monarch* sailed into the Mississippi River and anchored at 4:00 p.m. The converts would shortly begin the process of gathering on American soil. There were more delays. The Danish emigrants would not arrive in New Orleans until March 17. At that time, they pooled their resources so they could go together by steamboat to St. Louis, and from there to Keokuk, which was across the river from Nauvoo—the city that long since had been abandoned. In Keokuk they found outfits ready for crossing the Great Plains and were schooled in handling oxen and living in tents and wagons. They commenced their journey in mid-May and arrived in Kanesville, Iowa, across the Missouri River from what is now Omaha, Nebraska, by June 25. They rested there for a week. I like to imagine their wonder at crossing the continent as they followed the trail day after day for 1,400 miles, advancing only ten or fifteen miles per day. How did the ever-stretching land seem to my ancestors coming from small Denmark where no place in the country is more than thirty-five miles from the sea? How did the Rocky Mountains seem to them when the highest point in Denmark is only a little above sea level?

On the evening of September 30, they entered the Great Salt Lake Valley and were met by Erastus Snow, one-time companion of G. P. Dykes, who had converted so many of Niels Peter's fellow emigrants in Denmark. Apostle Snow re-baptized the immigrants "to wash them of the sins of the journey and renew their covenants. It was a visible token they had come out of the world; they were in Zion, and what was past for them was merely prologue."[36]

Niels Peter and Else and their daughter Caroline proceeded to Sanpete County in central Utah, where they settled in Manti. From December 1852 to October 1853, they had been in transit to Zion. What had sustained their faith? What had enabled them to proceed without fear? What had consoled their losses? Perhaps the answer lies in Niels Peter's own words from his autobiography, *"I believed the Gospel."*

How many times did Niels Peter and Else repeat those words as they sought to define the eternal verities introduced to them by Mormon missionaries? In the comparative ease but increasing complexity of the present, I try to define the eternal verities also. I, too, send off missionaries, my second son gone before my first returned.

After sharing a room in our home most of their lives, Jeremy and Chris would not see each other for almost four years as Chris departed twenty months prior to his brother. Chris went to Caracas, Vene-zuela. Prior to leaving, he would study Spanish for two months in Provo at the Missionary Training Center. As his departure approached, I spent six hours a day in a high school faculty workshop, relieved to fill my mind with the "other" in my life—books and students and lesson plans and objectives, to be with people who did *not* know that Wednesday, June 8, was "the big day" that was alternately anticipated and dreaded by me when my son would leave home for two years.

But each day when I returned home from the workshop, reminders surrounded me. Mission instruction letters and information covered the dining room table: *Check your driver's license and other documents to make sure they will not expire during your mission. Complete all the listed vaccinations and inoculations. ...* The list of vaccinations was worrisome. I remembered when Chris was about twelve and ripped off his catcher's mask at a baseball game to reveal lips starting to swell. When we got him to the emergency room, his eyes were swollen. A shot reversed the reaction to—we never knew what. A momentary fear gripped me. What if *something* in Venezuela triggered a reaction? What if there were *no* emergency room? What if ...

In nineteenth-century Nauvoo, women sent husbands and sons off without any inoculations. Their faith in medicine was replaced by faith in God's power to heal. As the riverboats disappeared down the Mississippi and the faces of departing missionaries became blurred, did these women have second thoughts? Did they return home and pray for their loved ones? Did some remember and cherish how a son looked just before departure as I did?

The day before Chris left, I watched him from our upstairs windows as he put on a maroon helmet, arranged his tall muscular frame on a three-wheeler, and conscientiously called out, "I'll be on the West Mountain up by the radio tower, but I'll be home before dark." He pushed his foot hard to start the engine, then he roared off. I watched his childhood trail behind him, knowing I wanted to hold him back, wanted him "home before dark" to *my* home, not to somebody else's home, each night. I remained at the window long after vision and sound had disappeared. I stood and looked at the empty road just as a century and a half ago, Nauvoo women must have looked from their windows at the vacant river.

Two months after our son left Richfield, we met him at the airport before his departure for Venezuela. He seemed like the old Chris of two months previous, animated and active, still displaying a helpful attitude, attentive to his new "missionary companion" whose parents were two states away. I was glad we could be there in person. Chris talked constantly. I wonder if he thought his chatter would keep me from crying. Whatever he thought, the constant flow of information occupied my mind enough to stifle some of the emotion I felt. I was busy getting last-minute photos: Chris with his companion, with his grandma, with his brother and sister, with his dad so we would each have a memory of our moment with him.

We gave Chris a few small gifts that he could carry in his backpack. I gave him a copied section from his great-grandfather's mission diary. E. P. Pectol had left Salt Lake City for New Zealand exactly eighty-seven years to the day before Chris's departure for Venezuela. Port Pectol traveled by train to Vancouver and then made his way by ship from there. Maybe it was better to have weeks of transition rather than hours. I wanted Chris to read the carefully penned words of his great-grandfather and know that, although technology changes, the human heart remains the same.

He left, not on a train, not on a Mississippi riverboat, but on a jet plane destined for Caracas. I picture him in my mind, how he looked before disappearing into the tunnel ramp leading to the airplane, so grown-up and slender-appearing in his dark suit. Used to seeing him in a basketball uniform, football pads, or casual school clothes, I kept peering after him, hoping to savor the memory of this new missionary son and my last two hours with him for two years. Those missionaries who waved from riverboats and the women who waved back from the dock at Nauvoo must have shared many of our feelings.

As our son's plane was leaving, my husband said, "We forgot to ask Chris if he needed any money!" Two hours to say and do all the important things, and we sent our son penniless to a foreign country. We were both amazed at our lack of foresight. All the "don't leave home without it" credit card ads and their facsimiles flashed before my eyes. Then I calmed down, knowing that we could wire money to Venezuela through our local bank. Chris didn't have to travel like many of the early missionaries "without purse or scrip."

The women who sent husbands or sons on missions from Nauvoo must have had the same bittersweet feelings I experienced: a pain of separation and a fear of the unknown offset by a joyful conviction that their missionary was doing the good work and growing personally in the process.

I had similar feelings as my son Jeremy departed for Oklahoma City. As we took Jeremy to the Missionary Training Center in Provo, we were comfortable with the familiarity of what would happen in a way we hadn't been twenty-one months earlier. Now I knew that the crowds would be large, that lines would take my missionary and his helper (my husband, in this case) and luggage one direction while I was kindly waved another way, and that they would rejoin me in an enormous hall of assorted Mormons— old, young, fat, thin, tall, short—who had come to "see our missionary off."

The orientation was blessedly brief, allowing little time to get emotional or to remember how empty our home would be when we returned, how quiet without a CD player filtering movie soundtrack music through the rooms, how full the refrigerator would stay without a nineteen-year-old fixing snacks in between meals, how lonely a weight set would seem without a muscular teenager working out on it.

That the MTC is a place dominated by youth was emphasized by a report on cereal consumed per year in the MTC—hundreds of pounds of Lucky Charms compared to sixteen pounds of All-Bran. Perhaps youth is the best time to venture into the world, when you still believe you can markedly make a difference. I thought of Thoreau's quote, "The young man gets together his materials to build a bridge to the moon ... and at length the middle-aged man concludes to build a woodshed with them." I thought about my own practicality, my own preoccupation with whether things will work, if they are feasible, and how much effort is worth the possibility of success. I contrasted that with the idealism of my son who really believed he could build a bridge, if not to the moon, then to people who could benefit from a better way to live.

I thought about the painful partings of my life and counted this a happy one because, at the MTC, my son would be with people who cared about his welfare and wanted to prepare him to be a force for good. I left him in a place which emphasized high ideals and lofty goals. I left him with the hope that in the process of trying to be a good example for others, he might grow in self-discipline; that in trying to explain his beliefs to others, he might deepen his own convictions; that in working hard against rejection, he might learn perseverance; and in seeking spiritual guidance, he might learn to counter self-pride. As I thought about other mothers who were seeing their missionary sons and daughters leave for two years, and of those who had done so in the past, I felt a bond across time and space.

I remembered a day on our trail trip in Illinois when darkness had descended over the Mississippi River and minute lights blinked on and off, momentarily glittering here and there in the grass. They were fireflies, one spark and then another and another dancing along the grassy shoreline. The red and gold of sunset had faded from the sky and the moon shone, its rays making a silvered path on the water. Stars were pinpoints of light in a velvet sky, seeming as tiny as the fireflies around us. I wondered at the easy distortion of our perceptions.

3.

The Women's Garden

My husband and I drove to the Mormon Visitors Center at Nauvoo and toured the displays, then entered the adjacent Monument to Women Garden. Sculptured statues, lighted only by soft illumination and framed by foliage, took on a spiritual aspect. During our slow stroll along the garden paths, we were unusually quiet. We sat on a bench, held hands, and remained silent, consumed with our own thoughts.

Neal interrupted my reverie. "Let's walk around one more time."

Viewing the statues the first time had triggered memories of events in my life that came back with vividness: the statue of Emma and Joseph Smith had recalled when my husband and I first fell in love, the trust I had had in him and the hopes I held for our future. The woman in a circular dance with children reminded me of when I had played ring-around-the-rosie with my own small children. The young woman sitting erect, long hair soft on her shoulders and back, an open book in her lap, had made me think of my daughter Kirsten, who from childhood had read constantly *The Secret Garden*, *The Box Car Children*, *Heidi*, and other books that I, too, had loved as a child. These were exchanged for more grown-up books over the years, books we had talked about together.

During our second tour of the garden, my husband and I stopped at a statue of a small child toddling on unsteady legs from one parent to another. Neal said, "Remember when Kerri took her first steps. I was at work and you called to tell me she had walked alone. I'm glad you were there to see her steps. I wish I'd been there."

"I wrote the date in her baby book," I said, feeling a tinge of guilt as I added that I hadn't been as good with the younger children's books.

I started to move on, but Neal pulled me back. Directing my gaze, he said, "Look where the child is in relation to the parents."

"Right in the middle, right between them. So, what's your point?"

"That's how it is, isn't it? Always children in the middle. I don't mean physically, but emotionally. You think I'm too harsh and I think you're too lenient with the children, and we never seem to be able to come to a compromise."

"It's especially hard with teenagers. Sometimes I wish they were little again and all we had to do was help them walk."

"Sometimes I wish that also," Neal said as he pulled me toward the statue of a woman, hands lov-

ingly rested on her son's shoulders. "I wish it were that easy for a father to be close to a son, to give him advice and have him really believe you know what's best, really believe you have his interest at heart."

"Mothers would like that same ease with daughters as well as sons. Sometimes children really trust parental advice, and sometimes they want to choose their own way." I hesitated and then said, "Maybe the problem comes when children see our mistakes and limitations. In the closeness of a family, you can't hide those things very well. Our children see our imperfections and think there's a better path."

"Maybe there is."

We moved to a sculpture of a woman molding a head of clay. I asked Neal, "What does this one mean?"

"I know what you want me to say—that women need a creative life, an avocation. Right?"

"And do you believe it?"

"That's what I've always wanted for you, Judy; you know that. It just doesn't work out in the real world. Something always has to give."

"And the woman is usually the one who gives."

Neal's words made me think about the vice of wanting too much, but I still felt the unfairness of it because it is usually women who feel guilty for want-

---

Emma Smith, memorialized here opposite her husband, was encouraged to "expound scriptures, and to exhort the church, ... and thy time shall be given to writing and to learning much. And thou need not fear for thy husband shall support you in the church; ... And thou shalt lay aside the things of this world, and seek for the things of a better [world]." —Instructions to Emma Smith, Doctrine and Covenants 25:5-10. *Cast bronze sculpture by Florence P. Hansen, photograph by Jed Clark © Intellectual Reserve, Inc.*

ing more out of life. Men who are dissatisfied with their opportunities or performance in a given area don't seem to feel guilty about wanting more. I thought about whether men could help women feel less guilt. I always quietly resented the phrase, "The mother sets the tone of the home." Why the mother? Why not the father, too? Why not the children as well? It seems to me that we're all in this together. On the other hand, children often feel a closer emotional connection to their mother, and that may imply a greater responsibility to set the tone.

In my work as a high school English teacher, I met thousands of young people who I admired for their good character. However, some students were selfish and unprepared for life even though their mothers had sacrificed to give them opportunities. Others felt abandoned by mothers who seemed too tired or self-absorbed to give them emotional support. It wasn't necessarily women who were working outside the home who were tired and self-absorbed. Stay-at-home moms could be emotionally absent. Being at home was not a foolproof plan for raising model children.

On my visits to the Daughters of Utah Pioneers museum in Salt Lake City, I have always liked to stop by the alcove display devoted to the accomplishments of Ellis Reynolds Shipp, a medical doctor and founder

in 1878 of Utah's School of Obstetrics and Nursing. I had read excerpts from her diary, 1871-1878, which traced "the striking metamorphosis from young mother with vague yearnings for wider horizons to medical doctor and teacher."[37] In 1866, when she was twenty-two, Ellis married Milford Shipp, a man eleven years her senior, whom she considered to be *ambitious, ardent, and energetic in all that was noble and laudable.*[38] Milford married three other wives in polygamy after his marriage to Ellis.

In October of 1875, Ellis's sister-wife Maggie entered the Women's Medical College of Pennsylvania in Philadelphia in the footsteps of another Utah woman, Romania Pratt, who had enrolled the previous year on Brigham Young's advice: "The time has come for women to come forth in these valleys of the mountains as doctors."[39] Maggie returned a month later, homesick. Ellis replaced Maggie at the school, leaving her three small children in the care of sister-wives. Perhaps the death of her infant son in 1868 and of a young daughter in 1873 made Ellis want to help others medically. She delighted in the stimulus of school, writing that *soon my interest was awakened and I began to feel my desire for knowledge increase as I began to see and realize how little I knew.*[40] Her sentiments are in contrast to feelings expressed three years earlier in

November of 1872: *I know that I am tired of this life of uselessness and unaccomplished desires, only so far as cooking, washing dishes and doing general housework goes, I believe that woman's life should not consist wholly and solely of routine duties.*[41]

During her schooling, letters from sister-wives were encouraging; but a conflict with her husband is apparent in a January 1876 diary entry: *I think he does not realize how almost harsh some of his letters seem, and did I not know him so well and understand his great desire for my success I should feel hurt at times. His words, though bitter and sharp, have a good tonic effect and urge me ever onward.*[42]

In June of 1876, advised by her professors to rest, Ellis went home for the summer. She returned to school in September, pregnant and with the added burden of paying tuition since her husband had informed her that he had no money to send. She took up dressmaking to help earn money and was helped by money orders sent from sister-wives. In May of 1877, she gave birth to her sixth child, a girl. A landlady looked after her infant while she served a summer residency. Despite having to juggle mothering, work, and schooling, Ellis delighted in her daughter, saying *it is to me the crowning joy of a woman's life to be a mother.*[43] She completed her degree in March of 1878 and re-

turned to Utah, where her income as a doctor allowed her sister-wife Maggie to return for a medical degree, as well as their husband Milford.

Rather than berate Ellis Shipp for being a working mother, modern-day Utahns praise her. Did *she* want too much? Did Brigham Young expect too much when he advised women to "enlarge their sphere of usefulness"? He said:

> We believe that women are useful not only to sweep houses, wash dishes, make beds and raise babies, but they should stand behind the counter, study law or physics or become good bookkeepers and be able to do the business in any counting house, and all this to enlarge their sphere of usefulness for the benefit of society at large. In following these things they but answer the design of their creation.[44]

I was educated at Brigham Young University in the same way that men there were taught to think critically, compete for grades, enjoy the intellectual rigor of class discussions, and feel pride in developing abilities to function in the world of adulthood. But when I married and had children, the message became one of reorienting my priorities, to put aside the characteristics developed at college, and to be a support for everyone else. I'm grateful that I, like Ellis Shipp, discovered my need for a life beyond "routine duties" and turned to education and a career for satisfaction in that area.

My career was linked to raising children as I taught all of my own children in high school. I remember the youngest, Noelle, born fourteen years after the oldest, telling me to "hold on till I get there" because she wanted me to be her English teacher. Well, I did hold on, and the memories of association with my children as a teacher are positive. In my idealized image of family dinners, I had pictured us sitting around the table discussing great books, but in reality, our dinner conversations were more along the lines of *Don't slurp your spaghetti* and *Please pass the peas.* In my classroom, we *did* discuss great books, and I could see my children among their peers, teenagers who became friends of mine as well as of theirs. Had I stayed home all those years, what would my children have lost? What would I have lost? And what might my husband have lost, living with a wife frustrated by "unaccomplished desires"? I think we all benefitted when I, like Ellis Shipp, "began to see my desire for knowledge increase as I realized how little I knew."

Thinking beyond my personal needs and continuing my walk among the statues in the garden, I considered the ideal love and family closeness portrayed in the statues through their poses and intimacy—something that our family achieved only intermittently. I felt a personal sense of loss. I'm sure other women, who are honest in viewing their own families, must feel the same as they stroll through the garden. I was comforted in remembering the humor of a cartoon I saw some years ago. In the cartoon, a family is posed for a snapshot on Temple Square in Salt Lake City in front of just such an "ideal family" statue. In contrast to the bronze figures who stand smiling, arms lovingly intertwined, the real family looks disheveled after the monumental effort of getting five children ordered into a line. A toddler stretches her mother's arm to its limit and tries to run off. Restraining the unruly child while balancing a baby on her hip, the mother manages a feeble, if vacant, smile.

I remember an attempt at family unity that failed markedly. Having read several magazine articles on the need for better communication as a tool for family togetherness, I decided that heart-to-heart conversing was the panacea for our family problems. I decided I owed my family at least the amount of planning and preparation I gave my students; so in a professional manner, I sat down at my school computer and typed up a neat form entitled "The Seven Cs to a Successful Family." It consisted of the following: Compliments, Complaints, Changes, Consequences, Checks, Coordination, Calendar. Six spaces were left under each heading to allow the six members of our family at home to express ideas.

As I typed, I was excited about the possibilities for discussions that would revolutionize our family. I actually started to feel that this form was an inspired stroke of genius. I daydreamed a little bit, imagining the future after this simple technique perfected my family. Of course, others would notice the change in our family and ask for the secret of my success. I would nobly share my secret with them. This would likely lead to seminars, locally at first and then state-wide. Eventually I would probably be asked to address a presidential council on family life. I could hardly wait to try out the Six Cs and begin the joy of true honest communication.

That evening I asked the family to join me around our kitchen table—an oak table, round like King Arthur's; but in this case, no sovereign, just a group of concerned citizens seeking the common good. Once we were seated, my face glowing with anticipation, I passed out the forms. My husband Neal glanced at his watch and asked how long this exercise would take. This was my first clue that all was not well in Zion.

We hurried quickly to the first section of the form, "Compliments." Everyone was given the opportunity to say something nice about other family members. Some of the compliments were a little stingy, of the "for a fat girl, you sure don't sweat much" variety. In any case, we got through the compliment section without too much difficulty.

The complaint section was next. Our rule was that after a complaint was expressed, everyone should sit silently for one minute, then we would propose solutions, selecting the best ideas to incorporate into our lives. At this point, Neal started to drum his fingers impatiently on the table. He wasn't used to discussion; he had his own variation of Spencer W. Kimball's motto, "Do it!" The finger drumming should have been my final clue that all was definitely not well in Zion.

To make a long and depressing story short, my son Jeremy, with all the breadth of his fourteen-year-old vocabulary, used the word *repulsive* about fifty times to describe our family dynamics. My husband threw his pen down and walked out, Jeremy following behind him. The rest of us toughed it out for a few more minutes before giving up. I sat wondering how I had produced such a catastrophic failure and began mentally revising my seven Cs to include Cuss, Crab, Criticize, Cut Up, Castigate, Cry, and Copout. I even decided to revolutionize the list to include the ABCs of a successful family:

A. Avoid discussing unpleasant issues. Eventually the children will leave home and the problems will solve themselves.

B. Bear up because this too will pass. What irritates you about others is probably about equal to what irritates them about you.

C. Count your blessings. Considering the variety of personalities involved and the number of things that go wrong each day, we all do about as well as can be expected.

What would the "ideal" pioneer family think anyway if they knew they were being held up for idolization in monuments to their perfection? Would they recognize themselves? Or would they struggle, as I did viewing the statues in the sculpture garden, at the divergence between the portrayal and the reality of family life as they knew it? The diaries of Mormon women living in Nauvoo from 1839-1846 give insights into the real lives lived there when streets were teeming with horses, wagons, livestock, busy workmen, hurried housewives, and racing children.

Bathsheba Smith's letters to her husband, Apostle George A. Smith, who was frequently absent on church missions, give glimpses of early Nauvoo and everyday family life. Her unconventional spelling lends a sense of the reality of education in her environment. In a letter dated *Sabbath morning Nauvoo July 16th 1843*, Bathsheba tells of their baby son:

> *George A has had the measels in addition to his coald and cutting teeth. ... I expect he was exposed to the measels on the fourth of July. I have not went to meeting sinse you left but stay at home. Sickness has kept me[,] if nothing else, but I think home is the best place for me [in] this hot weather.*[45]

In the same letter, Bathsheba escaped her concern about sickness by expressing her love for her husband:

> *It seems to me I could not wish to enjoy my self better than to sit under the sound of your rich and lovely voice and hear you unfold the rich treasure of your mind. Even the sound of your footstep would be music in my eare. I all most forget I am a lone, whilest I fancy to my self how happy I should be. The baby is waking. I must quit writing for the presant.*[46]

Other entries mention a lawsuit, concerns about money, a drought, the need to share well water, the fact that the house needed to be plastered, her hopes that her husband will return before the weather turns cold, the problem of the well going dry, more sickness for their baby, running out of flour, constant rain, concern about mail because the bridges were washed out, and the cellar flooding but at least water in the well again. Through all this, Bathsheba attempts humor when, in an August 1843 letter, she wrote: *Dr. Richards was here yesterday. Says to tell you we are all alive in Nauvoo only [except] those that are dead.*[47]

Even more serious problems are shared in a letter ten months later, dated June 15th, 1844, revealing a Nauvoo that is anything but peaceful or united. Writing of the destruction of the *Nauvoo Expositor* printing office, Bathsheba states that apostates William and Wilson Law and their associates *had printed one paper and a scanlelous thing it was.*[48] She then tells how *it was a newicence so the atharities went and burnt and disstroyed the press.*[49] As church historian William Bennett described the affair:

> Church apostates had purchased a printing press and prepared to publish a paper, *The Nauvoo Expositor,* for the avowed purpose of advocating "the unconditional repeal of the Nauvoo City Charter and to expose immoral practices in the Church." The only number appeared June 7, 1844. It was filled with slander against Joseph Smith and the Church leaders in Nauvoo. The charter was also bitterly attacked. The people in Nauvoo were incensed. The City Council met and declared the "Expositor" press a public nuisance. Under orders[,] the City Marshal, John P. Green, forcibly entered the printing establishment, pied [blotched] the type, and destroyed the printed papers. The conspirators, seeing what was done, set fire to their own building, and fleeing the city, circulated reports that their property had been destroyed and that their lives were in danger. The event was like a lighted match dropped in a powder house. The resulting conflagration swept the Prophet and his brother to their deaths and rocked the foundations of Church organization.[50]

In the aftermath of the destruction of the press, Joseph Smith and his brother Hyrum were arrested by officials of Hancock County, of which Nauvoo was a part, and incarcerated at the county seat of Carthage. However, they were not sufficiently protected from vigilantes, and as Bathsheba relates to her husband in a letter dated July 6, 1844, the brothers *were Kililled at Carthag on the 27 of June[,] and on 28 they weere braught home and such a day of mourning never was seen. It paines me to write such a painfull tale, but the Lord had comforted our harts in a mesure.*[51]

Following the martyrdom of the Smith brothers, the need to leave Illinois became evident, and Bathsheba describes how, in the fall of 1844, the city became "one vast mechanic shop."[52] Her own parlor was turned over to workmen as a paint shop for wagons. The reality of the historical Nauvoo, either in terms of civic or family life, was not the perfect scene of peace and harmony that visitors today experience when touring the city.

4.

The Scovil Bakery

Amidst the mild confusion of my normal home, I sometimes think that I would love to be back in restored Nauvoo: In the cleanness of a bakery never flour-dusted or ash-dirtied because nothing is ever baked there. In a nursery always uncluttered because no toys are ever scattered there. In a bedroom whose four-poster bed is neatly covered by a finely stitched patchwork quilt, never unmade because no one ever sleeps there. I would love to live in the order of a perfectly preserved past. Or would I? Would I miss the feel of dough on my hands, the yeasty smell of baking bread, the laughter of playing children, and the cozy warmth of cuddling, covered by tumbled quilts? Would I even miss the pain of a child's illness, of a loved one's absence, of a religious dream challenged? Yes, I think I would.

Still, there are moments in the clutter of my kitchen when I want to transport myself back to Nauvoo, to the fantasy land of the Scovil Bakery, a restored 1840s model designed to create the flavor of nineteenth-century goodies production. Hostesses give visitors gingerbread men to munch on as they mount the horse-drawn wagon that will take them on the tour of the other notable Nauvoo buildings. After commenting on the spotless kitchen, I was informed that the gingerbread men were baked elsewhere so they wouldn't "mess up" the bakery. No wonder women can stand in the confines of the small front

A fireplace oven of this type was used in Nauvoo, Illinois, in the 1840s, although the immaculate replica in Nauvoo fails to convey the sense of daily use. Gingerbread men given to tourists are baked off-site to avoid the appearance of untidiness. *From the Susa Young Gates collection, courtesy of Utah State Historical Society* room and idealize about how fun it must have been to roll pie crusts, cut cookie dough, and knead bread in the nineteenth century, popping the resulting delectables into a piping hot oven to bake and release savory smells throughout the house and neighborhood. Modern women conveniently forget the factors that make this vision of pioneer baking in the restored past seem so enjoyable: the replacement of hundred-degree summer heat with seventy-two-degree air conditioning and the replacement of long, incredibly hot dresses and petticoats with comfortable light-weight clothing.

Reviewing my own feelings about baking, I've always maintained that modern women made a mistake when they brought the cook shack, once located adjacent to the house and equipped with servants, into the main building. They should have kept runners bringing food *already prepared,* only to be *served* at the main table.

My personal history of homemaking could be a book entitled *Discovery and Disillusionment.* One chapter would definitely be entitled "Birthday Cakes" and would draw on my vast experiential resources. When my first child turned two, I, like any self-respecting woman in the 1960s, knew that good mothers made decorated birthday cakes, so I began a series of monumental failures that would make the Edsel look like a success.

One of my early disasters was a circus cake, which looked wonderful in the magazine's photograph of little plastic animals prancing around a center pole. I dutifully went to the dime store and purchased small colored creatures. I baked a cake, frosted it with chocolate icing, and proceeded to place the animals in a circle. They began sinking into the brown icing, ever deeper until they ended up almost completely submerged. I didn't have time to bake another cake, so I salvaged the situation by calling this one the "LaBrea Tar Pits," explaining to a rapt group of three-year-olds about how animals were trapped in the tar of prehistoric California, preserved for scientific study.

Another cake was white and was to have rose petals made from rolled, *pink* gumdrops and stems and leaves made from rolled, *green* gumdrops. In the process of being frosted, one side of the top layer caved in and, again, I was compelled to salvage it by saying it was supposed to portray an avalanche. The pink gumdrops were the heads of ill-fated skiers and the green stems were the legs of the even less fortunate, upturned skiers sinking head-first into the snow.

One year I made a snowman cake for a winter birthday party. I even bought a special pan to produce the right shape. It looked good until I piled on the frosting, and then things changed. The snowman began to look more and more deformed until I had to call this one "Bigfoot."

One year I was brave enough to try a castle cake complete with turrets, a moat, and a drawbridge. After four hours of work, the walls cracked, the turrets tumbled, and the drawbridge collapsed into the moat. We called it the "Sacking of a French Castle."

Not that all of my cakes were failures. There was one particular Halloween cake that involved simply cutting away parts of a rectangle to look like a ghost, applying fluffy white frosting, and positioning two half eggshells for eyes. Inside the eggshells, I placed two lemon extract-soaked sugar cubes and lit them, turning out the lights for effect. Admittedly there was an extra advantage to serving the cake in the dark.

One Father's Day I extended my cake baking skills, such as they were, into a new arena. I made my husband a cake. It was rectangular and was supposed to be a shirt and tie. I made the shirt yellow and the tie blue. Proudly, on the morning of Father's Day, I presented the cake to Neal. Our four-year-old, Kerri, beamed beside me. Neal viewed the cake from the top down, looked perplexed, turned it side-to-side and still looked confused. Next he turned it to view it with

the bottom at the top, shook his head, and went back to the horizontal perspective. "What is it?" he asked tentatively.

Being young and full of confidence, I said, "Guess." Peering at it closely, he said, "A whale? But why is the ocean yellow?" I positioned the cake to show him that it was obviously a shirt and tie, all the while exaggerating how much our four-year-old had contributed to this masterpiece. Would-be cake decorators, take advice from an old amateur and always involve a four-year-old in decorating. If it doesn't turn out, you can always say, "Look what *we* baked for you." What can a father, grandfather, or grandmother say other than "How sweet!" or "Isn't it cute?"

Looking back over the years, I have only one cake that has always been successful, and that is the "Bunny Cake." About thirty years ago, I clipped the recipe from a magazine; the egg, flour, oil, sugar, and food-coloring stains on the recipe card attest to its frequent use. Below, I offer instructions to young would-be cake decorators free of charge.

Mix the cake batter, placing half of it in a round, eight-inch cake pan and half in a square, nine-inch cake pan. After baking and cooling, cut out pieces from the square cake for bunny ears and a large bow tie, arranging these around the circular bunny face.

Spread Dream Whip frosting over the cake bunny and top with pink-tinted coconut.

If you have children like mine who can't stand coconut, omit that. You can make the bunny's eyes from sliced gumdrops or wafer mints or even large buttons if you haven't planned ahead, the nose from a gumdrop or large marshmallow, and the mouth from a curved string of red licorice (yarn in desperation).

My oldest daughter called to get this foolproof bunny cake recipe when she was about to give a birthday party for her two-year-old, my first grandchild; so I knew this cake had a bright future. The drawback with bunny cakes is that they aren't as popular after your children reach six years old. The solution thereafter is to call your local bakery. A friend, when requested to bring her favorite recipe to a bridal shower, gave the prospective bride the address of her favorite bakery and promised her that this was the key to a long and successful marriage. Over the years, our local bakery, Parsons, has been able to produce cakes that imitate soccer players, basketball teams, campers, scouters, ballet dancers, Disney cartoon stars, *Peanuts* characters, and graduates. This has saved me count-less hours and the mental turmoil of making up fanciful names for failed cakes.

When our youngest turned twelve, I hosted my last children's birthday party. After about fifty-five such events, I had earned a well-deserved retirement in my estimation. For this last birthday party, my daughter selected a bakery cake design featuring teens talking on telephones. The cake decorator produced a cake that brought approving *oohs* and *aahs* from Noelle's admiring friends. I shudder to think what my efforts would have produced. The girls would have mistaken my telephone lines for a giant squid's tentacles strangling the humanoid creatures at the bottom of the sea. I would have had to call the cake "Twenty Thousand Leagues under the Sea."

If you happen to visit the Nauvoo bakery or any other restored pioneer bakery, ask the docent to direct you to the real kitchen where they actually prepare the sample goodies. The lumps of cookie dough glued to the floor, the mass of sticky dishes and encrusted pans in the sink, and the pile of deformed and rejected gingerbread men will cure any illusion you might have about the good old pioneer days.

5.

Nauvoo

An early photograph of Nauvoo, its stately temple topping a hill in the distance, shows numerous wooden buildings—even what looks like an outhouse—in the crowded collection of structures in the foreground. These dwellings contrast with the statelier brick houses tourists visit in restored Nauvoo. In the brick structures, ample room, attractive furniture, a handmade cradle, or a skillfully carved toy suggests an ideal atmosphere for child rearing. In contrast to this ideal, one- or two-room cabins like those suggested in the photo often housed large families. Curiously, the *how* of raising children in such a small space is never explained in the pioneer diaries I have read, this amazing feat becoming another addition to the lore of pioneer ingenuity. The *why* of so many children is another provocative question seldom discussed in diaries of Nauvoo women or pioneer women in other parts of the West.

The nursery rhyme parody, "There was an old woman who lived in a shoe, she had so many children because she didn't know what to do," reflects a common belief about why pioneer women had large families. Victorian mores prevented mention of such things as pregnancy in diaries and journals. There are brief entries about "not feeling well" or being "put to bed," followed by the announcement of a boy or girl. Birth control is talked about even less. Historian Elizabeth Hampsten has probed the issue of pioneer family planning and quotes from confidential letters exchanged between women suggesting calendaring "safe days," using a preventative device called a *pessairre* which cost one dollar and was used to treat a tipped

33

uterus as well, and of nursing children until the age of two.[53]

For some women, pregnancy prevention required extreme solutions. Christina Neher, a German-Russian immigrant homesteading in Oregon in the early 1900s, received unsolicited help from an older and wiser German neighbor. After Christina gave birth to her second child, one year after her first, Frau Jäger set up sleeping quarters for Christina and her children in the Jägers' unused summer kitchen, then warned Christina's husband, Ludwig, to leave his wife alone. Less than two months after his wife's delivery, Ludwig complained about this separation by saying *die Natur verlangt's* ("nature demands it"), but was nevertheless barred from entry by Frau Jäger, who told him he should abstain: *Du sollst fasten* ("you should fast"). Christina returned to her own home when the summer kitchen was again needed by the Jägers. Seventeen months after the birth of Ottilia, Christina bore her

This early photograph of Nauvoo was taken by Lucian Foster in 1845 or 1846 from his studio near Parley and Hyde Streets. The crowded collection of structures in the foreground contrast with the statelier brick houses tourists visit in restored Nauvoo. Many large families lived in two-room cabins such as those visible in this photo. The *how* of raising children in such a small space is never explained in the pioneer diaries. *Courtesy of LDS Archives*

third child. Without Frau Jäger as a buffer, "nature" soon won out as Christina bore five more children. One wonders if she was happy about so many children or if she tried other methods of birth control which failed.[54] She may have followed a prominent nineteenth-century doctor's advice to restrict intercourse to the "safe" time in the middle of the menstrual cycle, a recommendation which might account for the high birth rate among pioneer women.[55]

I empathize with Christina because of my own fertility. Unlike many pioneer brides, I and my husband determined when to have children. Our first, Kerri, was born eighteen months after our wedding, Michael two-and-a-half years later, and Kirsten two-and-a-half years after that. The fourth child, Chris, was born after a reprieve of six years, as planned, and I became pregnant with Jeremy while I was nursing Chris. So much for that pioneer myth about relying on nursing as a prophylactic. My last daughter, Noelle, was conceived when I was thirty-six and Jeremy was one. Having confirmed that a sixth was on its way, I felt a need to tell my teenage daughter the news one day as I was standing by the dryer, folding diapers for my one-year-old. Trying to sound as casual as I could, I said, "Guess what? We're going to have another little baby at our house."

Kerri eyed me with disbelief and burst out, "You've got to be kidding!" A few weeks later, my mother, visiting and newly aware of my "condition," asked, "Don't you know where babies come from?" My students must have had similar thoughts. Teaching sophomore English in three different classrooms on my half-day assignment, I navigated crowded high school halls, balancing books on my abdomen as student whispers followed me. "Is she pregnant again?" they said in disbelief. In a little more than three years, I had borne three children. Pioneer fertility, with or without planning, doesn't surprise me.

My husband was present in the delivery room at the births of our last three children, something not allowed in the 1960s California hospitals where our first three children were born. I was comforted by the blessings he gave to me during each of my labors. His strong hands lay on my head and his reassuring voice seemed to calm my fears about imminent delivery. I think pioneer women in Nauvoo were calmed by blessings they received in the upper rooms of the temple beginning in December of 1845 as they prepared to abandon Illinois. Perhaps blessings of health and protection made pregnant women feel immune from the difficulties of delivery during the westward trek.

Historian Wallace Stegner says that most of the women would not have had to bear their children along the trail in wagons or tents if they had not chosen to do so: "No one actually is pressing them this hard: they could stay a week or a month and have their babies under a roof. But it is as if they covet the opportunity to drop their young like animals in any crude shelter available to God's chosen people."[56] Eliza R. Snow reported that nine babies were born in the ice-bound tent town of Sugar Creek across the Mississippi one night in February 1846.[57] Eliza's biographer, Maureen Beecher, feels that the "nine babies born" statement made years later in the 1870s may have been an embellishment to engender public sympathy. Beecher clarifies that many women did, in fact, stay behind to have their babies in the city, coming west later. The case of Diantha Clayton is cited as an example. But for women who chose to travel in late pregnancy, delivery in a tent or wagon, rather than in a home in Nauvoo, may have been a demonstration of faith and dedication and defiance in the face of persecution.

After leaving Nauvoo, my husband and I drove across Iowa. I rested on a bed in the back as our van creaked and rattled along a rough stretch of road. For a few minutes I imagined being a pioneer woman in labor, pushing to deliver a child. In doing so, I contrasted my own hospital births, made bearable by anesthetic, with the painful birthing of days gone by. The matter-of-fact nature of pioneer women's accounts amazes me. Nancy Hunt, a woman traveling overland to California, writes: *While the young folks were having their good times, some of the mothers were giving birth to their babes.* When I first read this statement, I wondered if a cause-and-effect relationship was unwittingly implied. Hunt continued:

> *Three babies were born in our company that summer. My cousin Emily Ibe ... gave birth to a son in Utah, forty miles north of Great Salt Lake, one evening; and the next morning she traveled on until noon, when a stop was made and another child was born—this time Susan Longmire was the mother made happy by the advent of little Ellen. The third birth [was to] the wife of my cousin Jacob Zumwalt who gave birth to a daughter while traveling in the Sierra Nevada. To this baby they gave the name of Alice Nevada.*[58]

Roxana Cheny Foster, a woman of thirty-six traveling to California in 1854, tells of stopping with no other wagons near: *We set up our tent and before twelve o'clock a baby boy was born to us, probably the first person born in Ogden. We rested three days and then went slowly on.*[59] The entry is so brief, I question what details remained unsaid. Roxana expressed no concern about bearing a child with only the help of her husband, no longing for another woman who had borne children and could understand her pain. She mentions no sense of relief at the child's first cry, that he had survived delivery, or that she no longer had to worry where and when and how her child would be born.

I prepared for the birth of my first child by getting regular pre-natal care, taking supplemental vitamins, quitting work in my sixth month, and avoiding long trips after the seventh month. I also took classes in preparation for childbirth. Each subsequent pregnancy was equally protected. My mother came to help after each birth. My daughters have had sonograms during their pregnancies, and I have been there to help them after deliveries. Pioneer diaries chronicle pregnancy as wholly unremarkable if even mentioned. Historian Lillian Schlissel says:

> Childbearing did not in any degree alter the determination to emigrate. The decision to make the journey rested with the men, and farm men of the early nineteenth century were not inclined to excuse women from their daily responsibilities to prepare for the occasion of childbirth. Women were expected to be strong enough to serve the common needs of the day, and strong enough to meet the uncommon demands as well. The society of emigrants yielded little comfort to frailty or timidity—or for that matter motherhood.[60]

I believe my maternal great-grandmother, Kirstine Sandersen Sorensen, was "strong enough to serve the common needs of the day, and strong enough to meet the uncommon needs as well," at least until she died in childbirth along with her sixteenth baby. When I was so young that I had not yet asked how babies came to be, I can remember my mother and her sisters maligning John Sorensen, their grandfather and my great-grandfather. They talked about him as if he ought to have been tried for the death of his wife.

I visited the small town of Æbelnæs on the Isle of Møn, south of Zealand, the island on which Copenhagen is located, where Kirstine was born in 1843. A large yellow stucco, thatch-roofed house looked so old that I wondered if it could be the very one she passed by on her way to work every day as a servant when she was a young girl. The open fields must have looked much the same then, grasses waving in the wind and brushing her long skirts as she made her way across the pastures.

Parish records show that she was *dobt* (baptized) into the Lutheran Church on Sunday the 17th of December 1843 in Damsholte. Her *daab* (christening) was witnessed by several Æbelnæs men, who were blacksmiths, and their wives. On a June morning in 2000, the sun just drying the last drops of a spring rain, I visited the parish church where this christening occurred. It was hexagonal and of the same yellow stucco as the thatch-roofed house, beautiful in its symmetry, set in the midst of a *kirkegård,* the Danish name for church garden or cemetery. Inside the chapel, a miniature ship hung from the high ceiling, poised above the pews. Ships like these were typical ornaments in Danish churches because parishioners were often seafarers looking for protection in their work. I wonder if Kirstine walked along the seashore not far from Æbelnæs prior to her emigration and contemplated the possibilities of her new life in Zion.

She was baptized into the Mormon church at the age of twelve in 1855, having possibly heard about this new gospel preached in the home of her employers. Being poor and illiterate, she had likely begun working as a scullery maid or nursery maid when she was ten or eleven. Her parents and other members of her family were baptized later than she, no doubt partially through her influence. At age nineteen, she shows up on immigration records traveling in 1862 with the Fredrick Christiansen family. Since she did not borrow money from the Perpetual Emigrating Fund, the Christiansen family may have paid her passage. They embarked in the early spring, going from their home to the island of Lolland where a steamboat carried them to Kiel. I wonder, once in landlocked Utah, if Kirstine remembered her last view of the Baltic Sea and if she longed for the brush of salty breezes on her cheek and the smells of a beach.

No autobiography explains her experiences, but a great-granddaughter, Norma Sorensen Taylor, has reconstructed Kirstine's life, using marriage and birth records as well as historical records and events of the time period. It is a chronicle of hardship in birth and death as Kirstine became a polygamist wife and mother of sixteen under difficult circumstances, finally dying in childbirth at age forty-two.[61]

Following their arrival in Kiel, a railroad trip took the emigrants across the German peninsula to the seaport of Hamburg, Germany. On Wednesday, April 9, 1862, they boarded the ship *Humbolt* under the direction of Captain H. B. Boysen; they set sail with 323 emigrating saints in the care of Elder Hans C. Hansen. Elder Hansen had been laboring as a missionary in Scandinavia and was returning to his home in Zion.

The *Humbolt* crossed the Atlantic in a scant five weeks, arriving in New York Harbor on the 20th of May 1862. As other immigrants then, Kirstine was processed through Castle Garden before being allowed to enter the mainland. The company of Saints was met by American elders who served as agents to help them further their journey.

As the Danish Saints who came in 1862 were soon to learn, New York was not America, but it was part of the spirit of America—big, garrulous, bustling, noisy. The great buildings, massive piles of masonry blackened with soot, filled a narrow neck of land skirted by two rivers that poured into the ocean to form a natural harbor; it was impressive. It is doubtful that the Danish emigrants, hard pressed by their own problems, had more than a vague realization of the bloody Civil War raging in the land of their adoption. They had their own appointment with destiny and no time to lose.

The *Humbolt* was the first ship of the four ships carrying Danish saints to arrive in New York that year. Passengers of the four ships would eventually meet in Florence, Nebraska, to continue their journey to Utah. The passengers of the *Humbolt* began their journey by railroad to St. Joseph, Missouri, and from there by steamship up the Missouri River to Florence.

Florence was a bustling frontier camp located on the west bank of the Missouri River at a point now known as North Omaha. Here, for the time being, was one of the spots where the East and West met face to face. On one side were the railroads and civilization; on the other, vast stretches of wilderness, Indians, deserts, mountains—the great land of the future. As might be expected, the place was seething with people: scouts, traders, freighters, home seekers, soldiers. With the Civil War raging, the demand was limitless for horses, mules, oxen, cattle—everything used for transportation or food. Needs were increased by the constant stream of Mormon emigrants going west. The half-bewildered Danish Saints were confronted not only by many strange people but also by strange conditions. The area contained thousands of head of livestock. Wagon trains were being outfitted by Mormon scouts and plainsmen, some of them sent directly from Salt Lake City.

The Danish saints from the *Humbolt, Franklin, Athenia,* and *Electra* were reshuffled into four companies for crossing the plains. Two companies were organized from those who had financial means to buy all their necessary equipment. These were placed under the leadership of Elders Hans C. Hansen and Ola N. Liljenquist. Kirstine and the Fredrick Christiansen family were members of this wagon train, which broke camp at Florence on July 14. For several days they had trouble learning to drive the oxen. Not only were the drivers inexperienced, but also, the oxen didn't understand Danish. It has not been recorded which had to learn a new language, the oxen or the drivers, perhaps both, for they came to understand one another and the journey resumed successfully.

The journey across Nebraska and Wyoming and into the Salt Lake Valley was accomplished in the heat of summer. Food was scarce and everyone able-bodied enough walked beside the wagons. They reached the Salt Lake Valley on the 23rd of September 1862.

A great many Danish saints were sent to Ephraim, and that is possibly where Kirstine met John Sorensen [twenty-two years her senior, an emigrant who, with

his wife Else Marie, had left Denmark in 1854 and apparently lost three children on the journey; three more children were born to them in Utah, but only one lived to adulthood]. Kirstine and John were married for time and all eternity on the 27th of December 1862 in the Endowment House in Salt Lake City.

John and Kirstine settled in the area now known as Gunnison. During 1862 and 1863, the two settlements previously called Chalk Hill and Kearns Camp were being amalgamated into one settlement on the present site of Gunnison to be safe from spring floods. Most homes were built during the spring of 1863; winter must have been difficult in temporary housing.

Kirstine was a plural wife, for John had married a woman named Hannah Andersen. Hannah was also a Danish immigrant but much [sixteen years] older than Kirstine, which must have caused some friction. Else Marie, John's other wife, isn't listed in the Gunnison Ward records ... and ... the 1870 census doesn't list Else Marie [who apparently died sometime between censuses, joining two of her children who died]. An eleven-year-old daughter of John and Else, Mary Christine, is listed on the census.

On November 11, 1863, Kirstine gave birth to her first child, a daughter she named Maria. Sadly, Maria died on the 23rd of December 1863. On the 9th of February 1864, Hannah had her first child, whom she named Hannah. Kirstine and Hannah must have struggled to establish a home in the newly settled area. ... On the 7th of November 1864, Kirstine gave birth to a son they named John after his father. She must have worried she would lose her second child when winter marked an outbreak of smallpox, but John beat the odds and lived to adulthood.

Indians that had been camped near Gunnison contracted smallpox and they blamed the settlers. War was inevitable because of the anger of the Indians, so plans were devised to protect everyone. For three years, Indian raiding parties plagued the Gunnison settlement, which was located halfway on the three-hundred-mile battlefront.

On the 25th of May 1866, Kirstine gave birth to a daughter they named Christine. During this time the Indian raids were particularly frequent so Judge Peacock came with directions from Brigham Young to build a fort. Cabins were to be moved in line for the outside walls of the fort. With ready obedience, the people set to work enclosing four city blocks. Walls between the cabins were rocked up to a height of seven feet with peepholes near the top. At each corner, circular structures with many lookouts served as small camps for the watchmen. There was a substantial gate on each side in line with the cross streets. In less than a month's time the fort was in fair condition against attacks. During July of 1866, in the midst of all this chaos, the baby Christine died. The Indian raids stopped during the winter to give the settlers a respite, but spring and summer brought renewed attacks.

Mary Ann, John's and Kirstine's fourth child, was born the 13th of June 1867. Hannah also gave birth to a baby girl, Maria, that year on the 14th of October 1867. A peace pact was consummated with Chief Black Hawk in the fall of 1867. Unfortunately some of his warriors weren't ready for peace, especially Jake Arapeen, whose father had contracted smallpox and died in 1864.

Fort Gunnison became a haven for settlers from many settlements during 1867 and 1868. A sense of normalcy was provided by organizing activities such as Relief Society, Sunday School and Priesthood quorums. Quilting bees, singing, dancing, as well as worship services, helped to balance the normal work of sustaining a family. Finally on the 19th of August 1868 peace was negotiated between Jake Arapeen and the other hostile warriors. The settlers decided to remain in the fort until spring.

In the spring of 1869, the people moved from the fort to their city lots; there they set out fruit trees, shade trees, planted gardens and made improvements to beautify their homes and make them inviting. During this beehive of activity, Kirstine gave birth to her fifth child, a daughter they named Minnie Martine, who was born on the 17th of June 1869. Peace brought many changes as men worked to make life easier by building a sawmill, a co-op store, and by establishing a cattle cooperative. Women kept their homes, tended the children, planted gardens, made tallow candles, and mended and performed the hundreds of little tasks needed to survive in a pioneer settlement.

A *Deseret News* article written in 1870 by Hans Thunnison, the postmaster, explains conditions:

We have but a small settlement of 90 families. The grasshoppers preyed heavily upon us the last years. The losses sustained from them and the burdens we had to endure during the Black Hawk War were equally severe, but we are improving. Our fields at present look barren and desolate, except about 250 acres planted with wheat, mostly late grain, which looks very promising and will, we hope—with addition of peas, potatoes, corn, etc., all of which appear to be doing well—suffice to feed the inhabitants of this place for the coming year.

A new rock schoolhouse 24 x 24 feet will soon be finished. With the good road now made up Twelve Mile Canyon we expect an abundant supply of lumber. The people appear to be well generally, the weather is fine and as soon as the grasshoppers get wings they take their flight to other parts.

On the 19th of February 1871, Kirstine and John were blessed with twin daughters, which they named Amelia and Emma Eliza. Unfortunately, these little spirits weren't long for this life for on the 14 of April 1871 Emma Eliza died and Amelia joined her twin on May 7, 1871.

On September 28, 1871, John and Hannah filed a mutual petition for divorce, which was granted. Hannah received custody of their two daughters, Hannah, age six, and Maria, age four, as well as a property settlement. On May 13, 1872, a daughter was born to John and Kirstine, whom they named Victoria ... but in August Victoria died. On December 24, 1873, a son named Christian Louis joined the growing Sorensen clan.

In 1874, John began farming in an area that eventually became known as Mayfield. Kirstine and the children remained in Gunnison during this time. On December 26, 1875, Kirstine gave birth to a son she named Sanders after her father. He died the same day he was born. Sanders was the last child born in Gunnison, for the family moved to Mayfield in the spring of 1876. It is possible that John and Kirstine were called by church authorities to Mayfield to participate in the newly organized United Order [a communal society], for they settled on the north side of the creek where it was being practiced. On the south side of the creek, another settlement was established by English immigrants who had moved from Ephraim. The settlement was called New London and they had a separate ward and bishopric until 1877 when the two settlements were combined.

During the rigors of moving, Kirstine was pregnant. She worked throughout the summer and fall to build a home. In addition to caring for her family and helping with hard work, she waged a constant war on lizards, snakes, and rodents that would share her dwelling in spite of all she could do. On November 9,

1876, Kirstine gave birth to her eleventh child, a daughter named Ricka Malinda [my grandmother].

In the newly emerging community, settlers found a need for recreation. In a delightful nook on a bend of the creek, all of the trees, shrubs, and turf were cleared of dead branches and a bowery was built. In this beautiful little park, called the Grove, both aesthetic and practical needs were satisfied. Meetings and socials were held in the bowery, picnics and games were enjoyed in the shade of the tall cottonwoods, and the "old swimming hole," screened by squaw berries and birch, provided pleasure on hot summer days. Here the family water barrel, mounted on a two-wheeled cart in summer and a bobsled in winter, was filled as needed from the creek. Baptisms were also performed here.

Brigham Young dedicated the Manti Temple site on April 25, 1877. The Twelve Mile (Mayfield) residents counted the milestones from twelve to one as they plodded by ox team to witness the groundbreaking ceremonies.

The United Order was disbanded in 1877 and sometime thereafter Kirstine and John moved to the south side of the creek and built a home. Four children were born to John and Kirstine in the next five years. Their twelfth child, David was born on January 4, 1879. A daughter named Ephalone was born May 27, 1881, and died on June 8, 1881. Louis was born August 27, 1882, and died a scant two and a half months later on November 2, 1882. Joseph Alma was born December 5, 1883. On December 17, 1885,

Kirstine died in childbirth [ten days short of her twenty-third wedding anniversary, and the child also died]. Her married daughter, Mary Ann, helped her mother in her struggle, but to no avail. At the age of forty-two, Kirstine Sandersen Sorensen left this life as she had lived it, struggling. She was buried in the Mayfield Cemetery, but unfortunately the location of her grave and the graves of her babies is unknown.

Apparently the original grave marker, assuming there ever was one, was made of wood and disintegrated. The cemetery records do not chronicle where Kirstine was buried, only that she was interred. Long after her death, a grandson had a granite marker for her placed next to his family plot. I can hear my Aunt Blanche, were she alive today, cursing John Sorensen for not putting a permanent marker on his wife's grave at the time of her death, one more insult to her. But how do we know what his feelings were at the time; perhaps he was overcome by grief, perhaps even by guilt and remorse. Without a diary or memoir, what can we know? No picture of Kirstine exists that I have been able to locate, so I cannot even visualize her appearance.

Considering the beliefs about the importance of raising posterity, was Kirstine a willing partner in the conception of sixteen children, children she believed would be hers "on the other side of the veil"? Was this "the why" of so many children? Did Kirstine and her husband rejoice in each birth; and after the death of each child, did Kirstine long for a new baby to fill the void, one to cradle in her empty arms, to nestle at her breast? Did she feel blessed to be free of the scourge of biblical women who begged for a cure for barrenness: Sarah before she bore Isaac, Hannah before she bore Samuel, Elisabeth prior to delivering John? Did Kirstine consider herself a handmaiden of the Lord as well as the wife of John Sorensen? And finally, did the women who lived in those small cabins visible in the photograph of Nauvoo consider themselves handmaidens of the Lord, finding Nauvoo beautiful because of their fulfilled calling to multiply and replenish the earth?

6.

Mt. Pisgah

We traveled west toward Mt. Pisgah, so named by Mormon apostle Parley P. Pratt. Mt. Pisgah was the second of the major way stations set up to provide food and shelter for the emigrating Mormons after their exodus from Nauvoo, in use between 1846 and 1852.[62] I thought about the biblical origin of the name: a hill in Moab opposite Jericho from which Moses saw the land of Israel he was not permitted to enter.[63] Perhaps Mormon pioneers saw Mt. Pisgah as a stopping place from which they could "see" the promised land ahead of them, although in actuality, the valley of the Great Salt Lake was more than a thousand miles ahead of them. It must have still seemed like an unattainable dream at this point of the journey. It made me think about all the "promised lands" at different stages of our lives and how repeatedly we anticipate a better time ahead, yet inevitably deal with unforeseen realities because we are blinded by our ardent hopefulness and longing. The moving from place to place of so many pioneers was their visible extension of a common longing for a better place.

Leaving Mt. Pisgah, driving comfortably on a highway, I thought about how it must have been slogging through the winter and spring mud of Iowa, comparable to biblical people plodding through desert sand. Wallace Stegner used a biblical comparison: "Every wagon train for many years was like a new flight out of Egypt. The Old Testament parallel was like a bugle in the brain; some of them probably even hoped for a pursuing Pharaoh and a dividing of the waters."[64]

Neal and I reached our next destination, Corydon, Iowa, wanting to see the museum's heroic-sized replica of a covered wagon and oxen, a portrayal of the supreme effort required to cross Iowa in the spring of

1846. In addition, the museum was a must-stop because of its extensive displays which cover an entire city block. When we arrived, we were confronted by a closed sign on the door. Walking to the service station across the street, we asked whom we might call.

"Try Wilma West," a clerk told the cashier, who looked up the number. After two rings, a vigorous and refined voice answered, "Wilma West speaking. May I help you?"

We explained our desire to see the museum before continuing on our journey.

"I'll meet you in twenty minutes," she answered. And she did.

With a name like Wilma West, she might have been a rodeo queen or a fictional Louis L'Amour char-

---

The faded wedding photograph of Charles Shell and Ida May Taylor is representative of the dim memories descendants have of them. Her parents are unknown and his parents are names and dates on census sheets only. Why do I search so earnestly for progenitors? Perhaps I want to know the past that made them so I can know the past that made me. I agree with William Faulkner: "There is no such thing as was. To me, no man is himself, he is the sum of his past. There is no such thing really as was, because the past is. It is a part of every man, every woman, and every moment. All of his and her ancestry, background is all a part of himself and herself at any moment." *Photograph in possession of the author*

acter, but she wasn't. She was better than that: a petite, dynamic, retired school teacher who had spent the better part of her life enlightening children and museum visitors with an enthusiasm that belied her years. She knew the museum backwards and forwards and took us on a quick tour that nostalgically reviewed the details of a past era. The extent of the museum made us wonder at the energetic devotion of this small community, enabling them to amass a 34,000-square-foot collection of superb memorabilia.

Stepping briskly to keep up with Wilma, Neal and I walked down a re-created nineteenth-century street scene. In the general merchandise store, I imagined a pioneer woman shopping for a dill pickle, calico, and a new bonnet in one stop. Today's superstores try to offer a variety of merchandise on an even grander scale.

The doctor's office, where one person—the doctor—examined, diagnosed, filled prescriptions, wrote a bill, and collected payment for a low fee, was in complete contrast to today's medical clinics with extensive staffs, high fees, and a confusing paper-load of insurance filings.

In a toy shop we viewed wooden wagons and china-faced dolls that had belonged to children of the nineteenth century. I thought about the value of toys to children who would have had few belongings, and how my children, with mass-produced toys available to them, preferred the dolls my mother made for them. I remember watching my first child, a daughter, play lovingly with the tiny doll furniture we had saved for her. I thought of boxes of special toys put away as childhood ended for my sons and daughters, things to be offered later to grandchildren as a connection to the past.

As we viewed two other building replicas, a church and a jail, I thought about how they encapsulated some of the basics of civilization. We moved on to a transportation section which featured an old postal wagon, once drawn by a horse in a day when the post office was a connection to those left behind—to people who were often never seen again. An open-sided school bus, decorated with autographs of those who had ridden it to simple prairie schools, reminded me of how education had served to Americanize immigrants from so many countries. As a teacher, I wished that more children and parents today saw education as a vital link to a better life.

Neal and I both lingered in front of some railroad trunks, the names of Scandinavians along with their Iowa destinations painted on the sides in beautiful script. "I wonder if my grandmother had a trunk like that," Neal mused. "I don't remember having seen one."

"I'd love to find something like that from my Great-grandmother Schell. I don't even have a picture of her. Imagine coming from Austria and settling in Wyoming as a twenty-three-year-old cook."

Leaving the museum, I thought some more about Great-grandmother Schell, or Barbara, as she is listed in the 1870 census. From the record, I knew that she married Charles Schell, a man from Prussia ten years her senior and listed on the census as a "leaborer." Ten years later, he was listed in Colorado as a "landlord," so they accumulated property as their family expanded with the addition of four children. I wondered if, when they married, they scraped together enough to pay for a formal wedding picture and how my great-grandmother might have treasured it. A photo of their son Charles, my paternal grandfather, is my only visual link to them. Charles stands tall by his bride, Ida May, on their wedding day in 1896. The picture has dimmed with the years, but Charles is noticeably handsome with neatly combed dark hair, a groomed moustache, and a dark suit that accentuates his straight, slender frame. To create a mental picture of Barbara, his mother, I imagine that Charles must have resembled her, just as my olive-skinned, dark-haired son resembles me. I close my eyes and picture a sepia-toned wedding portrait of a fragile-looking bride, upswept hair caught by flower buds, expression serious. Deep-set eyes might have complemented the smoothness of her high cheek bones, her figure accentuated by the fit of an embroidered bodice. Standing, she might have rested her hand on the shoulder of her intended groom as women often did in such pictures. He would have sat tall and straight-backed, possibly anticipating the imagined promised land of marital bliss. What would my great-grandparents have looked like in a fiftieth anniversary photograph and how would their reality compare with their earlier dreams, I wondered.

One major part of a married woman's life, not perceived by lithe young girls in wedding dresses, is caring for the sick: the child with croup, the neighbor with pneumonia, the husband with a broken leg, the parent with cancer. My mother, wizened by her years, often said, "I like to take care of people, rub their legs when they hurt or massage their shoulders when they're tense."

I remember times when I was ill, mother fluffing my pillow and smoothing the sheets until they felt just-off-the-line fresh, placing a clean towel across my lap, bringing a tray of hot chicken soup, strawberry Jell-O, and cold milk—even patiently feeding me when I was really weak. Maybe her care is why there is a pleasurable side to my memories of being ill.

I recall waking up one morning when I was seven and calling plaintively, "Mom, there's a lump on the side of my neck." She sleepily called back, "It's okay. Go back to sleep." However, Mother soon came to check on me. It was the mumps. I got a new Uncle Wiggley game, and Mother sat with me on the edge of the bed for hours as we moved our markers, seeing who could get Uncle Wiggley home first. For some reason, I usually won.

Memories of chest colds and sore throats make my nose twitch as I recall the pungent odor of Mentholatum. Mother would scoop some out of the can and spread it under my neck and across my chest, her strong hands stroking and massaging so thoroughly, I could feel the ointment penetrate skin, muscle, and bones, it seemed, to get to the very source of my illness.

After a rub down, Mother always placed a clean "rag," as she called it, a scrap from an old flannel blanket, around my neck and fastened it with a large safety pin, making me look like a turtle cautiously poking out its head. Enveloped in the healing vapors of Mentholatum, I knew I was on my way to recovery.

When I graduated from high school and prepared

to leave for college, my delight at soon being free and on my own blinded me to my mother's held-back tears. About three weeks after my arrival at Brigham Young University, my elation was dampened by my first illness. I had a terrible cold and my roommates didn't seem to care. In fact, no one noticed, let alone sympathized.

I called home. Hearing Mother's voice, I burst into tears and cried, "I'm sick and nobody cares." Mother's warm voice across the miles was almost as healing as her strong hands. I felt better.

As the years went by, Mother was still there in times of sickness, always noticing what needed to be done. I never had to say, "My neck feels cramped lying this way" or "The covers are knotted" or "Some ice-cream would be good." She always knew. She never asked, "Should I do the wash while you're ill?" She just did it.

After recovery, I'd go to the kitchen and open cupboard doors. Pans would be stacked neatly in order of size, no longer balanced precariously in uneven piles. The kitchen sink would gleam, every crevice scoured with an old toothbrush. My mother took care of things as well as she did people.

She also took care of herself. I recall when she was a vigorous seventy-nine and still shot a forty-four in nine holes of golf, how shocked family and friends were when an angiogram showed three major heart blockages. Wanting to "have at least ten more good years," she chose open-heart surgery. While she was recovering, I knew just what to do. I fluffed her pillow and smoothed the sheets until they felt just-off-the-line fresh. I placed a clean towel across her lap and brought a tray of hot chicken soup, strawberry Jell-O, and cold milk, but independent as ever, she fed herself. I helped her to the promised land of recovery just as she had done for me so many times.

Thinking about the care my mother has given me and I, in turn, gave her, I wonder how many children my father's grandmother, Barbara Vaich Schell, nursed through sickness. Did she help her aging husband as well? Who took care of my great-grandmother in her later years? Was she ill for a long time? How long did she stay poised on some Mt. Pisgah waiting for entrance to a *final* promised land? I don't even know the date or circumstances of her death.

7.

Winter Quarters

Neal maneuvered our van to Council Bluffs, Iowa, then across the state border to the site of Winter Quarters, now Florence, Nebraska. Many Mormon pioneers spent the winter of 1846-47 here after a hasty exodus from Nauvoo, while others remained strung out all across Iowa. We toured the Mormon Visitors Center, then visited the adjacent log cabin and covered wagon, representative of the hundreds like them that had lined the banks of the Missouri River in the mid-1840s. Here 500 log cabins and 83 sod houses had been hastily built to accommodate some 3,000 people. By spring, there were twice that number of people in Winter Quarters, and people had to sleep in wagons. In such dire circumstances, more than 600 died.[65]

Across the street from the cabin and wagon, on a rise above the city, lay the Winter Quarters cemetery.

As my husband and I walked among the graves, we spoke in hushed tones, noticing the many epitaphs and dates on gravestones identifying children buried there. I told my husband about a woman I had studied, Martha Magdalene Keller Brown, described as the "beautiful Maggie Keller," a southern belle, before her marriage.[66] She was not Mormon and had never been at Winter Quarters, but she experienced her own trial of faith and personal winter in the deaths of her children. I told Neal how I had identified with her feelings as I had read her story.

She gave birth six times, as I did. Her first child, Mattie, was born in 1878, mine, Kerri, in 1963. Maggie followed her doctor husband to Colorado in 1881, while I followed my teacher husband to Japan in 1969. Maggie's husband searched for silver mines in the West while mine taught chemistry in foreign countries.

Maggie crisscrossed the country four times—sixteen thousand miles, twenty-four moves in twenty-seven years—and I had crisscrossed the world four times—twenty-five thousand miles in four moves over the space of eleven years. Maggie left five small graves. I left one. In Rincon, New Mexico, in 1886, Maggie tended seven-year-old Mattie, watching her child's scarlet fever rage for five days. She told of her daughter's funeral:

She was dressed to look as natural as possible, lying a little on one side with her doll Aunt Mary gave her in her arms just as when she went to sleep Sunday night. She would have me undress her doll & give it to her when she went to bed. I can't fully realize I won't see her here any more.[67]

In 1887, Maggie gave birth to a son and named him James Albert. In letters otherwise heavy with the news of Western destitution, his antics become the joyful focal point of her reports. On May 14, 1888, she wrote, *Albert squeals and laughs a great deal & is perfectly happy when he can get hold of his papa's whiskers & pull; so is his papa, who thinks there is no boy like his.*[68]

Harvey Andrews with his family in Custer County, Nebraska, 1887, at the grave of a dead child. Solomon Butcher's photos say in images what might have been difficult to convey in words. *Courtesy of Nebraska State Historical Society Photograph Collections, nbhips 12871*

On December 22, 1890, another son was born, christened John Daniel. Three months later Maggie, ill with influenza, arose from bed to nurse her two children who were also sick with "la Grippa," as Maggie's biographer details:

Albert caught it first, then Johnnie. Albert was terribly ill with it and Maggie, realizing he had a very short time to live, said, "Oh, Albert, do you have to leave us?" He looked up at her and said, "Yes Mama, and Johnny too." Johnnie was not yet sick at that time, yet in five days both children were gone.[69]

Three years later, Maggie buried a stillborn child, her second stillborn in ten years. When she gave birth to a two-pound baby in 1894, it was so tiny, a silver dollar could cover her eyes, nose, and mouth and a ring could fit on her arm. But this child, Mary Augusta, was Maggie's only child to survive to adulthood.[70] Discussing the nineteenth century's high rate of infant mortality, some have suggested that the commonness of it made it easier to bear. I doubt this. A sepia-toned photograph of Maggie Brown, her lips pursed and her eyes vacant, is epitaph enough for her children's graves.[71]

Losing one child was enough sorrow for me. Six months after our one-year-old was diagnosed with leukemia, our hematologist told us the last medicine was not helping. I told Dr. Shore, "Let me take Michael home. Don't give him another shot, another bone marrow test, don't poke him for blood samples or tie him down for transfusions. Just let me hold him and rock him. Let him go in peace surrounded by love."

Michael grew weaker each day and slept more. His skin paled till it had the appearance of parchment, clear, flawless, almost translucent. Knowing my baby was dying meant rocking him to sleep, watching his eyes close, knowing that soon they would close for the last time. I would wind up his small musical dog and listen to "Lullaby and Goodnight" until it slowed to silence. I wondered what my baby felt when he looked at me with his pale blue eyes, perhaps questioning why I held him so tightly, why I cried, and why he felt so very tired. I treasured his efforts to patty-cake for me, wanting to remember just how he touched his palms together, stretching his small fingers. I told people I was doing fine. I made efforts to fill every hour so I did not have to think. In the middle of that long week, one night while Michael slept, I got out of bed and sewed a wool skirt for my four-year-old daughter. The up and down movement of the sewing machine's needle, the straightness of the stitches on the fabric, seam after seam, were a way to return to the kind of predictability that I needed.

Facing death, an adult has a philosophy or religion and some means of coping. But how is it for a baby who has had so little of life? Some might say it is easier because he does not anticipate anything. But how do we know what goes on in a baby's mind, what he feels, what he senses, what he knows? On my child's last day, I sat in the yard with him and said, "Look at the world. See the grass, see the butterfly. Feel the soft wind on your face; enjoy the warm sunshine. Look around so you won't forget." That evening, Michael started whimpering. I held him tightly to my chest and swayed my body to calm him. He started to breathe heavily and I prayed for God to let him go peacefully. I laid him on his stomach in his crib and patted his back. He took a few shallow breaths, turned his head to one side, gave two sighs, and lay still.

At the Winter Quarters Cemetery, standing before Avard Fairbanks's statue of a mother and father grieving as they bury a child connected Neal and me to the other parents who had wept at a child's death. We talked about Michael's funeral, trying to control our voices. Our words were few because our feelings were tender.

"Do you remember how Michael looked in that small casket?" my husband asked as he put his arm around my shoulder.

"Of course. I'll never forget. He seemed to be peacefully sleeping."

"His skin had paled so much with the leukemia, but he had color again."

"I remember when I touched his hand, I missed the warmth and the way he liked to rest his head on my shoulder and the feel of my cheek against his silky hair."

Neal pulled me closer, his arm tightening around my shoulder, and asked, "Do you remember what I said when we stood by Michael's casket?"

"Of course," my voice catching as I struggled to continue, "you said that Michael should be on his tummy with his little thumb in his mouth."

Holding hands, we left the cemetery. Glancing back at the quiet scene, I thought about the sobs that must have broken the silence a century and a half earlier as Mormon emigrants buried their children.

Later, as I continued to study pioneer women, I discovered that more than one-third of the Winter Quarters deaths recorded were of children under the age of two.[72] Considering the terrible living conditions, one wonders why the child death rate was not even higher than it was. One woman, whose husband died while marching with the Mormon Battalion, wrote of her difficulties:

Winter found me bed-ridden destitute, in a wretched hovel which was built upon a hillside; the season was one of constant rain; the situation of the hovel and its openness, gave free access to piercing winds and water flowed over the dirt floor, converting it into mud two or three inches deep; no wood but what my little ones picked up around the fences, so green it filled the room with smoke; the rain dropping and wetting the bed which I was powerless to leave.[73]

Lucy Meserve Smith, a plural wife of Apostle George A. Smith, described the desperate situation in which she lived:

We moved down to Winter Quarters when my babe was two weeks old. There we lived in a cloth tent until December, then we moved into a log cabin, ten feet square with a sod roof, chimney and only the soft ground for a floor and poor worn cattle beef and corn cracked on a hand mill for our food. Here I got scurvy, not having any vegetables to eat. I got so low I had to wean my baby and he had to be fed on that coarse cracked corn bread when he was only five months old. We had no milk for a while till we could send to the herd and then he did very well till I got better. My husband [would take] me in his arms and [hold] me till my bed was made every day for nine weeks. I could not move an inch. Then on the 9th of February I was 30 years old. I had nothing to eat but a little corn meal gruel. I told the folks I would remember my birthday dinner when I was 30 years old.[74]

Lucy not only had to deal with her own sickness,

but also with the sounds of her baby's crying: *My dear baby used to cry till it seemed as tho I would jump off my bed when it came night. I would get so nervous, but I could not even speak to him. I was so helpless I could not move myself in bed or speak out loud.*[75]

After recovery, Lucy still faced problems:

When I got better I had not a morsel in the house I could eat, as my mouth was so sore. … Then my companion would take a plate and go around among the neighbors and find some one cooking maybe a calf's pluck. He would beg a bit to keep me from starving. I would taste it and then I would say oh do feed my baby. My appetite would leave me when I would think of my dear child. My stomach was hardening from the want of food.[76]

Despite giving up food for her baby, she eventually lost her child to illness: *The next July my darling boy took sick and on the 22nd, the same day that his father and Orson Pratt came into the valley of the great Salt lake[,] my only child died. I felt so overcome in my feelings. I was afraid I would lose my mind, as I had not fully recovered from my sickness the previous winter.*[77]

Like many women, both pioneer and contemporary, these women depended on their belief in God to sustain them through the "winter quarters" of life.

8.

Platte River Road

Our journey from Winter Quarters to our next stop, Grand Island, Nebraska, took us along the Platte River, described by pioneers as "too thick to drink and too thin to plow." I thought of the thousands of emigrants for whom the Platte River Road was their highway to the West. The Stuhr Museum of the Prairie Pioneer in Grand Island devotes acres to recreating a typical pioneer settlement. One large area we visited contained a life-sized replica of a covered wagon and section of trail. In the sandy dirt which wound along two walls, possessions were scattered— a heavy black trunk, an ornate Victorian chest of drawers, an oak side chair, a treadle sewing machine— as reminders of the flotsam that littered the trails when oxen were unable to continue to pull their heavy loads. Discarded items were sometimes selfishly de-stroyed and sometimes left for the taking, but few travelers had room to scavenge.

When I was a child, we moved fifteen times in sixteen years, often selling or "giving away," as my mother called it, our possessions. We hunted for cardboard boxes behind grocery stores and wrapped things in newspaper that could be taken. For some reason, out of all the items we packed, what I remember most is tucking some protective paper around a small ceramic goose my mother keeps now in a curio cabinet. Of all the things left behind, I remember a white pine bedroom set and my mother weeping when it was sold, as well as tears years after when she remembered the incident.

Now whenever I try to discard things, even outgrown clothes or old dishes, I hesitate. It is as if the

THE PIONEERS.

losses of childhood days and my mother's hurt come back, making the giving away a betrayal of maternal loyalty. I feel that without my possessions, I have no self. Our house is filled with physical memories of travels—a conch shell from the beach at Acapulco, wooden statues of Don Quixote and Sancho from Madrid, a four-season silk screen from Tokyo, and on and on. Family memorabilia are displayed in cases. We have my grandmother's wedding dishes, my father's golf trophies, my mother-in-law's salt shaker collection. With rooms so full of things that they almost crowd out the potential for growth, I sometimes, in desperation, imagine being free of anything that requires arranging and dusting and protecting.

Then I think about Margaret Dalglish, an immigrant Scotswoman, who put her meager possessions in a handcart in 1856 and walked to Utah, unfortunately joining the immigrants under Captain James Willie.

An illustration of "Mormon Pioneers Crossing the Great Plains" from T. B. H. Stenhouse's 1873 *Rocky Mountain Saints.* As William Mulder has written, the trail "presented an amazing litter of dead animals, strewn wagon parts, clothing, and equipment, the shambles left by gold seekers. ... Emigrants who could not bear to see such waste overloaded their wagons each day with their finds ... only to be forced to abandon them all again before nightfall."[78] *Photograph courtesy of LDS Archives*

After leaving Iowa City in late July, the company was caught in Wyoming's early October snows. Her stomach as empty of sustenance as her cart, Margaret watched an immigrant girl in the flickering firelight die in the act of raising a cracker to her mouth.[79] A day later she saw eighteen of her companions buried together in the snow. Margaret reached Emigration Canyon, stoically pulling her pitiful handful of possessions, then tugged the cart to the side of the road and pushed it over the edge, watching it fall, tumble, crashing and finally bursting apart. She walked into the City of the Saints empty handed, with nothing but her own strong body to define herself.[80]

I envy her freedom at that moment when she decided she would no longer be defined by what she owned. When women visitors to log cabins say "How did they keep house with so little?" I want to respond with "How do we keep house with so much?" But I don't. I remember a mountain weekend, and memories of a possessionless place dance through my mind like dust ghosts stirred by a feather duster.

↝

I'm sitting on a cabin porch at Fish Lake, noticing the pleasant smell the cedar boards emit, like a rare far-eastern perfume. The rails, in the early morning sunlight, cast long shadows that angle across wood grains.

The nearby brook babbles soothingly and the sun touches my face with warmth. A chain lies curled on the deck like a thin, steel python—perhaps more dangerous because of its subtlety. To me it symbolizes the restraints which limit my communion with nature: staying in Richfield linked to house and job, sleeping in and arising to confusion rather than quiet, repetitively taking care of things and more things, continuously putting doing ahead of feeling.

A brown-gray mirage silhouetted by morning sun rays bounds lightly over the dew-laden grass. It is a squirrel threading its way between the sparkles suspended on slender blades of grass. It mounts the steps, leaping in jerks like a wind-up toy, its nose quivering like that of a high school biology teacher who comes to mind—the brunt of much teenaged imitation. The squirrel's black eyes are intent on discovering a morning meal as it shifts and darts about our cedar porch. Sighting the woodpile, the squirrel mounts it in an easy leap; but finding wood chips unpalatable, it jumps down and nibbles at the steel chain used to confine a dog yesterday. Leaping back to the woodpile and then to the porch railing, the animal curls its tail over its back, then motionless and attentive faces east like a devout sun worshiper in morning prayer. After another furtive exploration of the deck, including clicking its claws on the aluminum chairs, the squirrel leaves, leaping downward from step to step in mechanized jumps, gone to search for food in a more bounteous place.

The white sun, squint bright, rises high in the sky, creating a diamond-shaped reflection in the water, a map-wedge pointing the sun's westward path for the day. As if imitating the V of the ever-climbing sun, boats make their own Vs, gray-blue against the darker slate blue of the rippling water. They head for the far shore, which looks as pristine as a nineteenth-century Winslow Homer landscape; however, these present-day boatmen are accompanied by the purr of modern motors rather than the dip and splash of oars used by past boatmen who, like their oars, are long since silent.

Humans have always longed for other habitations, ever intrigued by water and air. I too am intrigued as I watch white gulls dip in ballet-like grace above the rippling liquid of Fish Lake. Another bird, framed between two porch rails, stands motionless like an Audubon illustration. I wish it bore a label or that I had knowledge enough to call it something other than the generic *bird*. It flicks its tail and moves a quarter turn like a model seeking to show just the right angle to an intent artist. I think about Emily Dickinson's poem "A Bird Came down the Walk" and understand how she found the world in simple observations.

The murmur of the nearby water draws my attention. Yesterday, the stream's call was answered by the children who lined its banks and leaped from rock to rock. I like to see rocks in a stream because they represent resistance in the face of pressure to change. As the water surges by with its myriad messages, the rocks stand firm, unmoved—their vantage point of being above the rush, rather than within, lending them their strength. Their firmness gives refuge to leaping children, and adults as well, seeking new places.

Two life preservers rest in a corner of the porch beside fishing poles, their work done for a while. These few days at Fish Lake have been a life preserver for me, nurturing the core within that wants to stand with little children and pitch a hundred rocks into the lake with no hurry to complete the task and no quota to pitch more and no stigma for pitching less; with time to walk between rows of quaking aspen and pause to hear birds trill in various tones, pitches, and patterns; with time to listen to the rain beat a message on a shingled roof or release the pungent smell of sage from brush; with time to listen to the musical note changes as a stream eddies around rocks and over stones; to really see green in the quiver of aspen leaves, in the dark splendor of pine needles, in the fragile tentativeness of long grasses.

At Fish Lake, I own everything because I own nothing. The rented cabin, deliciously bare of things I own, allows me time from taking care. Nature, public property, asks no effort on my part but to enjoy and not to sully. This being Sunday, I'll go to the religious service at the lodge, but I've already heard my sermon and already said my prayer of thanksgiving.

9.

Sod House

*I*n the outdoor section of the Stuhr Museum, a replica of a sod house rises literally out of the ground. Pioneers used the strength of several yoke of oxen to pull a special grasshopper plow or sod cutter to slice strips of sod from the earth and then, with a sharp spade, chop the strips into blocks. Each block weighed about fifty pounds and was generally one foot wide, two feet long, and four inches thick. The sod bricks were hauled in a wagon to the building site, which had been prepared by clearing the grass and packing the soil down hard to make an earthen floor, and stacked one layer at a time around the perimeter of the site. No mortar or nails were used.[81]

Pioneer settlers built earthen houses, each block of sod weighing about fifty pounds—one foot wide, two feet long, and four inches thick. Isadore Haumont, a Belgian emigrant, erected an elegant two-story sod house, nineteen feet tall. *Photograph by Solomon D. Butcher, courtesy of Nebraska State Historical Society Photograph Collections, nbhips 10735*

Solomon Butcher's revealing photographs of Nebraska's prairie families show settlers standing or seated before such sod houses. One photograph shows the Sylvester Rawding family arranged before a house built into a hillside, a cow grazing on its grass-covered roof.[82] In another photograph, the outline of a turkey has been etched onto the roof, perhaps portraying the family's Thanksgiving wish.[83] Some structures seem to be just holes in hillsides, their fronts a façade of "Nebraska brick," as Solomon Butcher described the material used on the dugout he built in 1880.[84] In another picture, a family by the name of Hilton shows their "refinement" by the placement of a pump organ in their yard along with wagons, stock, and other signs of success. Mrs. Hilton had the items arranged in front of the house so her friends back east would not see the condition of her dwelling.[85] Other sod houses were sources of pride. Isadore Haumont, a Belgian immigrant, erected an elegant "two story sod castle which stood nineteen feet at the eves. ... The total construction cost for the house was five hundred dollars."[86] In another Butcher photograph, a black family, the Shores, are shown in front of their modest sod home.[87]

Standing in front of the museum replica, I close my eyes to imagine what the interior of such a house might have looked like in pioneer times. A rag rug might have covered the hard-packed dirt floor, maybe encircling a bed with spooled posters of polished wood grain. "Springs" of tied rope would have supported a striped straw tick, covered with a quilt. I add more details to my mental picture: a wedding-ring quilt with minute stitches piecing together fabric saved from a hundred sources; a chamber pot discretely peeking out from under the bed; a worn wooden table in the center of the room, two chairs flanking it. In my mind, a pot-bellied stove occupies one corner, a kettle mounted on its coal-blackened surface. A fry pan, a few bread pans, two pottery plates, and some flatware crowd a small shelf above the stove. A wooden trunk, augmented by two wall pegs, holds linen and clothing. On an oak dresser, a pitcher and basin rest on a crocheted doily. A razor strop hangs on the wall and a shaving mug rests on the shelf above the dresser.

I think about those bearded and moustached pioneer men in the Butcher pictures. Somewhere in a museum, I saw a moustache cup with a restraining bar inside to keep the hair out of the liquid. I next recalled the silver, communal sacrament cup displayed in a keepsake cupboard at home. It passed from hand to hand in Utah's Torrey Ward for decades until someone retired it as too unsanitary to use. I remembered my mother's story of a similar cup passed from person to person and pew to pew in the Mayfield Ward of her childhood. During the ritual, she would surreptitiously raise her eyes from their proper prayer-like position and glance down the row searching for moustached men, memorizing the position of their lips on the cup's edge. Finally grasping the silver handles herself, she would rotate the cup to a place untouched by those bristles.

I think about pioneer women watching their bearded or moustached husbands hitch their trousers over a poster and climb into bed, moving close under the crisp neatness of carefully stitched quilts, the husbands' facial hair tickling the cheeks of wives. I know that many nineteenth-century men were unshaven, from the photographs, which convinces me that I could not have been happily married in those days.

When my husband had back surgery, he didn't

shave for a week. Returning home from the hospital, he was still "under the weather" and not up to recommencing shaving. He seemed to be under the illusion that his lengthening gray beard made him look like Sean Connery. His winks and sly looks as I'd straighten his bed sheets were clues that he was becoming convinced of his metamorphosis.

I informed him that, although his beard gave him a Hollywood look, he resembled Gabby Hayes, not Sean Connery. His first reaction was disbelief at my blindness. He shaved off the beard but kept the moustache out of obstinance.

As he recovered and resumed his public life, one of my friends commented, "Neal looks handsome in a moustache."

I replied, "It might be nice to look at, but ever tried to kiss a scrub brush?"

One post-recovery day, Neal was squinting at a pair of socks, trying to determine if they were brown or black. "Can you tell me what color these are?" he asked.

I said, "Only if you kiss the back of my neck."

He said, "Only if you kiss me on the lips." We compromised; he brushed his moustache across my cheek and I told him the socks were black.

Inspired by my husband, I decided I needed a new look, too. No, not a moustache! I wanted a new hairdo, inspired by watching a film studio make-up artist preparing a woman in the ladies room of the Harold B. Lee Library. They were filming a short back-to-the-fifties piece. As I passed by, the make-up artist said, "Hey, could you be in our film? Your hair is perfect for the period."

I declined the offer and felt crushed to appear so out of date, at least in the eyes of young people. I decided to let my hair grow. When a daughter said, "How long are you going to grow it?" I said: "Do you think Crystal Gayle is too extreme? It would look nice alongside your dad's Willie Nelson style, don't you think?" Neal soon shaved off the moustache and I cut my hair, deciding that particular aspect of pioneer attraction was not for us.

As we left the sod house and walked toward our van, I patted my husband's smooth cheek.

"Why did you do that?"

"Just 'cause."

"'Cause why?"

"Because I love you."

"What brought that on?"

"I love a clean-shaven man."

Neal laughed and put his arm around my shoulder. "I like a clean-shaven woman, too."

10.

Earth Lodge

The Stuhr Museum in Grand Island, Nebraska, includes a reconstructed Pawnee Indian lodge as part of its exhibit. It is a dome-shaped, earth-covered structure thirty-eight feet in diameter that could house up to fifty people. In traditional Pawnee style, sleeping areas are located all around the interior perimeter, and a fire area in the center is surrounded by flat rocks. In this traditional dwelling, a hole above allowed for the escape of smoke and served as a skylight. A covered entrance leads into the structure. Originally, the door would have been made of buffalo rawhide stretched over a willow frame that swung inward and could be secured at night. Inside the lodge, one can imagine the people cooking, talking, making and repairing clothing, or fashioning implements, the room arrangement affording close and communal relationships. In the early 1800s, the Pawnee "were living in two to six principal towns. The towns ranged in size from 40-200 earth lodges," and until 1876, the Pawnee "were the most influential and populous of the native peoples of Nebraska."[89]

Construction of an earthen lodge began with ten to fifteen posts about six feet long, set in the ground ten feet apart. Beams were placed on the posts, then taller

"The Mormons were usually on good terms with the Indians. Their Winter Quarters were built on Indian lands. One of the tribes living in eastern Nebraska along the Platte and Loup rivers was the Pawnee. [William Henry] Jackson took this photo of the Pawnee camp on the Loup River. Many emigrants mentioned seeing and visiting abandoned Pawnee camps. In 1847 Patty Sessions wrote in her diary 'we pass the Pawnee village to day[;] it has been burnt by the Sues [Sioux].'"[88] —William Hill. *Photograph courtesy of National Anthropological Archives, Smithsonian Institution, no. 1249* posts, eleven to sixteen feet in height, were added at the circle's center. Willow branches, grass, and earth were placed in layers over the framework.[90] I assume that these earth-lodge construction techniques provided inspiration for white settlers to use naturally available materials and build their houses out of sod.

The inclusion of an earth lodge as part of the Stuhr Museum of the Prairie Pioneer is fitting because the westward expansion and settlement meant resettlement for Native Americans. As white settlers occupied more and more land, Indians were forced to leave, not only their tribal territories, but also their traditional way of life. I can imagine the profound sense of disorientation this produced. "The population of the Pawnee in the 1780s was estimated at 10,000. In the 1840s, with the opening of a trail through their country, European diseases, alcohol, and war with other tribes, their numbers were reduced to 4,500." Their people died, not only physically, but spiritually as "the influx of white missionaries contributed to the gradual abandonment of their ancient customs and religious ceremonies. In 1970, the number of Pawnee was just under 2,000 with most of them located in Pawnee County, Oklahoma."[91] The American government claimed the right to change everything that had defined meaningful life for these Native Americans.

One instrument for change, the infamous boarding schools, was fueled by the belief that a white education would "civilize" native children and improve their potential for productivity and success. Much has been written about the negative impact of what many consider to have been misguided attempts to re-acculturate Indian children. Were boarding schools good or bad for the children? What do public writings tell us? What do private memories reveal? Again, the question of perception is crucial.

During my twenty-five years of teaching high school English, I had the opportunity to know Native American students, mostly Navajo, who resided in a modern boarding school in Richfield. They lived at a residential hall and attended classes at either Richfield or South Sevier High. In teaching them, I came to learn something about their point of view and occasionally wondered why I was trying to teach the poetic structure of a sonnet to young people who had grown up with the poetry of their tribe's chants. I'm sure that some of the Indian students wondered this as well. In 1981 after attending a summer seminar at the University of Arizona in Tucson, I developed a unit called "Heritage and Self-Identity: A Study of Native American Literature." I included poetry by writers such as Nia Francisco, a full-blooded Diné-Navajo, and Paula

Gunn Allen, a Laguna Pueblo, to validate Indian culture, not only for my Native American students, but also for my white students. Discussions were designed to probe meaning, to find differences and commonalities, and to promote understanding.

Over the years we learned to feel comfortable with one another's cultures, even laugh at times, such as when I asked one of my Navajo students if he ever played cowboys and Indians. He responded yes, but that the cowboys were always the bad guys. As I taught hundreds of Indian students over the course of a quarter decade, I was pleased to see the inclusion in the standard American literature anthologies examples of Native American writings, from the "Navajo Origin Legend" and the "Iroquois Constitution" to contemporary stories by N. Scott Momaday, a Kiowa Indian. White students learned the important contributions of native culture to America without the need for me to devise a separate unit on Indian literature. Often I asked Indian students to teach native literature to the class to draw on their understanding, learned from within their culture, to help white students appreciate their perspective.

My students also benefitted from discussions of books like *Me and Mine,* introduced to me at the Tucson seminar. The book is about a Hopi woman and is subtitled *The Life Story of Helen Sekaquaptewa as Told to Louise Udall.* It was useful in generating provocative discussions about culture.

The book's inception was in Phoenix, Arizona, where Helen lived while her children attended high school and college. She developed a friendship with Louise Udall as once each week the women rode together to the Maricopa Indian Reservation southwest of Phoenix. The two would spend the afternoon there holding Mormon Relief Society meetings. They visited as they traveled, and as Helen explains in their collaboration: "I am talking. She is writing."[92]

In a chapter titled "To School at Keams Canyon," Helen, who was born at the turn of the century, shares her boarding school experience:

> Very early one morning toward the end of October 1906, we awoke to find our camp surrounded by troops who had come during the night from Keams Canyon ... The children would have to go to school. ... All children of school age were lined up to be registered and taken away to school. Eighty-two children, including myself, were listed. ...
>
> There were not enough wagons so the bigger boys had to walk. We were taken to the schoolhouse in New Oraibi, with military escort. We slept on the floor of the dining room that night.
>
> The next morning three more wagons were hired. ...

In each wagon the older boys and girls looked after the little ones. I was one of the little ones. One little boy was about five years old. They let him live in the dormitory with the big girls so they could mother him. Everyone called him "Baby," and he was still called "Baby" when he was a grown man.

It was after dark when we reached the Keams Canyon boarding school and were unloaded and taken into the big dormitory, lighted with electricity. I had never seen so much light at night. I was all mixed up and I thought it was daytime because it was so light. Pretty soon they gave us hardtack and syrup to eat. There were not enough beds, so they put mattresses on the floor. When I was lying down, I looked up and saw where the light came from just before the matron turned out the lights.

For the next few days we were all curious about our new surroundings. We thought it was wonderful and didn't think much about home, but after a while, when we got used to the school, we got real homesick. Three little girls slept in a double bed. Evenings we would gather in a corner and cry softly so the matron would not hear and scold or spank us. I would try to be a comforter, but in a little while I would be crying too. I can still hear the plaintive little voices saying, "I want to go home. I want my mother." We didn't understand a word of English and didn't know what to say or do.

Our native clothing was taken away from us and kept in boxes until our people came to take them. We were issued regular school clothes. Each girl had two every-day dresses, three petticoats, two pairs of underwear, two pairs of stockings, one pair of shoes, one Sunday dress, and two white muslin aprons to be worn over the dresses, except on Sunday. The dresses were of striped bed ticking, with gathered skirts and long sleeves. ...

Boys and girls marched to the dining room from their separate dormitories. Usually the bigger boys got there first. Meals were served on twelve long tables, family style. There were Navajos there, even though it was a school for Hopis. ...

For breakfast we had oatmeal mush without milk or sugar, and plain bread. ... At noon it was beef, potatoes, and gravy, with prunes or bread pudding for dessert. At night we had the leftovers, sometimes served with beans. ... Day after day the food had a sameness. How we longed for some food cooked by our mothers—the kind and quantity we were used to eating. ...

When you were sick, the matron put you to bed in the dormitory. She was sympathetic and tried to comfort you. She brought your meals on a tray, and there was enough food. The trouble was when you were sick you didn't feel like eating. ...

The months passed by, and then it was the last day of school that first year at Keams Canyon. Parents in wagons, on horseback and burros, converged on the campgrounds around the school, from all directions. They had come to take their children home for the summer. [My parents and some others] would not promise to bring us back to school in September, so I was left to spend the summer at the school along with other boys and girls of Hostile [a group of Hopis opposed to boarding schools] parentage. ...

Come September, 1907, all the other children were brought back to school by their parents. And we were back in the regular routine again. ...

As soon as they could, which was a year after we were taken away to Keams Canyon, some of the mothers came to visit their children. They came in a burro caravan of eight to ten. If one did not own a burro she would borrow or hire one on which she packed blankets and food for herself and as much as she could load on of piki, parched corn, dried peaches, and the like to give to her children. Mothers who couldn't make the trip would send bundles to their children. ...

I had never had my hair braided or tied before I went to Keams Canyon to school. ... Certain bigger girls were detailed to come and braid the hair of the little girls. ...

I was really serious at school, even from the beginning, but some of the teachers were unkind to me. Once when I gave the wrong answer, the teacher boxed me real hard on the ear. I had an earache after that, every night for a long time, and I can't hear very well out of that ear. If they had boxed somewhere else it wouldn't have been so bad.

Every Saturday morning the little girls had to go outside the dormitory and stay out while the big girls cleaned the rooms, no matter how cold it was. The ground was often covered with snow, and it seemed like my feet would never get warm.

Every Saturday afternoon it was hair washing time. At the sound of the bell all the little girls went to the wash room where a matron would be in charge. We lined up—seems like that was the first English we learned, "Get in line, get in line," all the time we had to get in line. First, the delousing treatment. You dipped your fingers in bowls of kerosene, provided by the government, and applied it to hair and scalp. Next we lined up, and each had a fine-tooth comb run through her hair. If it came out clean, you could shampoo and go out and play, but if the comb showed "nits," the word was [to] "go to the buggy bench."

On the long bench we sat. More kerosene was applied, fine-tooth combs were passed out, and the girls combed each other's hair or just picked nits from the strands of hair. It seemed like we just had to sit there all afternoon when we wanted to go out and play. After a while the matron would inspect again and some would be given a clean pass, and a bar of yellow laundry soap with which to wash the hair. It washed the kerosene out all right and helped to keep the lice away. ...

Most of our teachers were women. There was a certain teacher, a man, who when the class came up to "read," always called one of the girls to stand by him at the desk and look on the book with him while the others took their turns at reading, down the line. He would put his arms around and fondle this girl, sometimes taking her on his lap. Some of the girls seemed to like it. They laughed, and neither teacher nor pupil paid any attention [to] the reading.

I was scared that I would be the one next called to his desk. Finally I was. He called, "Helen, come to the desk while we read." When I got there, Mr. M put his arm around me and rubbed my arm all the way down. He rubbed his face against mine. When he put his strong whiskers on my face, I screamed and screamed and didn't stop until he let me go. I knew he was embarrassed. I ran out of the room before he could catch me, and to the dormitory.

They didn't punish me. When they saw me, they knew I was really scared. I didn't go back to school that day and they didn't force me. The other girls said his face was red all the rest of the day. ...

One, two, three, and four years passed by, and each spring we girls from Hotevilla saw the children from the other villages go home with their parents for the summer, while we were kept at school.

Helen explains how the fathers were given permission to take their children home in June of 1910 for two weeks "with the understanding that our parents would bring us back when school started on September first." She continues:

We made quite a caravan, about fifty boys and girls, each riding a burro, with the fathers walking beside us, all happy to be going home. It was a long day's jour-ney. ... When September came in 1910, our fathers did not take us back to Keams Canyon to school. I spent a year at home and enjoyed the old life, learning from my mother the things a Hopi girl should know. ...

In the chapter titled "Back to School," Helen writes: "The following September (1911) the children from Hotevilla were gathered up by soldiers and again loaded into wagons and taken back to school." She remained a student until she completed the sixth grade and described herself as a good student who learned quickly. After Keams, she attended the Phoenix Indian School, continuing her education. Her autobiography implies that her boarding school experiences, though difficult in some ways, allowed her to function in two worlds, resulting in her being able to make life choices with more freedom.

Boarding school experience became a part of life for generations of Indian students, as poignantly told in an essay written by a Navajo girl attending Richfield High School in the 1980s. These were her memories and feelings about being placed in a Tuba City boarding school as a young child:

I was about seven or eight years old when the government officials came to my grandmother's hogan where my father and mother and my two little sisters stayed. "They have come to take you away to jail because you are not in school," my uncle would tease me. My grandmother would scold my uncle for teasing me that way, but he would always say mean things to me. Later I did not find out what the government people came for, but my mother got me two pairs of funny looking things; I found out later they were pants. She also bought me one thing that looked almost like the Navajo skirt I always wore, but it was much shorter. It came above my knees. This was a dress; it was also new to me.

My mother was sick and my father was always out somewhere branding cows or breaking wild horses, so he was hardly at home. My aunt and uncle came in their funny car, [something fairly new to us,] but this thing was a lot faster than a wagon. We always got to Tuba City in one day in that funny-looking thing, but in a wagon it took one and a half days to travel to Tuba City. [While we were preparing for the trip,] my moth-er did not talk to me; she just hurried back and forth to put what little I had into my aunt's car. I did not know where I was going, and I wanted to find out, so I kept asking her and asking her, but she would not tell me.

I was the oldest of all my sisters, and I was the first child my mother ever sent to school. I guess she was sad, that was why she would not speak to me, because I was going away to school.

When my aunt and uncle were ready to go, my mother told me to go with them. Thinking that she was coming too, I got in the car, but she did not get in, and my uncle hurried and shut the door. We took

off before I even realized my mother wasn't coming. I looked back towards where the hogan was and saw my mother standing there looking after us. She looked so alone. Right then, I felt a tight feeling in my throat and deep inside me. I felt like it was so heavy that it almost hurt. I wanted to tell my uncle to stop the car so I could go back to my mother. Somehow, I knew that my mother would not want me to do this thing I was [contemplating]. I felt she wanted me to go where my uncle was taking me, so I sat there and looked to where my mother was standing until she was out of sight and I couldn't see her anymore.

It seemed like it didn't take very long to get to Tuba City, and we went to this place I'd never noticed before in Tuba City. My aunt got out the suitcase, which looked to me like a pretty box at that time. She told me to get out and go in with her, so I did.

We walked on the stones that led all the way up to the door of a big building. I felt my stomach begin to do funny things like it does when I ride the big wheels at the Pow-wow. I thought she was taking me to the hospital. The inside looked like a hospital. I thought, "Why is she taking me in to see the funny man with hair on his mouth when I am not sick?" But she never answered, because I never asked. All these things I thought to myself, but I never said a word because it seemed like this place was a quiet place where nobody talks. It felt like it was as sacred as my grandfather's ceremonies.

I wanted to be a medicine woman and help the sick

people just like my grandfather, someday. I wanted to be a medicine woman because I used to think what if one day my grandfather and all the other medicine people get old and go away. What will happen to my people when there is no medicine man to sing over them. When they are sick, will they all die?

In the meanwhile, we went into this one room. There were boxes that almost reached the high ceiling. There were some little boxes inside where clothes and shoes stuck out. There was a lady in there doing something, and my aunt said something to the lady that I didn't understand.

The lady motioned to something that had four sticks poking up from the ground, and on top of it, it looked like somebody was sitting on the four sticks, but it didn't have a head. She told me to sit on the lap of the thing that was sitting there. Later, I learned to call this thing a chair. My aunt was finished talking, so she was leaving. I got up to leave with her, but she told me to stay and that she was going to come back for me in a little while. I just sat back down, and the lady started talking to me. I didn't understand what she was saying. It sounded like she was making funny noises, so I just sat there and listened to her funny noises. I only smiled when she smiled, but other than that I just sat there and stared at her. My mother had told me not to stare at people, but since she wasn't there, I thought I'd do a little. Sometimes I'd just sit there with my eyes shut tight so I wouldn't stare at this strange lady and her funny sounds.

I wished my aunt would hurry and come back. She had not returned and it was getting dark outside. I tried not to think about her, so I just sat there looking at the floor. Then I saw that box my mother gave to my aunt; it was still there on the floor. I thought my aunt must have forgotten to take it with her, so I hurried over and picked it up. I went back and sat down, and I put it on my lap so my aunt wouldn't forget it again when she came back for me.

After what seemed like another long time, this lady led me into another room where there were lots of girls, but none of them looked like my sisters. They were all running around in funny long white things. They all looked alike. When the lady took me into this room, all the girls gathered around to stare at me, and I thought their mothers must have never told them that staring was not nice. But since I had done it to the lady, I thought I'd let them do it.

It was dark outside now, and my aunt still hadn't come back to get me yet and by now everyone was asleep. Here they didn't sleep on sheepskins, but they slept on one of the things my cousin had in her home. She called it a "bed." But these were much different. There was one a little bit off the ground and there was another one on top of the bottom one.

My aunt never came back for me, but I didn't want to believe that she lied to me, so I sat almost all night waiting for her. Three ladies came in and tried to get me to go to bed, but I wouldn't. I [finally] had to go to bed after a long time.

Many, many days later I got to know everybody, and I learned my ABCs. Then I learned to like school. It was easy to understand the strange sounds.

Every Friday most of the girls would have their parents or relatives come and see them or take them home. I never had anybody come to see me. This was probably because my mother and father didn't have a car. Besides, nobody hardly ever went to see my grandmother's hogan far, far away. I wanted to hear someone say, "You have a visitor." But I did not hear that for a long time. Every time I saw someone talk to her mother, I would hurry and go somewhere so I would not think of my own mother and father. I just wanted to cry or run away to my aunt's home. But I stayed at school because I knew my mother and father wanted me to stay there and learn. One day when I got back from school, one of the dorm mothers gave me a bag of candy. And she showed me a pretty new dress someone had left for me. I asked her, "Who brought it?" But she didn't know, so I never found out who came to see me that day, and that made me all the more anxious to see my mother and father.

After school on Friday, we used to sit in the living room and the parents would come and take their children home. Every Friday I would look for my mother or father. Then at five o'clock we got sent to our wing to change from our school dresses to pants. We used to wear dresses to school all the time.

When we got back into the bedroom, I would just sit on my bed and feel so sad, but I never cried. One Saturday I was just sitting in my locker thinking when someone called my name and told me that someone was here to see me. At first I was so happy I just jumped up, but then I thought what if it's not [for] me, but [for] someone else. So, I just sat back in my locker. After a few minutes I heard my name called again so I slowly got up. I knew I couldn't bear it if it wasn't [for] me. This one girl hurried in and she was so excited for me. I asked her if it was really me that someone had come to see. I got all excited again and ran out of the bedroom into the bathroom to a short-cut into the hallway to where I was told that someone was waiting. I slowed down at the bathroom door and slowly walked out. I was just so happy inside, I don't know what I would have done if it had not been [for] me. I walked out into the hallway and looked up and down the hallway, and I didn't see anybody. Something sank inside me and I felt sad again. Just as I was about to start crying, someone poked a head around the door outside and I saw my father standing there. I wondered why he didn't come in, so I went outside, and he was holding the reins of a horse. I thought it was so great that he had ridden a horse all night and half a day just to come and see me. I could tell he was tired, but I didn't know what to do.

I must have been the happiest little girl in the world at that time. I wanted to cry and hug my father, but I didn't because I knew he would not want me to cry. I don't know what he would have thought of my hugging him. I was the happiest person in the whole wide world at that time.[93]

This essay was signed simply "Richfield Navajo Dorm Student." Perhaps its anonymity is fitting because her story is representative of the experience of so many students rather than just of her own. Her writing captures well the tension that exists between wanting to remain home, in this case in a traditional hogan, fearing change and yet knowing that her parents wanted her to be educated at a boarding school.

As I have watched the annual Native American assembly at Richfield High School, one of the best assemblies each year, I have seen in the performances of traditional dances, the beating of drums, the recitation of stories, the explanation of tradition, and introductions in the Navajo language a retention of cultural values. Yearly, as I watch Indian students receive their high school diplomas, often wearing the family's treasure of turquoise jewelry over their graduation gowns, I see a future of choices before them, the ability to work and live in two worlds. In the snapping of pictures by parents and other relatives, I sense familial pride in this opportunity to choose, to retain one's birth culture but not to be limited by it. Perhaps this is best explained in a narrative poem written in 1986 by one of my students, Nelda Dugi, given as a graduation address:

OTHER THAN GRINDING CORN

Time sure flies fast
I remember …
It was only yesterday,
I was starting in grade school,
My first day in a school unknown to me,
In a boarding school
Where I had never experienced life before.
It was sad and lonely when Momma left me
Behind in a strange place
[So I could] learn something very valuable …
Other than herding sheep,
Shearing and butchering them,
Other than grinding corn or weaving a rug,
Other than living my traditions
For the long life remaining,
Something too precious
Just to look at and yearn for later on.
We shed a few tears
And hesitated a moment.
I then waved goodbye to Momma.
The school year ahead of me seemed endless …
I remember …

I used to look forward to Fridays
And wait for Grandpa to arrive
When he did, I'd run home in the bitter wind
Or in the ice cold weather.
After two days with my parents,
I would go back to school
Packed in a pick-up like a sardine,
Keeping warm with whatever I found,
Not knowing someday I would be here ...
Trying to find a way
To repay my parents and grandparents ...
Now I remember ...
Why Momma left me standing there
In a strange place with nothing
But a packed suitcase in front of me.
It was for my own benefit,
To show Mom I was brave enough
And had enough courage
To take my first steps
Into what life was really about ...
But I didn't realize these things then.
I was too young and too stunned
To understand why Mom left me. ...

Wanting the best for me, she
Left me there to make my life easier,
Much easier than it was in her days,
By giving me the opportunity for an education ...
After Mom walked out the door,
I started little by little
To understand what education meant.
I started making my own decisions,
Making sure everything I did was what
Mom expected of me.
I started and finished everything
Very carefully and ambitiously,
Step by step ...
Reminding myself
That this is my life,
Not Mom's and not Dad's or anyone else's,
Only my own.
This is what my parents planned
And did for me yesterday.
That is why I am here today.
This is why there will be
Another goal achieved tomorrow.[94]

Have boarding schools been good or bad for
Native American children—or good for some and bad
for others? If Indian girls had remained in hogans or
earth lodges, what would Indian women be like today?

11.

Red Cloud

From Grand Island, we drove an hour across the flat landscape to reach Red Cloud, Nebraska. On the town's outskirts, I stood surrounded by prairie. The land seems to undulate in a sea of grass in all directions. The breeze gusts to a steady hum, billowing the fields. As pioneer women passed this way, the grass opened before and closed after their covered wagons. Standing on this prairie, thinking of their destination, they may have shaded their eyes to make out a point on the western horizon, then looked back, re-membering the places left behind: Pennsylvania, Virginia, New York. I wonder if eastern winds reminded them of shorter grass where women in sheer white dresses swept across green turfs.

Did these pioneer women feel trapped when the long prairie grass entangled their cotton skirts, whispering *stay with me?* Their skirts were like blowing brome grasses too, and the women themselves were forever reaching for and then receding from a cycle of indecision, their ties of family loyalty, material hope, or religious zeal rooting them to this or that stretch of earth.

Under the dome of sky, I watch the clouds elongate and fade to mist. A century and more ago, women and men spent a lifetime here in conversation with the earth. Pioneers spoke in wide swaths with scythes, lined syllables straight with plows, their sentences

Annie Sadilek at seventeen. Cather scholar Marilyn Arnold writes that "Ántonia represents the pioneer woman, the immigrant who comes to this country and becomes one with the land. She becomes a type as well as an individual, and that is part of myth making. De-myth-ified, Ántonia would be her real life model, Annie Sadilek, and would have lost much of her power to inspire." *Courtesy of Willa Cather Pioneer Memorial Foundation and Nebraska State Historical Society* falling into even rows. Their checkerboard paragraphs touched those of other immigrants who spoke other tongues but communicated the same basic message in furrowed lines. Individual voices, gleaned from letters and diaries, seem to speak from this earth below the fields.

As we continued toward Red Cloud, we left the open prairie behind. A signboard caught our attention with its picture of a black plow silhouetted against a red-orange sun, the visionary plow described in Willa Cather's *My Ántonia*:

> On some upland farm, a plough had been left standing in the field. The sun was sinking just behind it. Magnified across the distance by the horizontal light, it stood out against the sun, was exactly contained within the circle of the disk; the handles, the tongue, the share—black against the molten red. There it was, heroic in size, a picture writing on the sun.[95]

I thought about Cather's heroic-sized pioneer women, Ántonia of *My Ántonia* and Alexandra of *O Pioneers!* and how I admired them. That admiration was deepened through my acquaintance with Cather scholar Marilyn Arnold. My college-aged daughter, Kirsten, and I rode with Marilyn to the Cather International Seminar held in Red Cloud in the summer of 1993. There was hardly room for our luggage in the trunk as it was filled with boxes of three-by-five cards, thousands of them, the life work of a man named John March who had researched Willa Cather's allusions. Marilyn was compiling them into a book. As she explained, "I've devoted ten years of my life to it!" Through conversations with Marilyn on the trip, hearing her presentation at the seminar, and later through a class she taught on female authors, I learned what it means to love what you study and to sacrifice other goals in order to make a contribution to the literary world and enrich others. I think Annie Dillard used an apt metaphor when she said that

> writing a book is like rearing children—willpower has very little to do with it. If you have a little baby crying in the middle of the night, and if you depend only on willpower to get you out of bed to feed the baby, that baby will starve. You do it out of love. Willpower is a weak idea; love is strong. ... You go to the baby out of love for that particular baby. That's the same way you go to your desk. There's nothing freakish about it. Caring passionately about something isn't against nature, and it isn't against human nature. It's what we're here to do.[96]

Another thing I learned from Professor Arnold was the power of myth. A major goal of my study was to discover the private attitudes hidden behind public images, to *de-myth-ify* pioneer women. Even so, I didn't want to lose the heroic-sized portraits and their power to intrigue and inspire. Marilyn Arnold helped my understanding of myth in this way:

A lot of people think of myth as the opposite of truth, [but] ... there's another kind of definition. Myths actually are things that keep reoccurring in cultures. Wherever you have people, you have the myths they live by, ... enduring truths that repeat themselves, patterns of life and thought, stories ... that keep coming up and therefore take on a symbolic cast as they don't just apply in one situation, they apply in many. The myth of the earth mother, or the corn goddess, those kinds of things appear in cultures all over the world. These same kinds of figures, these same kinds of attitudes and practices appear in communities totally isolated from each other. Since they are basic to human experience, they help people shape a world. Because we all live in the same world, there are bound to be some things about human experience that we see regardless of where we are. ... These are the enduring myths. ... These universal truths are another kind of reality, a deeper sort of reality.[97]

Ántonia and Alexandra, in their mythic presentations, become this "deeper sort of reality." Marilyn Arnold says that Ántonia "represents the pioneer woman, the immigrant who comes to this country and becomes one with the land. She becomes a type as well

as an individual, and that is part of myth making."[98] Marilyn explains that de-myth-ified, Ántonia would be her real life model, Annie Sadilek, and would have lost much of her power to inspire.

Because of conversations with Marilyn, I have examined the myths and realities that have gone into defining womanhood, in the process coming to see the value and limitation of each. Heroic-sized pioneer women capture our attention, just as Cather's heroic-sized plow does, enlarging the meaning of Western settlement. I believe, as did Cather, that the plow can be guided by the firm grasp of a woman as well as by the strong grip of a man.

One summer I sanded our deck, all 300 square feet, with an electric sander. The wood had grown ugly through its accumulated coats of varnish. The work of restoration made me feel powerful, even more than staining the siding had the previous year. Maybe it was the feel of a machine in my hand, a man's machine. I liked having the gritty sawdust ground into the knees of my Levis, sweat stains on my tee shirt, the challenge of my husband's "You can't do that" as he recuperated from a broken foot. Each day a wider patch of smoothly grained redwood emerged from the murky boards, and I felt stronger.

Women homesteaders felt powerful because of

their independence and masculine labors. Glenda Riley gives examples in her book, *The Female Frontier*. One is of Myrtle Yoeman who, writing from South Dakota, said, "There are [so many] old maids out here holding claims that a person must wonder where they all come from."[99] One woman homesteader was Elizabeth Corey, nicknamed "Bachelor Bess." Her brother said she had "fended off many suitors" for "the freedom and happiness that she found living on the plains."[100] Edith Eudora Ammons Kohl, who homesteaded with her sister, believed that a woman had more independence in the West than in any other part of the world. "When she was told, 'The range is no place for clingin' vines 'cause their hain't nothin' to cling to,' she felt it a challenge."[101] The hardship of wresting a living from the stingy soil of the Great Plains was "more than compensated for by its unshackled freedom." She added, "There was a pleasant flow of possession in knowing that the land beneath our feet was ours."[102]

Cather's literary creations, Ántonia and Alexandra, are earth mothers of two types: one who raises children and one who raises crops, making them interesting models for women today who must choose between home and career. Ántonia is described in earth tones. She is golden brown with plum color in her cheeks. In childhood, she survives the poverty of immigrant life and the suicide of her father. In adulthood, she survives and even prospers through hard labor in the literal sense of the word, her fertility proven in her large family. Near the end of the novel, narrator Jim Burden, now middle-aged, returns to visit his childhood friend. He describes the profusion of life he sees emerging from Ántonia's fruit cellar: "We were standing outside talking, when they all came running up the steps together, big and little, tow heads and gold heads and brown, and flashing little naked legs; a veritable explosion of life out of the dark cave into the sunlight."[103] The scene's birthing symbolism glorifies motherhood. Despite the rigors of bearing and rearing so many children, Ántonia still "had that something which fires the imagination, could still stop one's breath for a moment by a look or gesture that somehow revealed the meaning in common things."[104]

In my early twenties, newly married and first aware of the term *earth mother* with its accompanying connotations, I was attracted by the possibility of becoming one. I wanted to be the all-patient, all-sacrificing mother who could have numerous children clambering around her and remain pleasantly unperturbed while they called for her attention. Though I had previously found pigs disgusting, I began to see mother pigs in a new light. A sow, a piglet at each teat, relaxes into complete contentment at her ability to give to all the piglets freely without diminishing her plentiful self. This was worthy of admiration, I thought. Dedicating myself to child rearing, I wanted to reap the rewards of my offspring's adoration, my husband's love, and society's approbation.

But in reality, it didn't work out that way. Trying to prepare dinner with a crying one-year-old hammerlocked around my leg, I silently lost my temper. Trying to talk long distance while a three-year-old, safely beyond the telephone cord's reach, finger-painted a wall with chocolate pudding made me livid. With time I was able to simultaneously nurse a newborn gurgling in contentment, play giddy-up horsey with a two-year-old latched to my ankle, and read to a four-year-old snuggled by my side. I loved and enjoyed my children and found meaning in common things like Ántonia did: through comforting a child's hurt, having a son show off his musical talent, bustling in the kitchen with an older daughter's help and insistence that I rest for a minute, or simply having a little one lay her head on my lap in affection. But sometimes my children were less charming and more common than Ántonia's: they sometimes appeared with runny noses and soiled trousers, and running up stairs, sometimes shoved and cried "I'm gonna be first." Some days I yearned for a world beyond Dr. Seuss and Mother Goose.

After one child, I started secondary education courses. After three, I student-taught. After bearing five children, I became a half-day teacher. I went full-time when my sixth was in elementary school. With only two children left at home, I began a master's degree program. In these ways, I pursued Alexandra's choice in O Pioneers! where she is entrusted with the family farm. This is the wish of her dying father who has noticed her sensitivity to the earth: "For the first time perhaps since that land emerged from the waters of geologic ages, a human face was set toward it with love and yearning."[105] Because of Alexandra's oneness with the land, she is able to foster miraculous growth; she senses in "her own body the joyous germination in the soil."[106] The crops become her children, replacing the babies she never bore, just as careers can replace or supplement families for many modern women. Sometimes I imagine what my life might have been with Alexandra as my sole role model. I imagine a door plaque at a major university reading "Dr. Judy Shell." Inside the room, a collection of my writings lines an oak shelf. I confer with a book company representative about the schedule for publishing my next book. In my wilder dreams, I answer the telephone and agree to an interview on Good Morning America.

It would have been a long shot, and it might have meant abandoning my Ántonia-choice, the "big and small, tow heads, and gold heads, and brown"; and in that sense, I'm glad it's not the choice I made.[107]

In *O Pioneers!* Alexandra attributes the success of her crops to the land rather than to herself: "It pretended to be poor because nobody knew how to work it right; and then, all at once, it worked itself."[108] Contrary to Alexandra's experience, my land has not "worked itself." Though teaching colleagues respect me and many students enjoy my classes, and sometimes I even receive awards, none of this is the result of miracles, just hours of extra effort balanced against the same extra hours and added effort my family has required and still requires. When people compliment me on my children's success, I think about what the cost has been—but I don't resent the expenditure. I am also aware of my children's setbacks, the prerequisites to any success. I like my combination of earth mother and earthly mother. I like my role in nurturing growth in the narrower world of family, and I like turning over fresh soil in the wider world of my career. I'm no longer perplexed by Willa Cather's heroic-sized Ántonias and Alexandras. On my good days, they give me something to emulate as an ideal, and on my bad days, they give me something to avoid as unreal.

12.

Pavelka Farmhouse

Not far from Red Cloud is Annie Sadilek Pavelka's farm home in which she and her husband and children lived. The home's white-painted exterior gleams in the Nebraska sun. A red barn stands nearby. In *My Ántonia,* Willa Cather used details from her adult visits to the Pavelka farm for her fictional Ántonia and her husband Anton Cuzak. The book's narrator, Jim Burden, says: "Set back on a swell of land at my right, I saw a wide farm-house, with a red barn and an ash grove, and cattle-yards in front that sloped down to the highroad."[109] He sees a plum thicket by the side of the road and notices two young boys there bending over a dead dog. They are Ántonia's sons, and after Jim introduces himself, they lead him to the barn by the windmill to tie up his team. Jim describes approaching the Cuzak house:

Ducks and geese ran quacking across my path. White cats were sunning themselves among yellow pumpkins on the porch steps. I looked through the wire screen into a big, light kitchen with a white floor. I saw a long table, rows of wooden chairs against the wall, and a shining range in one corner.[110]

After greeting Jim warmly and proudly introducing her children, Ántonia visits with her childhood friend, then shows him her well-stocked fruit cellar. Some of the children point out their mother's bottled fruit by tracing "on the glass with their finger-tips the outline of the cherries and strawberries and crabapples within, trying by a blissful expression of countenance to give me some idea of their deliciousness."[111] Jim and Ántonia exit the cellar, followed by the children, who come running up the steps, amazing in all their variety to the childless Jim Burden.

Ántonia's husband and oldest son are absent until the following afternoon, so during supper that evening, Ántonia sits at the head of the table filling plates and passing them to her children. Each older sibling takes responsibility for a younger one. After supper, the family goes to the parlor, one child remarking that they will get a parlor carpet if the wheat sells high. As there are not enough chairs, the younger children sit on the bare floor. Ántonia gets out a box of old photographs and she and Jim reminisce as the children look on. One son plays the violin, and a young daughter dances barefoot to the music.

The images are idyllic scenes of order, cleanliness, conservation, concern, pride, politeness, and family closeness. In the memoirs of Annie's and John's descendants, we read similar praise for two hard-working, caring people. Annie is particularly lauded for her cooking and quilting skills, as well as for other homemaking abilities. Yet, I wonder how Annie and John handled the crises of daily life when they were raising ten children in their house. Was every day as idyllic as the day described when Jim Burden visited Ántonia?

Probably not. To reduce fighting, Annie's daughter Antonette reports, the girls slept downstairs with their mother and the boys upstairs with their father. Besides the normal problems of children squabbling, there was the pressure of economic survival. John said "there were times when he wished he had never started to farm because the weather could ruin the whole planting with one giant hailstorm, or perhaps a drought would wreck havoc on them. Sometimes the grasshoppers were so thick that they shaded the sun. The grasshoppers could also ruin an entire crop in one day."[112]

In a letter to Willa Cather in 1936, Annie wrote, "If we could only raise some crops. The wind is blowing and we don't get rain, only some blizzards." Barry Turner explains:

In the same letter Annie was happy with a five dollar check from Cather. She said that she applied it to the purchase of a gas-powered washing machine, with a good wringer. She needed it badly because she said her old hand-run wash machine that she purchased second-hand, ten years ago, had worn out. She was currently using an old hand wash board. The children

In *My Ántonia*, narrator Jim Burden describes Ántonia's children coming out of her fruit cellar: "We were standing outside talking, when they all came running up the steps together, big and little, tow heads and gold heads and brown, and flashing little naked legs; a veritable explosion of life out of the dark cave into the sunlight." The passage's birthing symbolism glorifies motherhood. *Photograph by R. Bruhn, courtesy of R. Bruhn and Nebraska State Historical Society* did not like to see Annie using a hand washboard, since she had huge loads of washing and ironing to do daily. Annie exclaimed that she was working all the time, from early morn' till late at night, but still it seemed to get her nowhere.[113]

How did the Pavelka farmhouse look in the reality of daily existence? Probably like many farm dwellings housing large families today, clean but cluttered with the things of living: boots left on the back porch, clothes needing washing, pans to be scrubbed, beds to be made up, furniture to be dusted, and school books waiting to be read.

I have this recurring dream, or perhaps a night-mare, in which I return to my home of many years but find I don't belong there because other people now occupy it and have changed the way it looks inside. They are polite and yet convey to me a distinct sense that I don't fit in there anymore. I wonder if pioneer women returning to their "restored" homes would have the same sensation. Would the absence of winter laundry drying on lines stretched across the parlor, of coal dust scattered on the fireplace hearth, and of the pungent smell of baby soakers not yet washed and chamber pots not yet emptied be confusing to the returning pioneer wife?

In 1976 our home in Richfield was in the Junior Culture Club Home Show. This had a great fringe benefit because five hundred people toured my house thinking I was a perfect homemaker. It had a devas-tating effect in that I came down with Better Homes and Gardens Syndrome and wanted the house to look that way always. The jarring disparity between the ideal and the real still unnerves me.

I know that an entry hall sets the tone for a home, and mine was oriental to reflect our two years living in Japan. The flower arrangement attested to my fond-ness for *ikebana*, and the bubble gum stuck to the side of the vase attested to my children's indifference to it. The carefully raked sand garden in the entry was to inspire meditation, concentric rippled lines intended to promote the harmony of the soul, but the tennis shoe footprints trailing through the ripples interrupted my tranquility.

At the heart of the home is the kitchen, and it should reflect cleanliness and order. That is why I was bothered by the flour-dusted floor, victim of an attack of the cookie bakers; the Rorschach-style Kool Aid stains on the counter, a tribute to the business debut of Punch Stands, Inc.; and the assorted bees, beetles, and bugs freeze-drying in my fridge for a fifth-grade science project.

A refuge from the chaos inside was our back porch

deck, its redwood boards arranged in an artistic pattern to add to the beauty often notably diminished by numerous muddy paw prints from our poodle, which the children liked to take wading in irrigation ditches. I would arrange the deck chairs and lounges in conversational groupings, which the children would commandeer as battle fortifications until in exhaustion they collapsed into cocoon-like clumps for sleep-overs. On some mornings the sleeping bags still contained the un-metamorphosed bodies of neighborhood children when I went out to enjoy the tranquility.

Of course, a playroom is a must for a house of many children. The shelves were originally built for selected toys but were soon filled with treasured bits of wire, string, "genuine" Indian arrowheads, discarded bullet casings, and bird feathers. To navigate the room, I had to tiptoe precariously among blocks, wood chips, rocks, and tiny figures of a boy-made *Star Wars* world, as well as different sets of intermixed cards arranged in a follow-the-yellow-brick-road pattern.

Actually, this play-room paradise turned into a booby-trapped no-man's-land for vacuum cleaners. In ten years, I went through three of them: a Hoover, a Rainbow, and an Electrolux. The Hoover succumbed to strangulation by a jump rope. The Rainbow was asphyxiated by chemicals from a Junior Genius science kit. The Electrolux tried to digest one too many Tinkertoys and died of over-eating.

Sometimes in desperation, I wanted to live in Wonderland, to shrink Alice-like and slip quietly into the pages of *Better Homes and Gardens*, where life could be one eternal Home Show; but I was always pulled back by the laughter of bubble-gum chewers, cookie bakers, and Dorothy, going somewhere over the rainbow.

Given a choice, I wonder if Annie Pavelka—or any pioneer woman, for that matter—would have substituted the quiet sterility of a perfectly restored home for the noisy tumult of real life as they knew it, lived in the original structure. On the other hand, how many female visitors would linger in a restored home that mimicked the disorganized reality of their own houses?

13.

Ogallala

After leaving Red Cloud, my husband and I continued across Nebraska, stopping at Ogallala, a name as unintelligible as the feelings I experienced there. We camped in our van, and by ten o'clock it was rocking like a small boat in an ocean squall. I recalled pioneer stories of relentless prairie winds, gusting and dusting, until women went crazy at the unremitting sound of wind whistling down the chimney, scratching on the windows, squeaking around the doors, groaning through the walls, rasping along the roof to produce a relentless cacophony of misery.

Neal opened our van door, bracing it against the stiff wind. "I'm hungry. I think I'll get a hamburger. Do you want anything?"

"Don't leave me here," I pleaded, firmly clutching his arm. My anxiety was unnerving, so completely out of character for me.

Neal stared hard at my face. "You're acting crazy. See the café? You can see it from here. I'll just be gone a few minutes."

I tightened my grip on his arm. "I'm serious. Don't leave me here alone," I said, carefully emphasizing each word. "I don't know why I feel this way. Maybe it's the wind. I just don't know."

My husband drove us the half-block to the café. Encased in the van's warm security, I watched his tall

In Harvey Dunn's painting, *The Homesteader's Wife*, we see an earthy woman who, down from the wagon of Koerner's *Madonna of the Prairie,* takes her place in the fields. Notice how she tugs a recalcitrant ox and the taut rope crosses her dark skirt and crumples her white apron. She cannot escape the drudgery of survival, the premature aging in the prairie's summer heat and winter cold. Yet, in the crucible of her life, she exudes a kind of power. *Courtesy of South Dakota Memorial Art Center* figure through the plate glass windows, unsettled by my loss of confidence. Recalling pioneer diaries and memoirs I'd read, I tried to picture myself as a widow, my husband dead from exhaustion, cholera, ague, or accident, on a moonless night on the prairie after campfires and lanterns had been extinguished. Neal and I returned to our own campground. Just before sleep, I curled my smaller body into the comfortable S-pattern of my husband's larger one, natural after more than thirty years of bed-sharing.

In October of 1856, struggling toward the Rocky Mountains with the Martin Handcart Company, Elizabeth Kingsford had become alarmed when her husband was not able to "swallow his morsel of supper."[114] Wrapping him in blankets, she lay down nearby. In the night, reaching to embrace him to give her warmth, she realized that he was dead. She cried out, but no one answered. Dry-eyed, she lay till morning, arms around his stiffening body.[115]

I thought about another pioneer woman, a Norwegian, who took fifteen or twenty days to cross land we can cross easily in one day. In *Giants in the Earth*, Beret, a young wife immigrating in the 1870s, hears the sound of the parting grass day after day: "*Tish-ah ... tish-ah, tish-ah.* Never had it said anything else— never would it say anything else."[116] Arriving in the Dakota Territory, she told her husband, Per Hansa, "I'm so afraid out here! ... It's all so big and open ... so empty."[117] The presence of several Norwegian neighbors was not comforting to her. She wondered how anyone could live there with no place to hide. Even the sod house her husband built did not protect her. Beret stuffed the windows with family clothing, one garment after another, in an effort to create a sense of intimacy and coziness, her attempt to shut out the stretching emptiness.

Comforted by the warmth and confinement of our van, I pictured Beret gazing at an old Norwegian chest carted across the plains and crawling inside it with a quilt and pillow. When Per Hansa returns from a three-day supply trip, he finds her cradling their infant, curled up in the chest. Though coffin-like, the chest gives Beret security, forms a link with Norway, a tie to civilization that can keep her safe in some way. At the novel's end, Per Hansa, lost in a winter snowstorm, is frozen to death; his face is ashen and drawn, his eyes set toward the west. Since the story concludes here, Beret's response is hidden. Thinking about Beret's reaction to this final abandonment, I move closer to my husband, one arm resting on the smooth surface of Granny Pectol's quilt that half encircles his cocoon-like body.

How would I have reacted to losing my husband? I might have crawled into some narrow space, or maybe I would have become more determined to work the land with my children's help. Maybe I would have married a man I didn't love. Perhaps I would have lived with relatives and become a quasi-servant. I might have returned east, blotting out the prairie's loneliness. Tempered in the Western crucible, I might have decided to live alone, no longer fearful of the approaching prairie dark.

Considering my earlier anxiety when Neal wanted to leave the van to purchase food, I was grateful not to have faced the testing of my independence. I curled more tightly into my husband, wanting to completely touch him, my head resting against his back, my feet extra soles curled under his, and slept.

The next day Nebraska faded behind us as we entered Wyoming. Halfway across the state, we left the Platte River, which had been our companion for several days. The river is shallow and dotted with small islands as it winds its way across Nebraska into Wyoming. Pioneer women by the thousands walked the roads that lined its north and south banks as they immigrated west more than a century ago. They drank the Platte's water, used it to bathe perspiration and trail dust from their weary bodies. They washed their clothes and hung them to dry on the river's banks. I tried to visualize the women's faces, but this was difficult because art had stylized pioneer women so much that caricatures were ingrained in my mind.

I kept seeing Koerner's *Madonna of the Prairie,* painted in 1921.[118] His pioneer subject personified the myth of the frontierswoman, the gentle follower who faithfully journeyed west. The doe eyes of Koerner's madonna suggest timidity, as her heart-shaped face suggests love. Her forehead is circled by chestnut curls and is unspotted by perspiration that might smudge her penciled eyebrows. She looks like a silent screen star, a kind of pioneer version of one of the leading ladies of the screen such as Mary Pickford, who reigned for so long as America's sweetheart. Two generations too soon for the movies, Koerner's production lives only in canvas and oil, her bowed lips unable to mouth even a captioned exclamation. But she seems to have just stepped out of the makeup room, no trail dust dulling the sheen of her dark dress. Her milky collar remains closed with a cameo brooch, a nursing infant curiously absent. Her tired, placid face reflects patience, a quality essential for one who must sit poised on a wagon seat, going nowhere, west or east, because she never really existed. Koerner's pioneer madonna seems hallowed by the wagon's canvas oval, which reinforces her spirituality while limiting her reality. Circumscribed in her primitive ellipse, she is trapped by her idealization just like her Victorian counterparts in gilt frames.

How would she compare with the real women who trudged along the Platte River Road. I wonder who her prototypes were. Were there any pioneer mothers so carefully groomed and nobly enduring, so touchingly sad and patiently silent? I wanted to know what real pioneer women thought and felt. I didn't want madonnas to worship; I wanted women to understand. How many willingly came west? How many bore children on the trek? How many watched children die of disease or accident? How many watched children grow strong in the Western openness? Beyond statistics, I wanted stories.

Maybe real pioneer women looked more like the subject of Harvey Dunn's painting, *The Homesteader's Wife*,[119] in which an earthy woman steps down from the wagon seat of Koerner's *Madonna* and takes her place in the fields. Hunched forward, she tugs a recalcitrant ox, the taut rope crossing her dark skirt and crumpling her white apron. Her sun-bleached hair is pulled back into a bun, keeping loose strands from her brow. Her blouse curves low, revealing a sunburned chest. She peers forward like Koerner's madonna, but the goal of this homesteader's wife seems only to get the ox to the barn one more time. The golden-grassed, saucer-flat land which stretches away from her on all sides confines rather than frees. Representative of many immigrant women, surrounded by open space, she cannot escape the drudgery of survival, the premature aging in the prairie's summer heat and winter cold. And yet, in the crucible of her life, she exudes a kind of power.

I think the real women who walked the banks of the Platte sought power as well, defined in a variety of ways, just as women today try to develop their varied strengths. Whenever I view pioneer art, I linger long enough to detect and then question the stereotypes. I measure what I see against what I have read in diaries and memoirs. Wanting diversity, I introduce alternate visions, still unpainted.

14.

Lone Tree

Lone Tree, Nebraska, was described in the diary of Frederick Hawkins Piercy, an artist hired by Mormons in England to record his journey to Salt Lake City. On Wednesday, the 13th of July, 1853, in a romanticized style, he wrote:

> In the guides there is a notice of a "Lone Tree." All through the journey the lone tree had been in my imagination and at last I had associated an interest, a sort of romantic idea, with it, which became quite exciting. I pictured to myself an old, weather-beaten, time-worn tree, standing in mournful solitude on a wide spreading prairie, having to encounter alone the attacks of the elements, with no companion to share the storm, or help to break its fury. I could imagine it on a cold winter's night with its arms bare of foliage, tossing them in sorrow in the wind, being desolate and alone. ... I started off ahead of the company with the intention of making a complimentary and therefore careful sketch of this tree, but I could not find it.

> Some unpoetical and ruthless hand had cut it down, so my hopes were blighted and my occupation was gone.[120]

The sense of emptiness Piercy captured in his journal entry is similar to what Willa Cather captured in My Ántonia, describing the Nebraska landscape as she first saw it. Her narrator, Jim Burden, coming as a child to his grandparents' home, muses: "There seemed to be nothing to see; no fences, no creeks or trees, no hills or fields. If there was a road, I could not make it out in the faint starlight. There was nothing but land: not a country at all, but the material out of which countries are made."[121]

Cather touches specifically on the absence of trees:

Trees were so rare in that country, and they had to make such a hard fight to grow, that we used to feel anxious about them, and visit them as if they were

persons. It must have been the scarcity of detail in that tawny landscape that made detail so precious.[122]

Solomon Butcher captures the absence of trees well in a photo of Lookout Point in Cherry County, Nebraska, near the Snake River. The alterations made in the photo, the etching in of trees on the barren hills, confirm the human longing for abundance.[123]

As pioneers experienced the westward trail, what words would they have used in describing the emptiness? *Sparse* is a word that could have defined much of the terrain. In some places mountains were nonexistent and hills were slight rises in the earth; trees were sparse, towns were sparse, and some of the people looked sparse. It is as though the region had planted a lesson in their physiognomy that things don't come easy.

So much of what one reads of pioneer households

The alterations in this Solomon Butcher photograph taken at Lookout Point in Cherry County, Nebraska, reveal a human longing for abundance rather than the barrenness that was the reality in Nebraska. As Willa Cather wrote: "Trees were so rare in that country, and they had to make such a hard fight to grow, that we used to feel anxious about them, and visit them as if they were persons. It must have been the scarcity of detail in that tawny landscape that made detail so precious." *Courtesy of Nebraska State Historical Society Photograph Collections, nbhips 10130*

speaks over and over again of *frugality:* tiny scraps from worn out clothes sewed into patchwork quilts, lard stored to be combined with the saved ashes from the fireplace to make soap, boys' suits made of cut-down men's suits, newspapers and magazines used to paper the inside walls of the sod houses which dotted the prairies.

Frugality is a word imprinted on my psyche even though I am three generations removed from my pioneer ancestors. My parsimonious ancestors engraved the phrase "Waste not, want not" deep into the minds of their children. When the Depression, which began with the stock market crash in 1929, engulfed their children and grandchildren, the latter were ready to "make do or do without." Memories of the Great Depression linger in my memory, not because I lived those years, but because the experiences of that time were so indelibly stamped on my mother's mind. Her subsequent words and actions inevitably influenced me.

When I was a child, to be frugal was a high virtue. Gifts were carefully opened, hands delicately loosening the tape so the wrap could be neatly removed and folded to be used again. A ball of string graced our kitchen cupboard; it was made up of hundreds of shorter pieces tied together. Thanksgiving week we were never done with the turkey until soup had been made off the bones. Catsup bottles were always turned upside down to coax out the final drops, and even then the residue was rinsed out, the last diluted juice added to a meatloaf or spaghetti. Nylons were never thrown out because of holes: small runs were stopped with clear nail polish, larger holes mended with special nylon thread that was colored to match the various stocking shades. Cotton and wool socks were stretched over a worn out light bulb and darned to prolong their use. Eggshells were saved to crush and spread in the garden soil. Rags were precious, to be spread with Mentholatum for sore throats or used to make rag rugs; better cloth was cut up for quilt squares. Printed chicken feed sacks became skirts; flour sacks became underwear. The phrase "Use it up, wear it out, make it do or do without" was a household aphorism.

My mother was raised in the rural Utah community of Mayfield in Sanpete County. The family had a nice home and plenty to eat. However, financial difficulties arose for the family when land and farm prices fell during the Depression. Her father farmed in the summer and fed sheep in the winter trying to survive financially, but as the Depression worsened, he lost more money every year. He finally defaulted on his home loan and sold his farmland at a loss. My mother recalls that initially she didn't realize what it was to be

poor, because everyone around her was poor, until she ventured outside the county. One of her high school teachers invited her to go to Provo. Excited, she borrowed her mother's rayon stockings and black coat. She didn't realize how impoverished she looked until a comparison was made with the girls in Provo. Her face reddens with embarrassment still today, over seventy years later, if reminded of that realization.

My mother recalls Christmas when an orange in a stocking was a valued gift. One Christmas she received a compact with a mirror in it, something her mother had obtained as a bonus from the Watkins man for having bought spices over a period of a year. That was the sum total of my mother's Christmas. At least there were gifts of some sort in my mother's family. My father recalls a Christmas when the only gift for eight children was a white-frosted Christmas cake— the red candy horse that adorned the top of the cake being given to the baby. And that was Christmas.

When my mother's parents and siblings sought employment in Salt Lake City, my mother stayed behind to finish her sophomore year of high school in Manti. She lived with her aunt and, like so many other young people of the time, was fortunate to have a relative to "take her in."

She followed her family to the city in the summer

of 1932, attending South High School. Of those years, she recalls regularly borrowing her older sister's clothes so she would look fashionable. Her sister had a job and left for work before my mother left for school. Mother would then choose a stylish outfit from the closet to wear to South High. It wasn't until years later that she confessed to her sister.

Following graduation, she got a job as a counter girl at Woolworth's, later pleased when she was promoted and could order items for the notions department. In a time of economic uncertainty, she felt fortunate to have a job. It was at this time that she indulged herself in her first luxury, a seal skin coat. She recalls, "It cost a hundred dollars and I had to save for a whole year to afford it."

Entertainment during the Depression was of necessity inexpensive. My mother has pictures of canyon cookouts as typical dates for young people. It was on a blind date in 1936 that she met Ken Shell and became engaged to him at Christmas of that year. There was no money for a stylish wedding. She and her mother journeyed to Virginia City, Nevada, where she joined her fiancé for a ceremony performed by a Mormon bishop. My father had moved to Nevada because work was available with the mining companies in Virginia City.

Later my parents moved back to Salt Lake City, still later to California, searching for decent employment, which was the focus of their lives for many years. My mother recalls her desperation in Salt Lake when she once sold one of my father's white shirts for fifty cents to a brother-in-law to get some money for food. Her mother-in-law sustained their family for a time. My mother recalls, "Ken's mother would go to the store and on the way home drop off a half pound of hamburger and a few potatoes. That would be our dinner." She remembers her longing to buy a Coke, which cost a nickel then, and her inability to do so. One of her daydreams was making a fruit salad and eating as much as she wanted, a daydream that would not materialize for many years.

My father had a job as a hod carrier, pushing a wheelbarrow laden with cement, helping build an addition to Granite High School in Salt Lake City. Numerous other men, unemployed, lined up to watch and "wait for one of us to quit or drop dead," as my father explained.

My mother remembers one hot summer day when she observed, from her small rental house near Granite High, my father walking quickly with determination away from work. As he entered the house, she awaited his inevitable words: "I quit my job; we're going to California." They proceeded to load their meager possessions into their car and join so many others seeking economic salvation in California. My parents, like many other people before and after, lived with relatives until they could get a job.

My father found work with the Pinkerton Detective Agency and began patrolling the busy docks at Long Beach. Eventually my parents left California and returned again to Utah, where I was born, and then later resettled in California. On December 7, 1941, the day Pearl Harbor was bombed, my parents were on the road. Stopping at a service station in Nevada, they were shocked to learn of the attack. The entrance of the United States into World War II was, ironically, in one way a blessing for U. S. citizens. They went back to work. My father apprenticed in automatic fire sprinkling, a war-essential job, and was never again unemployed even after the war ended.

Despite my father's new economic security, we never relaxed our vigil of frugality; we always needed to "save for a rainy day." For those who lived through the deluge of the Great Depression, another flood of hopelessness might be lurking on the horizon.

15.

Black Hills

The Black Hills of Wyoming, which should not be confused with the Black Hills of South Dakota 150 miles distant, is where a trail crossed Horseshoe Creek, according to pioneer diaries.[124] Wallace Stegner calls them "the dreary Black Hills" in his book, *The Gathering of Zion.* The phrase *Black Hills* made me think about how many connotations there are to the word *black,* one of them being *dreary.* I thought about how the terms *colored* or *Negro,* once commonly used as racial descriptors, had been replaced by *black* and later *African American* as more affirmative racial indicators. I thought how little I knew about black pioneers.

One of Solomon Butcher's photographs shows a black family by the name of Shores posed in front of a sod house, two women and two men seated on chairs as one man stands, a dog seated on the chair in front of him. Jerry Shores was one of several former slaves who settled in Custer County, Nebraska. He took a land claim near his brothers, Moses Speese and Henry Webb, whose different surnames reflected their former owners' names. I wonder what the lives were like of the women in these photographs, how the transition from slavery to freedom changed their perceptions, how this played out in their existence, and what their new life came to mean to their descendants. I thought about the consciousness-raising for me as I learned about black history.

One of the black pioneers who is of interest to me is Jane Elizabeth Manning James. Kate B. Carter tells of her life in *The Story of the Negro Pioneer.* Margaret Young and Darius Gray have used her as a character in their book *Standing on the Promises: One More River to Cross.* On her journey to Zion, Jane would have come close to the Black Hills of Wyoming.

She was born a free Negro in Connecticut in 1822. When she was six, Jane was sent as a servant to work for a wealthy family by the name of Fitch and was well trained by Mrs. Fitch in household work. Jane had a child out of wedlock when she was a young woman. Family gossip identified the father as white. However, Jane never talked about the circumstances of her son Sylvester's conception. The infant stayed with its grandmother while Jane returned to work in the Fitch household.[125]

Jane heard Mormon missionary Charles Wandell preach in October 1841 and was favorably impressed with his message. That night she had a vision of the prophet Joseph Smith's face, although she did not know whose face it was until she later met him. Soon after hearing Wandell preach, Jane was secretly baptized and left the Presbyterian faith, which she had joined only eighteen months earlier. Her minister warned her against the Mormons, but this was not enough to dissuade her. About three weeks after her baptism, she experienced the gift of tongues. She also converted other family members, and in October of 1843 they made plans to travel together to Nauvoo, where the Latter-day Saints were gathering.

As explained in *One More River to Cross*, "The Manning journey plan was simple: canal boat to Buffalo, New York, where they'd meet up with the other Saints; river boat to Columbus, Ohio, where Charles Wandell would help them pay their fare; steamer to Nauvoo, Illinois."[126] However, as the Mannings were not able to produce the necessary passage money at Buffalo, they were not allowed on the boat. Jane's trunk had been already loaded and, to her later dismay, was lost or stolen. Undeterred, she and her child, her mother, brothers, sisters, and a brother-in-law and sister-in-law walked 750 miles to Nauvoo, enduring many hardships including a challenge to their status as free Negroes.

When they arrived in Nauvoo, tired and worn from difficult travel, they were directed to the Mansion House. Joseph and Emma Smith received them with caring words and open hospitality. Jane stayed on at the Mansion House as a servant; her brother Isaac became the Mansion House cook and taught dancing at the Masonic Hall. Others of the party found work

In this Solomon Butcher photograph of 1887, we see the family of Jerry Shores (seated right) in Custer County, Nebraska. Left to right: Minerva (with infant), the Rev. Marks Shores, Rachel (wife of Jerry), and their son Jim (standing). What impact did the transition from slavery to freedom have on these men's wives, and what did their new life mean to their descendants? *Courtesy of Nebraska State Historical Society Photograph Collection, nbhips 10527* elsewhere. In her dictated autobiography, Jane spoke of Joseph Smith with reverence. His political platform during his 1844 presidential campaign, which included "tak[ing] off the shackles from the poor black man,"[127] must have been particularly appealing to her.

After the martyrdom of the Smith brothers by vigilantes in 1844, Jane moved to the home of Brigham Young and was there married to Isaac James, who had come to Nauvoo after his conversion in New Jersey. Isaac was delighted that a "colored" woman had come to Nauvoo so he could marry. Jane, Isaac, and Jane's son, Sylvester, trekked west with other Mormons, leaving Nauvoo in the spring of 1846. Jane bore another son, Silas, in Iowa, assisted by the prominent pioneer midwife Patty Sessions. Jane spent the winter of 1846-47 at Winter Quarters and then left for the valley of the Great Salt Lake with the Isaac Haight Company in June 1847.

The family arrived in Salt Lake City in September. The next year Jane bore another child, Mary Ann, and bore at least five additional children over the next twelve years. The family was able to improve its economic conditions through the accumulation of livestock and other possessions and became one of the more prosperous families of the First Ward where they resided. In late 1869 or early 1870, Isaac left the

household, perhaps due to marital difficulties. The family subsequently moved to the Eighth Ward and experienced economic decline that left Jane among the poorest of the ward's residents.[128]

Despite problems, Jane's loyalty to her church remained steadfast. She worked in the Relief Society of the Eighth Ward, contributing to its charitable causes. In later years, she and her brother, Isaac L. Manning, had specially reserved seats near the front and center of the Salt Lake Tabernacle for Sunday services.[129] Jane maintained her church activity despite the fact that the church had come to deny priesthood to black males and excluded blacks from Mormon temple worship. Sadly, Jane was not living when this policy was changed by church president Spencer W. Kimball in 1978. She would have rejoiced to find black members enjoying full equality and fellowship with other members of the church.

Joseph F. Smith, LDS president in 1908, spoke at Jane's funeral. An article in the newspaper described Jane in the following way: "Few persons were more noted for faith and faithfulness than was Jane Manning James, and though of the humble of the earth she numbered friends and acquaintances by the hundreds."[130]

I know about Jane Manning James because of her autobiography and other bits and pieces written about her, but I like to think that in some ways I can guess her feelings as a mother, as someone displaced from her native land to the Western frontier, and as someone who bore up courageously under the weight of racial prejudice. In 1963 I became aware of the frustration of blacks when I became a social worker in California, with many clients living in Compton and Watts. As a new Brigham Young University graduate, I had entered these enclaves like Mary Sunshine dispensing advice about keeping a positive mental attitude and needing to pull their lives together. A twenty-two-year-old Pollyanna, I was filled with naiveté born of my white, middle-class, Mormon upbringing and limited by my then childless, newly married perspective.

In a culture that considers you subordinate because of your skin color, how do you "think positive thoughts"? The "Black is Beautiful" movement of the 1960s began altering blacks' views of themselves as well as the predominant culture's view of blacks. As a social worker, I visited my clients' homes quarterly. In one instance, I observed a teenage boy with a nylon stocking over his head and asked what he was doing. From the mumbled response, it was clear that he did not want to answer me. It was decades before I learned what he was doing, through an essay titled "In the Kitchen" by black writer and activist, Henry Louis Gates Jr. The young man was attempting to straighten his hair. Gates describes the process:

> A stocking cap was made by asking your mother for one of her hose, cutting it with a pair of scissors about six inches or so from the open end, where the elastic goes to the top of the thigh. Then you'd knot the cut end and behold—a conical-shaped hat or cap, with an elastic band that you pulled down low on your forehead and down around your neck in the back. A good stocking cap, to work well, had to fit tight and snug, like a press. And it had to fit that tightly because it was a press; it pressed your hair with the force of the hose's elastic. If you greased your hair down real good and left the stocking cap on long enough—*voila*: you got a head of pressed-against-the- scalp waves.[131]

How fortunate that there were more thoughtful blacks who realized the harm of denying a part of one's identity. They said "black is beautiful" in a variety of ways: the popularizing of the Afro hair style, wearing dashiki African-style shirts, and taking names that originated, not from the poverty of Southern slavery, but from the wealth of African heritage and achievement. As African melodies and rhythm flourished in soul, blues, and rock and roll, whites began to imitate some of the styles and fashions of the black culture.

How important it is to have identity validated by seeing people like yourself reflected in the arts and in other fields. In my elementary years, I attended an integrated school in Long Beach, California, in the mid-1940s. At that time, I did not think it strange that no black children were pictured in our readers. Dick and Jane were white and so were all their friends. No blacks appeared in magazine advertisements I saw and none appeared in commercials our family viewed on our ten- inch-screen television. What would it have been like to be black and seldom see anyone like yourself in the media, only as a negative stereotype? It was as though you did not exist beyond the ghetto, as though schools assumed you had no stories to tell, as though businesses assumed you used none of their products, and as if you had little to contribute to society.

From 1956-58, I attended Long Beach Polytechnic, an integrated school, although you would not have known it from the pictures in my yearbook. One page shows the officers of our canteens where activities such as dancing, ping-pong, pool, television, and other recreational activities were held. Whites went to the Poly Hutch, named after our school mascot, a rabbit; blacks went to the Teen Tavern. Although some of the school sororities included Asian-American girls, no blacks were Pi Sigs or Scarabs. Pictures of administrators, counselors, and teachers and of office, custodial, and kitchen workers showed an all-white staff.

My memories contrast with the reality of today, where school social clubs separated by race are prohibited, where school staffs are multi-racial, where blacks are common in television commercials and news broadcasts and in sports and other areas. I recall my ten-year-old daughter watching "The Bill Cosby Show" with a friend in 1988 and commenting, "Wouldn't it be fun to have Bill Cosby for a dad." That made me feel good to know that blacks were desirable role models for white children. However, when I began to feel positive about the progress in racial equality, I remembered one black comedian's tongue-in-cheek remark of years back, "If you think we're integrated, try to buy a flesh-colored Band-Aid." I still notice subtle signs of the preferential treatment Caucasians receive.

During the Civil Rights Movement of the 1960s, my husband and I tried to encourage racial understanding in some small way. We had moved to Long Beach in 1964, choosing to live in an integrated neighborhood that consisted of whites, Asians, Hispanics, and blacks. At our home, we held a series of what were called "black-white dialogues," although people of other ethnicities participated as well. One of the participants was the first black bus driver in

Long Beach. I can still vividly recall him sharing that experience.

He told about some people stepping back and deciding not to ride his bus when they saw he was black. Later a second black bus driver was hired, and he was able to tell hesitant riders, "The driver behind me is black too." He recounted with pain how an older woman had placed a handkerchief in her hand to receive the change he gave her. The incident made me think of lines from "Any Human to Another" by Countee Cullen, a black poet of the Harlem Renaissance. In one stanza, he pleads:

> Your grief and mine
> Must intertwine
> Like sea and river,
> Be fused and mingle,
> Diverse yet single,
> Forever and forever.

As prejudice develops, people become immune to any kind of empathy for those who constitute the "other." I remember feeling hope in the 1960s when I encountered children who had not yet learned prejudice. One day I was substitute teaching at an integrated elementary school and a white girl about seven years old ran up and pointed toward the rings, saying: "That girl pushed me." I asked, "Which girl?" to which she replied, "The girl in the green dress." As I looked at the line of children by the rings, only one girl was wearing a green dress and she was a black child. I thought how fortunate it was that this white child distinguished her classmate by the color of her dress rather than by the color of her skin.

Another day, while substituting in a fourth-grade class, I was concerned that I use the right language, so I said to a little girl, "Would you rather I call you black, colored, or Negro?" She replied, "How about just calling me Mary Ann?" The lesson about seeing people as individuals rather than as part of a group came from a nine-year-old child who knew this instinctively.

In 1972, teaching at an American high school in Frankfurt, Germany, I had to develop a black literature unit to expose my students to a class of writers who had not yet been included in the curriculum. Later, teaching in Utah, I noticed the gradual inclusion of more and more black writers in our texts from 1976 on. I could assign the writings of Langston Hughes, Countee Cullen, Gwendolyn Brooks, and Alice Walker from the standard classroom texts. Black identity had become an integral part of the American experience.

I wonder what Jane Manning James taught her children about racial identity as they grew up in a predominately white society. I wonder how Jane would relate to the black women I served as a social worker. The names of my women clients of 1963 have long since left my memory, but the faces remain indelibly etched on my mind, not of stereotyped "women on welfare" but of individuals. One was a particularly gracious woman, tall and slender, soft-spoken, her skin the color of creamed coffee and her dark hair framing fine features. Her small home was furnished in lovely pieces of old furniture. I still recall the glass lamps with their fluted shades sitting on mahogany end tables. Divorced, she had worked as a maid for the wealthy of Hollywood and had perhaps acquired their discards as the source of her décor. I recall her telling me in a clear and cultured voice, tired with the strain of surviving health problems, of rearing children without a father, of having a limited income, and of being in a neighborhood where illegal activities of various sorts flourished only a few doors away.

The second image I recall is of a woman who lived in a wooden frame house furnished in an excellent manner with secondhand furniture of all ages and types. She was small, wiry, and energetic. Working days and going to school evenings, she was trying to break the cycle of welfare, her lot as a woman divorced from a man who was not paying child support. She verbalized her worries about leaving her children home in the evenings when she attended school, concerned about the alcoholism and drug abuse that were so close. But what choice did she have?

The third image is of a massive woman, filling a wide armchair with her body. Almost defiantly, she cradled two small children in her ample arms. The victim of poor judgment and repeated alliances with men who had deserted her, she was trying to provide sustenance for the five children she had borne. I wondered if her defiance was enough to give her and her children any hope in life.

The fourth image I hold in my head is of a young-looking grandmother, an attractive woman in her late thirties. She had lost the battle to keep her own teenage daughters from the poor choices that had brought her onto welfare. Now they were surviving on state assistance too. One of the girls lived with her infant daughter in a dilapidated house behind her mother, a house completely bare of furniture except for a caved-in couch and a cradle.

The fifth image is one of the few women I visited whose husband lived in the home. Injured in a factory accident and partially paralyzed, he sat in an upholstered chair, useless legs resting on a hassock. The many-windowed living room was unusually bright in the California sun, but no dust specks were revealed by the soft rays entering the neat room. Despite setbacks, the couple had a happy family. The woman was gentle with her husband, a man who, from his background of little education, had determined a different course for his children. The wife beamed with pride as she introduced me to her children, one a recent high school valedictorian, the other attending college on a scholarship. These were children who had beaten the odds. How would I have mothered such children in South-Central Los Angeles? How would Jane Manning James have done so? How do you raise children when all the normal family supports of a secure neighborhood, a strong husband, economic viability, and exemplary peers for your children are missing?

Each January, we observe Martin Luther King's birthday. Around the country the day is remembered in various ways, paying tribute to a man who has had a profound effect on how black people are treated in America because he was able to articulate his "dream" of a better world. This world would be much different than the one he and I, and Jane Manning James before us, had grown up in. What Dr. King envisioned was not a white man's world, not a black man's world, but one in which "justice rolls down like waters and righteousness like a mighty stream."[132] I think Jane Manning James, were she alive today, would applaud Dr. King's words and join with him in the realization of that dream.

16.

Devil's Gate

The weather was unseasonably cold near the Nebraska-Wyoming border. Snow dusted the ground and sifted itself like powdered sugar over the spire of Chimney Rock. In Wyoming, after the Black Hills, we continued on past Fort Casper, the Buttes on the Sweetwater, and Independence Rock to the landmark known as Devil's Gate. The wind was relentless and whipped my light coat around me. I braced myself and made my way to the historic marker, steadying myself to read the scant details of the agony experienced by the Willie and Martin handcart parties, who had become enveloped in unexpected snowstorms. I thought about the mothers in those companies, women who could not cease to nurture children who were beyond toddling and prattling, women who had to make an effort to preserve their adolescent and adult children as well. One such woman was Amy Britnell Loader, a mother of thirteen children, who converted to Mormonism in England in the winter of 1850-51, immigrating to America in February 1856 along with various family members. Amy, her husband, five daughters, and one son, as well as in-laws, were all members of the ill-fated Martin Handcart Company. Leaving Iowa City in mid-July of 1856, the group became stranded in early October-November snows. Amy's daughter Patience wrote a reminiscence that

Patience Loader, shown at age ninety, reminisced about traveling with the Martin Handcart Company in 1856: "We had to travle in our wett cloths untill we got to camp and our clothing was frozen on us. ... It was too late to go for wood and water. ... The ground was frozen to[o] hard. We was unable to drive any tent pins in. As the tent was ... somewhat frozen[,] we stretched it open the best we could and got in under it untill morning." *Photograph courtesy of Drusilla Loader Smith family, Pleasant Grove, Utah* begins after the death of her father and ends on November 30 when the Martin Company reached Salt Lake City. Her description is poignantly real: *About the beginning of October we had the first snow storm. We was then at the black hills. We halted for a short time and took shelter under our hand carts.*[133]

She describes the realization that Brother Jonathan Stone was missing: *He was sick and laid down to rest by the road side. He fell asleep it was supposed. Some of the breathren had to go back in seach of him and when thay found him, he was dead and nearly eaten by the wolves.*[134]

Patience tells how she and her sisters almost drowned trying to pull their cart across a river:

The water came up to our arm pits. Poor Mother was standing on the bank screaming. As we got near the bank I heard Mother say for God sake some of you men help my poor girls. Mother said she had been watching us and could see we was drifting down the stream. Several of the breathren came down the bank of the river and pulled our cart up for us and we got up the best we could. Mother was there to meet us. Her clothing was dry but ours was wet and cold and verey soon frozen. Mother took of[f] one of her under skirts and put on one of us and her apron for another to keep the wett cloth from us. ... We had to travle in our wett cloths untill we got to camp and our clothing was frozen on us. ... We had to make the best of our poor cercumstances and put our trust in God our fa-

ther that we may take no harm from our wett cloths. It was too late to go for wood and water. The wood was to[o] far away that night. The ground was frozen to[o] hard. We was unable to drive any tent pins in. As the tent was wett when we took it down in the morning[,] it was somewhat frozen so we stretched it open the best we could and got in under it untill morning.[135]

Besides the weather, another problem was getting food:

I was always on the look out for anything that I could get to eat not only for myself but for the rest of the family. We got of[f] the skin from the beef head [and] chopt it in pieces the best I could [and] put in into the pot with some snow and boiled [it] for along time. About four o clock in the after noon we was able to have some of this fine made broath.[136]

She describes the death of a fellow traveler, an English tailor, who had left his wife and nine children in England until he could earn enough to bring them to America. The Loaders were kindly in sharing their tent with him, but found him dead and frozen in the morning.

Patience recounts the arrival of a rescue party from Salt Lake, which included Joseph A. Young:

Seeing us out there Br Young ask[ed] how many is dead or how many is alive. I told him I could not tell. With tears streaming down his face he ask[ed] whare is your captains tent. He call[ed] for the bugler to call everybody out of ther tents. He then told the captain Edward Martin if he had flour enough to give us all one pound of flour each and said if there was any cattle to kill and give us one pound of beef each saying there was plenty provisions and clothing coming for us on the road.

Wallace Stegner, describing the rescue, writes:

It is hard to imagine ... the emotions of rescue, the dazed joy of being snatched from the very edge of a snowdrift grave, and then the agony of being forced to put out more effort when the whole spirit cries to give up and be taken care of. It is hard to feel how hope that has been crushed little by little, day by day, can come back like feeling returning to a numbed limb. It is hard even to imagine the hardship that rescue entailed—the jolting, racking, freezing, grief-numbed, drained and exhausted three hundred miles through the snow to sanctuary.

As only the sick and dying could ride in wagons, Patience and her sisters continued to pull their hand-cart. Of this ordeal she says: *One day I well remember we had a very hard days travel and we came to Devels Gate that night to camp. The snow was deep and terrable cold freezing.* She describes her joy when George Grant told them *all to stand back for he was going to knock down one of those log hutts to make fiars for us. For he sais you are not going to freeze to nigh[t].*[137]

Trials continued, and even with help from the val-

ley, many were still not saved from death. Patience tells how *many of the stout young men went out and got raw hide and anything thay could get to eat* while the company was camped on the Sweetwater for nine days. One of those mornings, Patience and two of her sisters, Tamar and Maria, freezing and starving, refused to get out of their snow-covered quilts. Mother Loader said, *I believe I will have to dance [for] you and try to make you feel better.*[138] She started to sing and dance and then slipped down in the snow. The three girls, afraid their mother was hurt, jumped up. Patience further explains in her memoir what happened next:

She laugh[ed] and said I thought I could soon make you all jump up if I danced [for] you. Then we found that she fell down purposely for she knew we would all get up to see if she was hurt. She said that she was afraid her girls was going to give out and get disscuraged and she said that would never do to give up.[139]

Amy's actions remind me of a time when my life seemed fragile, when my mother's actions and words told me that it "would never do to give up." When I was in my early forties, I suffered a major depression. I used to go to the swimming pool because the doctor said exercise would help. I'd float to the middle of the deepest part and want to sink, to see the water closing over me in a gentle embrace that would stop the hurt.

Sometimes driving in the car with my husband on a cliff-edged mountain road, I'd wish for the door to open so I could free-fall into the air, soaring until the emotional pain ceased. Watching my children laugh at some game or television program, I'd wonder how anyone could laugh and if I would ever laugh again. I didn't want them to see my tears and didn't want them to believe that life was as sad as I had come to think.

When I told my mother about my depression, she came to help. When I cried about my worthlessness, she would stroke my hair and tell me all the things of value in my life. She said, "You're the best thing that ever happened to me. You're the reason my life was all worth it." As I lay on my bed and mother sat on the edge, we talked of my childhood, and image after image filled my mind. I tried to tell my mother what I saw.

"I'm four years old. You're holding me close in the middle of a room in a small frame house in Ogden while a wild thunder storm is raging outside, rattling windows and sending shrieking wind under the doors. I'm terrified, but you're holding me, and that makes me know everything will be all right."

"I remember how long that night seemed until your daddy came home."

"I remember when I was six, the way you ironed my cotton dresses, making sure every ruffle stood out starched and creaseless. I remember leaving for first grade each day, feeling crisp and clean. My lunch box was exciting to open each day, just to see what you had tucked into it."

"Remember how I used to cut your peanut butter and jelly sandwiches in triangles?"

"And wrap them in wax paper. There were little carrot sticks, too, and on cold days, you'd put tomato or chicken noodle soup in my thermos."

Mother nodded.

"Remember how, when I didn't go to school, you'd write an excuse note. I was always proud to hand your note to my teacher because you wrote in round, sweeping whirls like a note was too important to be anything but a work of art. ... And when I came home from school, remember how we'd play jump rope and you'd turn the rope while we chanted 'Mable, Mable, set the table' and speed up and laugh as we said 'And don't forget the red hot pepper.'"

"There was the one about 'Mother called the doctor, and the doctor said. ...'"

"And 'Three little monkeys jumping on the bed.' You know what else I remember?"

"No, what?"

"Our house. Whenever I see hardwood floors, I remember how shiny ours were and the smell of wax when you'd just polished them. In the back yard, I'd hand you clothes pins from an old cloth bag as you hung wash on the line. I can still smell that freshness in the sheets when we gathered them in. And I remember the ironing board set up in the front bedroom and you ironing sets of Daddy's khaki-colored work pants and shirts."

"Yes, I ironed them like someone would iron a tuxedo today."

"Remember the kitchen and how I'd help you with the dinner dishes."

"Yes, I'd wash and you'd dry."

"And no matter how fast I worked, I could never keep up with you. Sometimes you'd let me wash. ..."

"But you never wanted to scoop the garbage bits from the drain. You said they were 'icky.'"

"So you'd do it for me."

Voices came from the playroom: "You wrecked my puzzle." "It was an accident." "No, it wasn't." I started to raise myself off the bed.

"No, you rest. I'll take care of it."

I turned and curled into myself. Already halfway across the room with her quick steps, Mother turned and came back to the bedside, stroked my back, and said, "Judy, remember how strong you've been for all your children. ... And you can be strong again. Don't let anyone tell you that you can't." My mother said healing words over and over until I knew "it would never do to give up" and until I could believe it was worth living again.

My husband's mother was a healer, as well. When she was dying of lung disease and complications from hip surgery, she chose to spend each of her last few months with a different child, even though moving from house to house and city to city was painful. She, like Amy Loader, lived the message that "it would never do to give up." Golda left some needed hope in each home. It was difficult to see her weaken with each passing day because my memories said she should always be strong. When she and her husband, Stiner, celebrated their fiftieth wedding anniversary six years earlier, I read a tribute to her:

If a theme song were selected for my mother-in-law, some who call her "the little general" might choose "Charge of the Light Brigade," but I'd choose "Food, Glorious Food."

One of my earliest memories of Golda was at deer hunt camp. She'd prepare bacon, eggs, pancakes, and hot chocolate for ten (or twenty) on a two-burner Coleman stove, serve it all steaming, and not even look flustered. Deer hunt food also included the ever-present pot of spicy chili kept warm on the back burner, ready to feed children, grandchildren, various in-laws, and indigents who might want to mingle with the family for a free meal.

Every family get-together meant food ... and more food. Although Golda sometimes expressed concern for the over-weight, she never failed to serve them pumpkin pie smothered in whipped cream, skimmed from the top of milk pans on the service porch. Of course, if someone asked for "just a small piece, please," she'd give them a sixth of the pie instead of a fourth.

Golda had a magical ability to produce food. Like a magician pulling scarves from a hat, she'd pull plates of good things to eat from her new refrigerator in the kitchen and her old one on the service porch; and, amazingly, she could fit the leftovers back in, too.

From her two freezers came decorated sugar cookies, raisin-filled cookies, and carrot pudding sometimes served with flaming sugar cubes. Along with the main dish at each holiday meal were at least two salads, three vegetables, and a couple different desserts. The drop-leaf table expanded to accommodate the bounteous offering.

Golda planted a garden each year, which was bounteous too. The family attributed this to a spring ritual, which she religiously followed, blaming her husband for poor prospects. After seeds began to sprout, Golda would chant in a loud voice, "Stiner didn't plant the beans right." This spell guaranteed abundant crops in the summer and fall, enough to supply relatives, neighbors, and friends, so much so, that in September another ritual was called for which consisted of lining up in front of the Jack-in-the-Bean-Stalk vines and shouting, "Die, vines, die."

Golda taught me to can. I remember good times, warm times, close times, of snapping beans, peeling apples, and slipping beets, talking and laughing and sharing. Rows of brightly-colored bottles lined her cellar shelves and my basement as well: pickled red beets, green beans, sun-yellow peaches, wine-red cherries, almond-colored pears, multi-colored relishes, and an array of jams and jellies in hues of amber, orange, and red.

One time when I was young and uninformed, I noted Golda's variety of pans. Typical of this odd assortment was a well-dented triangular one with no handle. My husband and I remedied this deplorable situation by giving her new pans for Christmas.

For years I wondered why she didn't throw the old ones away. But now I'm older and wiser and know why. Those dented relics were not just pans, they were a hanging on to the past, a cherished part of life just like her family histories and genealogy.

The expansive holiday meals were the physical extension of an emotional giving. The variety of food—all warm on the Coleman stove—was like Golda herself, balancing children, husband, employment, church service, genealogy, and club work in a life where everything was "served up hot" and ready to go.

During her final weeks, I watched as Golda, her small frame steeled, leaned on her walker and slowly slid one foot after another down our long hall, conquering an impatience developed in her years of demanding activity. Each day after school, my fifth-grader would crawl into bed beside her grandma, who would listen as Noelle slowly sounded out the syllables of hard words in her reader, her determination to read mirroring her grandmother's determination to walk.

When Golda could no longer bathe herself, she accepted my help as I'd accepted hers so many times. Stroking a washcloth over her soft skin, I considered how hard it is to die gracefully, to give up one ability after another without screaming at the loss. I remembered Christ's advice to Peter when he was reluctant to have Jesus wash his feet, "If I wash thee not, thou hast no part with me."[140] I thought of how giving is always dependent on the graciousness of the receiver. I thought about Kahlil Gibran's words:

> See first that you yourself deserve to be a giver, and an instrument of giving.
>
> For in truth it is life that gives unto life—while you, who deem yourself a giver, are but a witness.
>
> And you receivers—and you are all receivers—assume no weight of gratitude, lest you lay a yoke upon yourself and upon him who gives.
>
> Rather rise together with the giver on his gifts as on wings;
>
> For to be overmindful of your debt, is to doubt his generosity who has the free-hearted earth for mother, and God for father.[141]

17.

Rocky Ridge

In Wyoming emigrants traveled along the banks of the Sweetwater River, then entered a small canyon where they cut up over rocky terrain. William Clayton described the "Rocky Ridge" as "dangerous to wagons" and warned that it "ought to be crossed with care." In such a remote area, one can imagine the emigrants' anxiety rising with the possibility of bad weather, limited food supplies, accident, or illness, being miles from any store, livery, or doctor. Retracing the trail, I sensed their desperation.

Even today Wyoming is still filled with so much empty space, it is hard to imagine the concern about the population explosion—emptiness stretching for miles in all directions. For those who live in crowded cities, how freeing this space must seem: room to breathe deeply the clean air, to shout with no one to complain about the noise, to run and not be blocked by pedestrians or traffic. How freeing ... unless you are suddenly injured or ill. Then the confinement of open space, blocking quick access to emergency care, can be frightening. Back home, the hospital is one mile from our house. The EMT center is across from the hospital. An ambulance could be at our home in minutes. My neighbor Luzon Peterson is a retired school

There are only two known portraits of Patty Sessions, this one thought to have been photographed near the time of her death. Susan Sessions Rugh wrote that Sessions's "legendary 3,977 deliveries earned her the title of 'Mother of Mormon Midwifery.' However, ... from an historical perspective perhaps her most significant contribution is her diary, which presents a fascinating account of the Mormon exodus from Nauvoo and the early settlement of the Salt Lake Valley." *Photograph courtesy of Daughters of Utah Pioneers*

119

nurse and was a quick resource when any of my children had a cut and needed a butterfly bandage, the littlest one calling her "Wu-zon" as if she were a Chinese healer. If a child had an unfamiliar rash and I wondered if it might be measles or roseola, Luzon could tell me. She could also check my husband's progress after surgery when I was unsure about his appearance, saving us a six-block trip to our family doctor.

But what did pioneers do when a doctor was twenty miles away by wagon or one hundred miles away, if available at all? In Lander, Wyoming, I found an interesting book, *The Oregon Trail Cookbook: A Historical View of Cooking, Traveling, and Surviving on the Trail.* Apart from the recipes for Western fried squirrel and Big Blue beaver tail soup, I found a section on home remedies as interesting as it was frightening. I've joked with people about keeping such a book on their person at all times in case they ever get marooned away from their local pharmacy. I tell them they can concoct their own cures or decide that survival may not be worth the effort ... or, for that matter, the risk. Some suggestions in the book include:

Nose bleed: "Take a small piece of lead and bore a hole in it. Put a string around the hole, tie it and wear it around your neck. Your nose won't bleed again." Of course, you might die of lead poisoning.

Worms: "Take shells of a hen's eggs and bake them until they turn brown and brittle. Crumble them up fine and mix the particles with syrup and butter. Feed this to the sick person every morning for one week. The particles cut the worms to pieces. This remedy also works for dogs and other animals."

Asthma: "Suck salty water up your nose."

Arthritis: "A magnet draws it out of the body." I think this one still has credence with some people.

Chest Congestion: "Render the fat of a polecat. Eat two or three spoonfuls. This brings up the phlegm," not to mention what else it might bring up.

Burns: "Put hot coals on the burned place and pour water over them. The steam will draw the fire out." Fight fire with fire, in other words.

Headache: "Smear brow with crushed onions." Wow, what an effective addition to "Darling, I've got a headache tonight."

Spider bites: "If bitten by a black widow spider, drink liquor heavily from 3 p.m. to 7 p.m. You won't get drunk, you'll be healed"—or at least die happy.

Rheumatism: "Carry a buckeye or an Irish potato until it gets hard."

Sores: "Put butter around the sore so a dog will lick it. The dog's saliva will cure it." This requires a very devoted pet.

Nightmares: "Place a Bible under your pillow and you will never have nightmares,"[142] unless of course you're worried about someone using an old pioneer cure on you.

I've always been appalled at the high death rate among pioneers, but now that I've seen their remedies, I'm amazed that so many survived. Though I poke fun at them, I have to seriously ask myself what I would have done without the ready availability of professional medical help. Historian Lillian Schlissel writes:

> The remedies against illness were pitifully few. Laudanum (tincture of opium) and camphor were sometimes carried, but the women's diaries give little evidence that the emigrants were well supplied. Catherine Haun's diary tells that her family had with them such medicines as quinine for malaria, hartshorn for snake bites, citric acid for scurvy, and opium and whiskey for everything else. "A little of the acid mixed with sugar and water and a few drops of essence of lemon made a fine substitute for lemonade." Elizabeth Geer's diary confirmed that "no one should travel this road without medicine, for they are sure to have the summer complaint. Each family should have a box of physicking pills, a quart of castor oil, a quart of the best rum, and a large vial of peppermint essence."
>
> Home remedies such as herbs and water baths were common. There were commercial medicines, usually useless, but most of the time the emigrants had nothing at all. One either recovered, or did not.[143]

The Mormon community, faced with the absence of medicine and professional medical help, relied on faith healings. They had confidence in these prayers by priesthood holders or family members and found a great source of strength in the ritual. Giving healing blessings continues today, although usually in conjunction with medical help. I personally find this type of blessing to be comforting. My husband and sons are elders in the church with priesthood authority to give blessings. In our family, we do not resort to blessings lightly, only when the need is most direly felt, such as before each of my imminent deliveries. When labor began to convulse my body, the strong and comforting hands of my husband laid on my head and a petition offered to God for assistance gave me courage. These spiritual and mental assurances actually made my body relax and prepare for its birthing function. I have benefitted from blessings when I have had surgery and when I have experienced mental anguish. I have seen people in the last days or hours before death find comfort by being blessed, even if the promise was not one of healing but of release from pain.

My husband, Neal, contracted polio as a young man of fifteen. He spent six weeks in the polio ward of the county hospital in Salt Lake. During this time, a Mormon apostle, Matthew Cowley, visited to check on Neal's roommate, an eight-year-old boy whom Apostle Cowley had blessed when the boy was still in an iron lung. As the apostle was about to leave, the boy gestured toward his roommate and said, "Wait a minute, don't forget my partner." As a result, Neal also received a blessing and went home shortly after that, gradually returning to normal activity and firmly believing that he had experienced a miraculous healing experience.[144] We don't often talk about this in our family. It is a quiet thing that exists as a substantial underpinning to our daily life, a reserve and a strength.

Women do not hold the priesthood in the Mormon church as men do, but in earlier days, Mormon women were active in giving blessings, particularly to other women and to children. Pioneer midwife Patty Bartlett Sessions delivered thousands of babies and regularly visited the sick, and her diary is interspersed with numerous references to formal blessings, given and received. On March 17, 1847, she wrote in her diary, *I then visited the sick. Mr Sessions and I went and laid hands on the widow Holmans step daughter. She was healed.*

On February 4 that year, Patty's birthday, she wrote

of asking Eliza Snow to bless her. On June 1, 1847, Patty wrote about a gathering of women: *I blessed sister Christeen by laying my hands upon her head and the Lord spoke through me to her great and marvelous things. At the close I thought I must ask a blessing at sister Kimbals hand but it came to me that I must first bless her.* Her accounts of blessings and healings are juxtaposed among entries about such common things as *Not well* or *Picked some wool* or *I commenced [k]niting a comforter.* Perhaps as isolated as these women were from expert medical care and filled with the joy of their beliefs and at having escaped hostilities from antagonistic neighbors in the Midwest, blessings seemed as natural as daily chores.

Serving as a local Relief Society president, I try to live the motto "Charity Never Faileth." I have comforted the sick, sat with dying people, listened to the laments of the bereaved, and helped with funerals, but I am grateful that I do not have medical responsibility for those I visit and that I have not had to wash, lay out, and clothe the bodies of the dead as pioneer Relief Society women did. I sometimes wonder what my life would be like in this role if I had lived a century and a half ago, and I ask myself if I would have been equal to the task. Would my tendency to value the logical and the provable, to try practical solutions before moving on to powerful prayer have been a barrier to the exercise of faith?

Perhaps my practicality is one reason I do not long to give formal blessings as some Mormon women do. When situations arise that require my deep prayer, I turn to private communication with God. I remember praying for the healing of a teenage son's arm night after night. When doctors and sophisticated medical technology could find no explanation for the loss of motion, I went to the temple in Manti, Utah, to gaze on a painting of Jesus blessing the children and pray for my son. I put his name on the prayer roll. At night, lying beside my husband in our room above that of our son, I would pray for whatever it was that was limiting his mobility to leave his body so he could play football and basketball again. My husband gave a blessing to Chris. After a time, movement returned to Chris's arm and we felt that our prayers had been answered.

In Latter-day Saint temples, I continue to put the names of sick relatives or friends on the prayer rolls and sometimes participate in prayers that these people might receive special healing blessings. Those I care about seem to feel strengthened when I tell them I have put their names on the prayer roll and receive it as another loving gesture in addition to stopping by with a casserole, holding their hands, and listening to words that grope to explain pain and loss.

Were I about to embark on a perilous journey as the Nauvoo pioneers did, I would do just as they did—going first to the temple before making the long walk down Parley Street and being ferried across the icy river to begin the trek to a strange place in the West. This would have given me the assurance, as William Clayton penned it, that "all is well."

I understand the renewed faith of pioneer Mormons, their increased assurance once they had partaken of holy ordinances. Each time I go to the temple, I am renewed in body and spirit. I love to enter the temple, to be in a holy space. I leave my worldly cares behind, and as kind people dressed in white surround me, I feel a communion, a joining of hearts. Because we are all in white, we have a sense of equality. We are not, as in the outer world, distinguished by the quality of our clothes, the price tags of our possessions, the models of our cars, and the sizes of our homes. We are one.

Sometimes in the temple I like to look at the hair colors, the only thing in contrast to the white clothing. In their various shades, the colors seem to represent our differences, some extreme, from white to jet black, some minor like the shades of blonde that seem so infinite in this setting. Sometimes I notice hands, from the smooth tapered fingers of young women to the gnarled arthritic ones of old women. Or the hands of men, those of strong young men about to embark on missions to the calloused hands of the older men who have farmed our rural land for decades.

This sense of oneness is joyful, particularly in a world where division is so common, as we separate ourselves according to young and old, rich and poor, beautiful and plain, educated and uneducated, strong and weak, and the list goes on. Of course, in the temple we are all those things, but we are also all seekers after spiritual nourishment, and so our differences are minimized. The *rocky ridge* of being part of the "other" can be smoothed by the similarity of religious conviction. This in and of itself is healing.

18.

South Pass

As we traverse barren stretches of Wyoming, I turn to my books on pioneer life to break the boredom. *Cholera, malaria, childbed fever, black canker ...* were all included in lists of pioneer ailments. Curious, I check the indexes of several resource books and realize that I cannot find *cancer*. Why? Was it called something different back then? Did doctors not know how to diagnose it? Was emphasis placed on common and quick-death diseases so that cancer seemed less worrisome? I wanted to find some mention of cancer because I wanted to stretch back across the years and find pioneer women with whom I might identify in this illness.

Later in my seeking, I did find a pioneer woman who had cancer, Louisa Beaman Young. After losing five children in death along the Mormon Trail and in the Valley of the Great Salt Lake, she suffered an affliction she described this way: *I comenced the first of May to docter my breast, at times. It is quite painful which makes me feel verry miserable indeed; most of the time I can do a little[. W]e are a trying to draw it to a head [but] it get[s] along slow.*[145] Louisa died on May 15, 1850, mercifully released from suffering in a world unaware of how to treat her disease. She was only thirty-five.[146]

That day in Wyoming, I did not know of Louisa. I closed my eyes and remembered a day in early November of 1978 when I stood lecturing to my third-period English class and an office assistant entered the room to hand me a note. It read, "Call Dr. Greenwood." The color drained from my face. I glanced at the wall clock and was relieved to see that the bell would ring in two minutes, thus ending my half-day teaching assignment. Somehow I managed to con-

tinue talking for those interminable two minutes. As the students left, I rushed for the car, tears welling up in my eyes as I drove the few blocks to the clinic. I knew what was wrong.

I parked at the back of the clinic and used the emergency entrance, purposely avoiding the waiting room. I mumbled to the nurse, "I had a message ..." My choked sobs muffled the rest. She put her arms around me and led me to the doctor's private office.

Dr. Greenwood, who two days before had performed a biopsy assuring me it "looked benign," entered. Compassionately he said, "You must know, the tumor is malignant. The breast will have to be removed."

"I don't care about that," I said, "if only the cancer hasn't spread."

Driving home, the word *cancer* echoed in my ears. I felt angry and frustrated. A microscopic nothing was

An artistic depiction of South Pass emphasizes the openness of the area. Susan Nobel, remembering her immigration in 1847, recorded a similar impression. "We had heard so much of the South Pass that we thought, of course, a dangerous and difficult climb was before us. One can hardly imagine our surprised feeling when we found the Continental Divide as a long broad easy upland valley with splendid trails. It was hardly believable." *Painting by William H. Jackson, photograph courtesy of Utah State Historical Society*

tearing away at my body, tearing away at my life, and I felt powerless. I called my husband at work. As soon as I heard his voice, my control crumbled and I said just two words, "Come home."

Within minutes, he arrived and I shared the crushing news with him. The next few hours were a jumble of frantic efforts to prepare to leave for Salt Lake City, all paling against the background of the overriding thought, *I have cancer.*

The most difficult moment came as I said good-bye to the children. I had never had surgery before and had a fear of going under the anesthetic and never coming back. It could happen. Ordinary moments of every day suddenly took on great significance: Noelle flashing her two-tooth smile as her chubby baby hands grasped for a definite no-no; Jeremy swiveling his small, snake-like hips, flipping around to explode in "kyuu, kyuu, kyuu" sounds of mock attack; Chris in four-year-old seriousness examining a record player to see where the sound came from; Kirsten bouncing down the stairs with golden hair flying; Kerri in her room writing volumes in her journal, the problems of being almost fifteen engulfing her. Would I ever share those moments again, and if I couldn't, who would?

Neal and I drove to Salt Lake, talking quietly about the good past and the possible future. We checked in at the hospital and were directed upstairs. Edged with dilapidated looking foliage, an upper-floor lounge provided the perfect opportunity for the comic relief we both so desperately needed. Neal quipped, "I hope the patients do better than the plants." I gratefully laughed.

Bordering the lounge were bookshelves filled with notably non-best sellers. A large sign proclaimed DO NOT REMOVE FROM THE HOSPITAL. Neal dryly commented, "I don't think there's any risk of that."

To divert my thoughts, I began to peruse some of the individual titles and joked with Neal that the person who selected these books for the hospital was sadistic. I giggled uncontrollably as I read aloud: *A Client is Canceled, The Blow at the Heart* (a great must-read for transplant patients), *Speak Softly of the Dead, They Buried a Man,* and *Deadly Joy.* At least there was a note of optimism in the last one. The laughter was therapeutic as it took our minds off the gravity of my illness for a moment.

That evening I turned serious as I penned some careful thoughts in my journal "just in case." I felt so much like Emily in *Our Town,* wondering why we didn't live life more fully when we had it. My husband gave me a blessing that calmed and prepared me for surgery. The next morning, a pre-operative shot relaxed me and made me sleepy. I recall the feeling of drifting and the ever-present fear of "Would I wake up?"

The next thing I knew, the surgery was over and I was in my bed, my chest bandaged, but I was experiencing no pain. Late in the night, an intern came to check me. Wanting reassurance, I asked him what the chance of long-term survival was for a person with cancer like mine. Being young and forthright, he assumed a clinical voice and quoted cold statistics. I cynically wondered if he was responsible for selecting *A Client is Canceled* for the hospital's book-of-the-month shelf.

The second day was difficult as I experienced relief that the operation had gone so well and fear of what the post-operative tests might show. When the doctor reported with an "all lymph nodes clear" result and said I would not need chemotherapy or radiation, I felt an overwhelming sense of relief. All that I had really feared losing was mine again.

Thoughts about my cancer receded as I opened my eyes again to the Wyoming scenery, bringing me back to the present. I was surprised by the sudden weather change. Sun had replaced the snow, which had gusted and soared outside the van's windows near the Nebraska border. Those snowflakes had been early and unexpected like my cancer. I remembered other snowflakes, dipping and rising in the autumn wind a few weeks after my mastectomy. Illuminated in the flood-lights of our deck, they were so individual, like cells viewed under a microscope. I had watched those flakes through a kitchen window and started to cry, relieved that I had lived to see another snowfall.

A few days later was Thanksgiving. As I stood chopping celery and onions for the dressing, my moth-er said, "Judy, let me help you." I said, "No, I want to do it myself." As I stirred the dried bread cubes, I breathed in the scent of sage, I tasted the tongue-tang flavor of the dressing, savoring it. That afternoon as my family sat around a dining room table dressed up with white china and silver rimmed crystal, I made my perennial comment, "Don't you love the variety of colors, the green of the peas"— and here all the children joined in with a refrain so familiar, they chanted it without hesitation—"the orange of the sweet potatoes, the brown of the gravy, and the red of the cranberry sauce."

Kerri said, "Go on, Mom, finish it. Tell the story of the fish head soup." To build gratitude in my children once more, I told about how Ivan Denisovich in Alex-ander Solzhenitsyn's novel of the Gulag longed for Siberian camp cooks to stir the soup before they dipped his portion so the fish heads would come to the top and he might get a little nourishment.[147] Usually after this story, the children would giggle, but this year they were silent as I cried, more grateful than Ivan Deniso-vitch for small blessings.

19.

Echo Canyon

Near the Wyoming-Utah border we stopped at Fort Bridger, paying tribute to my husband's great-great-grandfather, William A. Hickman, who had operated the fort for a time. Then we drove south into a familiar Utah landscape. As we passed through Echo Canyon, I thought about a pioneer woman who had made her way through this same canyon in the fall of 1848 when she was eight months pregnant, a woman whose voluminous diaries revealed to me the complex private attitudes of depression, doubt, and worry that lay beneath her public image of confidence and achievement. She was Emmeline B. Wells, the quintessential can-do woman. I could identify with Emmeline because, like me, she was a devout Mormon, a wife, a mother, a teacher, a journalist, a woman of strong ideas, a diarist; but more than that, she was a woman who longed for the companionship of a husband frequently preoccupied with business, civic, and religious responsibilities. Glancing sideways across the separation between the van seats, I traced my husband's strong profile and thought about Emmeline's desire for Daniel Wells's companionship.

I reached between the seats into the large cooler filled with books and typescripts and pulled out several books with sections about Emmeline Wells. I leafed through their pages, recalling some of the fascinating things I had read about this woman. Carol Cornwall

---

Emmeline B. Wells was president of the LDS Relief Society and an ardent promoter of women's rights. According to Patricia Eaton-Gadsby and Judith Rasmussen Dushku, Wells "was not universally loved, but she was universally respected. Her willfulness and instinct for self-preservation co-existed, almost incongruously, with a profound and sustaining faith in her God and a trust in her church and its leaders."[148] *Photograph ca. 1879, courtesy of LDS Archives*

Madsen's dissertation, "A Mormon Woman in Victorian America," supplied intriguing details about an almost mythical woman, sensitively exploring her inner feelings through her diary entries. I remembered holding a copy of Emmeline's diary in my white-gloved hands at BYU's Harold B. Lee Library and how close I felt to her as I read her words in her own script.

She was baptized into the Mormon church in 1842 when she was fourteen years old. Extremely bright, she became a teacher at age fifteen. Being barely five feet tall and sporting long curls, she must have looked like one of the students.[149]

She married James Harvey Harris on July 29, 1843, when she and her husband were both fifteen. Biographer Carol Madsen says the marriage seems to have been encouraged by Emmeline's mother, who wanted a way for her daughter to be tied to the church and be able to travel to Nauvoo with the well-to-do Harris family.[150] Years later, looking back at the romance, Emmeline described James as *so young and altogether unused to the world, we two so unsophisticated ... having no ideas of the stern realities of life.*[151]

Shortly after their arrival in Nauvoo, James's parents left the Mormon church and its city, encouraging their son and daughter-in-law to do likewise. However, the young couple remained in Nauvoo. Emmeline gave birth to a baby boy in September 1844, but the child died within five weeks. James subsequently left and journeyed down river to seek work. Devastated when he didn't write, Emmeline waited, hoping to see him return on one of the Mississippi steamers. She wrote on February 28, 1845:

Last night there came a steam boat up the river, O how my youthful heart fluttered with hope. With anxiety my limbs were affected. ... [N]ot all that has yet been said can shake my confidence in the only man I ever loved. ... I watched the boat and looked out at the door. I walked a few steps out of the yard. ... I saw a person approaching. My heart beat with fond anticipation. It walked like James. It came nearer and just as I was about to speak his name, he spoke and I found I was deceived by the darkness.[152]

James never returned. It was only years later that Emmeline found he had died in 1859 in Bombay, India, while working as a seaman on a whaling vessel.

Forty years later in 1885, Emmeline returned to New England, visiting relatives and her former mother-in-law, Lucy Harris. She visited the area again three years later, shortly after Lucy's death. A family story says that while rummaging through the attic of her mother-in-law's home, Emmeline came across a packet of letters James had written to her before his death in 1859, which his mother had never forwarded. According to a niece who was traveling with Emmeline:

> Aunt Em had Mother [Emmeline's sister Pallas] take her to the cemetery where Mother Harris was buried and there that tiny but mighty old lady stood with her arms raised over the grave and called down a curse upon her mother-in-law that made Mother tremble and no doubt caused the wicked one to tremble in her shroud.[153]

In a poem entitled "Faith and Fidelity," written in later years, Emmeline made reference to the discovery of these letters. Some excerpted lines reveal her emotions:

> *Was it not wonderful, that after weary years . . .*
> *These letters should have come to light again?*
> *The one who wrote them with affection long since dead;*
> *What satisfaction could they ever bring?*[154]

After the disappearance of her young husband from Nauvoo, Emmeline was invited to educate the children of Elizabeth Ann and Nauvoo's bishop Newel K. Whitney. Emmeline was treated well and particularly enjoyed her relationship with Newel's first wife, Elizabeth.[155]

The couple soon taught Emmeline the theology surrounding polygamy, and in February 1845, she was "sealed" to Newel as his second "plural" wife. According to Carol Madsen, it seems likely that the marriage was not consummated until two years later in Winter Quarters, as Emmeline did not bear a child until November 1848, one month after arriving in the Salt Lake Valley. Another daughter was born August 1850. A few weeks later, Newel died suddenly, a shock to his wives. Emmeline was only twenty-two years old and left with two small children.[156]

Emmeline wrote in her diary of her love and admiration for her husband, saying he was *as good a man as ever lived, a father to all within his reach and more than father to me.*[157] The fact that he was thirty-three years her senior seemed not to dim her affection for him. In her diaries, he emerges as a fine man who treated her with concern and sensitivity, encouraging her talents as well.

After Whitney's death, to support herself and her two children, Emmeline began teaching school. She explained the difficulty of this work:

> *I taught 65 children in a log house without desks, charts, blackboards, or scarcely two books of the same kind. The remuneration was likewise trying, [one] bringing a piece of salt pork, another a bucket of flour, a third perhaps a skein of yarn; to repay the ever toiling task of school teaching; the work was unceasing; the day spent in the school room and the night in planning and working for the morrow, whole nights being spent in cutting fancy*

patterns and writing verses in blue ink and working on bits of cardboard mottoes in various colored silks for rewards, to urge the children to diligence and good behavior.[158]

In 1852, likely realizing her precarious position as a single mother, Emmeline made an uncharacteristic plea for help. She wrote what she called "A Letter From a True Friend" to Daniel H. Wells, Lieutenant General of the Utah Militia and her deceased husband's friend. In the letter she explained her predicament candidly yet discreetly: She reminded Wells of his friendship with Whitney in Nauvoo and asked him to "consider the lonely state" of his friend's widow. She wrote that she had often hoped to be "united with a being noble as thyself" and requested him to return a description of his feelings for her.[159]

He did respond, visiting her, and accepted her proposal. Within six months she became his seventh (sixth plural) wife on October 10, 1852. Emmeline moved into the original Wells home, a small adobe structure, until 1856 when she moved into a home of her own.

Her strong feelings for Wells are expressed many times in her diary, as in an 1874 entry: *My heart gave one great bound towards him; O how enthusiastically I love him, truly and devotedly.*[160]

Her husband resided in a home on South Temple Street in Salt Lake City with several of his wives, but was otherwise preoccupied with business, civic, and church responsibilities. He later became a counselor in the LDS First Presidency. When he came to visit Emmeline, her frustration at not having a closer relationship came to the forefront, as expressed in her diary on September 30, 1874:

> *Oh if my husband could only love me even a little and not seem so perfectly indifferent to any sensation of that kind, he cannot know the craving of my nature, he is surrounded with love on every side, and I am cast out O my poor aching heart when shall it rest its burden only on the Lord, only on Him can I look.*[161]

Over a ten-year period, Emmeline had three daughters by Wells: Emmie in 1853, Annie in 1859, and Louie in 1862. Though she interacted with the other wives and visited the large Wells home frequently, she maintained her independence, living with other wives only in 1858 in Provo when the Salt Lake homes were temporarily abandoned for fear of an approaching altercation with the United States Army.[162]

During her life, Emmeline was editor of the *Woman's Exponent*, which for twenty years of its existence carried on its masthead the motto, "For the Rights of the Women of Zion and All Nations." Emmeline wrote numerous articles promoting women's rights. She journeyed to Washington and spoke before two presidents. She became prominent in the suffrage movement and a friend of Susan B. Anthony. Impressed with Mormon women's empowerment, though not understanding their allegiance to polygamy, Susan gave Emmeline a gold ring as a "symbol of the sympathy of two great women for one great cause."[163] Utah was the second territory to grant women suffrage, and Mormon women were the first to vote in America.[164]

In 1899, at age seventy-one, Emmeline attended the World Congress of Women in London, sponsored by the International Council of Women. On July 1 in Convocation Hall of Westminster Abbey, she presented a speech on the history and purposes of the Mormon Relief Society. She attended other meetings in London at the fashionable houses of English nobility, as well as a reception with Queen Victoria. On the ship returning home, writing in her diary on August 8, 1899, she commented: *My life seems so wonderfully changed and developed. What further changes are yet to come, I know not. Certainly a remarkable destiny and a most romantic life.*[165]

In 1876, Emmeline was asked by Brigham Young to organize Mormon women in gathering and storing wheat. The program was so successful that in 1918 President Woodrow Wilson asked Emmeline and her committee "to provide Europe with grain during the final stages of World War I. The organization's grain was donated to Europe, and Em was rewarded with a private audience with Wilson just before his death and hers."[166]

At age eighty-two, Emmeline became president of the church's Relief Society and continued in the office until 1921 when she was ninety-two years old. She died on April 25, 1921. On April 29 flags in Utah flew at half-mast in tribute to her, the first time this honor was extended to a woman.[167]

On initially reading Carol Madsen's dissertation, I couldn't help but think about how Emmeline's success in journalistic endeavors, political activism, religious leadership, and motherly devotion had not entirely filled her life, but that she longed for a man's steady companionship. I felt a kinship with Emmeline.

When we reached Provo, Neal said: "Why don't we go home by way of Manti. We could drive by the temple. Can you remember driving down there the day of our wedding?"

"Yes, do you think we were crazy to get married the day after graduating from BYU?"

"Not really crazy, just in love."

"Did we really know what love was then?"

"Do we know now?"

"That's a good question. This trip has given me a

lot of time to think. You know one way you really show love for me?"

"How?"

"By taking me places."

"What do you mean?"

"I don't know. There's a kind of security when you're driving. I don't worry about taking a wrong turn and getting lost or feeling anxious in snow or on twisty mountain roads or getting sleepy at the wheel."

"Is that what I'm good for, to drive you places?"

"It's not just the driving; it's the mental companionship along the way. It's not just mental either, and not spiritual exactly. Maybe *emotional* is the word I'm looking for, to know that what matters to me and generates feeling in me matters to you, too. May I tell you a story about Emmeline B. Wells? It has to do with the Manti Temple."

"Sure."

"Well, you know her husband, Daniel, was a polygamist, and lived separate from her in a house with other wives. He was prominent in government and church affairs. I've told you before how she wrote in her diary about missing him. Well anyway, in one entry—let me see if I can find it ..." I thumbed through Carol Madsen's dissertation until I came to the passage I wanted. "This was written in Emmeline's diary in March 1890. She wrote about visiting her husband in Manti where he was temple president:

O the joy of being once more in his dear presence. His room is so nice and we are so cosy by the large grate and such a comfortable fire in it. We are more like lovers than husband and wife for we are so far removed from each other there is always the embarrassment of lovers and yet we have been married more than 37 years—how odd it seems. I do not feel old neither does he—we are young to each other and that is well.[168]

Emmeline was sixty-two at the time and Daniel was seventy-six."

Neal turned his head toward me. "Do you think we'll feel that way when we're that old?"

"Oh, I don't think we'll feel embarrassed, but I hope the joy is there." I reached over and placed my hand on his knee, "And I hope we'll still feel like lovers."

"I think we will ... if we can keep from getting 'far removed' from each other."

I lifted my hand from Neal's knee and edged my fingers around his arm. "We need to work at that. In some ways it's going to be hard to go home."

20.

Emigration Canyon

After leaving Echo Canyon, we passed near Witches Rock, Hogsback Summit, and Willow Springs, then proceeded to Emigration Canyon, the entrance to the Salt Lake Valley. Emigrants came down the mountain here through the canyon, following the route opened by the Donners. The passage was difficult, but each succeeding party made the route a little better. I thought about Eliza R. Snow, who passed this way and "made the route a little better" for women who followed her lead in many aspects of life.

She kept a trail journal beginning in February of 1846. Earlier I had purposely stopped at a place called Bonaparte on the Des Moines River to connect with Eliza, who 147 years earlier wrote in her diary that she had *slung a tin cup on a string and drew some water which was a very refreshing draught.* At my stopping, the water was too dirty to drink.

Born in 1804, Eliza was baptized a Latter-day Saint in 1835 and moved from Ohio to Missouri to Illinois. She became a plural wife of Joseph Smith in 1842. After his death, she became a wife of Brigham Young in October 1844. When the Mormons were forced to leave Nauvoo, Young arranged for her to travel with the family of Colonel Stephen Markham from Nauvoo to Winter Quarters. Her diary of this period gives a vivid word picture of her adaptability and optimism. Besides writing in her diary, she creatively composed many poems to inspire and urge others forward.

She tells of crossing the Mississippi on February 13th and finding her brother Lorenzo camped on the other side. On the 14th, she, along with the wife of Colonel Markham, traveled in a buggy doing needlework *tho' the melting snow dripp[ed] thro' our cover.*[169]

On the 19th, to take her mind off the severe cold, she amused herself by writing "The Camp of Israel: A Song for the Pioneers No. 1," whose six verses were interspersed with a rousing chorus:

> *Tho' we fly from vile aggression'*
> *We'll maintain our pure profession—*
> *Seek a peaceable possession*
> *Far from Gentiles and oppression.*

On February 28th, she told of camping on Indian Creek: *We arrived here a little before sunset, and the prospect for the night seem'd dubious enough. The ground was covered with snow, shoe deep, but our industrious men with hoes soon prepared places and pitch'd the tents, built wood-piles in front of them and but a few minutes with many hands transform'd the rude valley into a thriving town.*[170]

On March 3rd, she passed through the town of Farmington, Missouri, where the inhabitants came out

---

Eliza R. Snow, in historian Maureen Ursenbach Beecher's words, "commanded such respect among the Mormon women of Utah that they celebrated her birthday, whether or not she was among them; ... They listened to her, quoted her, obeyed her, and found in her 'the president of the female portion of the human race.' She was a legend before half her effective life was done, and lived that legend for the rest of it." *Courtesy of Utah State Historical Society*

to look at them, manifesting *great curiosity and more levity than sympathy for our houseless situation.* At this time, the buggy in which Eliza and Sister Markham had been riding, *which serv'd me as sitting room & dormitory,* was exchanged for a wagon.[171] The two women soon found themselves *nicely seated in an ox wagon on a chest with a brass kettle and a soap box for our foot stools, thankful that we are so well off.*[172]

On March 7th, Eliza wrote: *The weather warm & the ox-teams seem'd almost exhausted. I got out of the wagon & walk'd for the first time on the journey.*[173]

On March 9th, commenting on the ability of the emigrants to organize at stopping places, she wrote: *At nine this mor. I notic'd but a few rods from our tent, a black-smith's shop in operation, and every thing indicated real life. Not a cooking utensil was idle. Sis. M. baked a batch of eleven loaves but the washing business was necessarily omitted for the want of water, an inconvenience the present location suffers more than any previous one. Had the pleasure of the first interview with Prest. Y[oung] since we left the City.*[174] Interestingly, though she was his wife, she addressed him formally as "President Young."

A few days later, Eliza wrote: *Quite windy. Our tent blew down & with other accidents upset a pail of potatoe soup which was intended for breakfast, but instead thereof we had coffee, fried jole [fish head] and jonny cake.* In a diary for March 14th, commenting on other food, she said: *Sis Y. sent us a supper of rich pot-pie made of wild game, rabbits, pheasants, quails, &c. which is the fourth dish of the kind on which we have feasted since we left the City, being 4 weeks yesterday.*[175]

Eliza also tells of using a washing vale and of making the wagon comfortable with coals. On March 22, just before crossing the Chariton River about halfway across northern Missouri, she was in an open area where she could count eighty wagons before her in one view. She composed another song, the second verse counseling:

Let us go—let us go from a country of strife—
From a land where the wicked are seeking our life
From a country where justice no longer remains—
From which virtue is fled & iniquity reigns.

The final verse concluded:

Let us go—let us go to the far western shore
Where the blood-thirsty "christians" will hunt us no
    more;
Where the waves of the ocean will echo the sound
And the shout of salvation be heard the world round![176]

Arriving in Davies County, Missouri, on March 25, she explained that twenty-five men decided to take a

job making rails, *for which they got 10 bush. of corn, which was distributed tues. night. They also got 100 [pounds] of bacon for the pioneers, 100 more paid for.* With characteristic optimism, she concluded: *Thus the Lord opens the way for his poor saints, thro' patience & industry to obtain the necessaries of life, as they journey toward the western wilderness.*[177]

Eliza reached Winter Quarters, Nebraska, in June 1846 and remained there for a year. Her second trail diary was begun in mid-June 1847. On the trail she noted her interactions with people, events, weather, scenery, and mileage, describing the experience of passing through Emigration Canyon and entering the Salt Lake Valley in October 1847:

Fr. 1st Left the carriage & an ox that gave out yesterday— I rode in the black wag. sis. P. M. & Edith walk—very, very dirty, thro brush & timber. ... [W]e then went slash mash down over stumps, trees &c. ... Thankful for our deliverance thus far.
Trav. 10 ms

Sat 2d Cross a stream 19 times—which is dry in some of its beds—the vegetation & shrubbery is very much chang'd; here is oak, maple, and elder, ozier &c. About 4 we come in view of the Valley looking like a broad rich river bottom —it rains & a breach made in the side of our [canvas. B]eing in sight of home we make our way to the Fort—I am too sick to enjoy the scenery but a good cup tea pre-

par'd by sis P. refreshes me, also a vis. from sis. Sess. Trav. 14 ms.

Su 3d This mor. seat myself by a doby [an adobe] fire-place outside the body of a log house ... have my things put in Clarissa's room who said Prest. Y wrote her that I should live with her. ...

Feeling dirty, sick, tired, and required to live with nineteen-year-old Clarissa, one of Brigham Young's other wives, did Eliza imagine that her life would improve in future years? Did she have any hint of the major role she would play in the lives of women in the State of Deseret in the years to come? Could she possibly have anticipated how a future historian might describe her life?

Poetess, prophetess, priestess, and *presidentess* are terms which her contemporaries applied with reverent awe to Eliza Roxcy Snow. This woman, this captain of Utah's woman host, commanded such respect among the Mormon women of Utah that they celebrated her birthday, whether or not she was among them; they took up a collection to pay her fare on a jaunt to the Holy Land; they turned out in numbers whenever and wherever she spoke on her many visits throughout the Great Basin kingdom; they listened to her, quoted her, obeyed her, and found in her "the president of the female portion of the human race." She was a legend before half her effective life was done, and lived that legend for the rest of it. She was aware of her position and both played upon it and was plagued by it. "Sisters," she told an audience, "I occupy an honorable position, but the great responsibility attending it prevents my feeling proud."[178]

Historian Maureen Beecher believes that Eliza's life can be examined under the headings used to describe her: *poetess, priestess, prophetess,* and *presidentess.* The first is an apt description of Utah's first lady, her writing ability evident from childhood. Growing up in the Ohio territory, she showed an early talent for writing poetry, even putting her school work into verse when she became bored with mundane prose assignments. She later published lofty sounding verses in local newspapers, but her poetry became more than ornamental when she began to compose verses to inspire after her conversion to Mormonism. Though exposed to doctrines of the religion in 1830 or 1831 when she was in her mid-twenties, she waited almost five years to be baptized, wanting spiritual confirmation of the rightness of her decision. This she received the night following her baptism after she had retired to bed. "I saw a beautiful candle with an unusual long, bright blaze directly over my feet. I sought to know the interpretation, and received the following, 'The lamp of intelligence shall be lighted over your path.'"[179]

She journeyed to Kirtland, Ohio, where she served as governess in the home of Joseph and Emma Smith. Later she was joined by her parents, sister, and brother. The family moved to Adam-ondi-Ahman in Missouri where Eliza became friends with Zina Diantha Huntington, whose family had traveled with and settled near the Snows. Later both families moved to Nauvoo, and it was there that the title "Zion's poetess" was given to Eliza by Joseph Smith. When the Saints abandoned their beloved Nauvoo, her verses encouraged the Camp of Zion, as it was called, as they moved across muddy Iowa in the winter and spring of 1846. One poem, written on Sunday, March 1, ends:

> *Where is freedom? Where is justice?*
> *Both have from this nation fled?*
> *And the blood of martyr'd prophets*
> *Must be answered on its head!*
> *Therefore to your tents, O Jacob!*
> *Like our father Abra'm dwell—*
> *God will exercise his purpose—*
> *Camp of Israel! all is well.*[180]

One of her poems, translated and later included in a Scandinavian hymnal, became a favorite with emigrants, perhaps even sung by my Danish ancestors as a warning against too much idealization:

> *Think not when you gather to Zion*
> *That all will be holy and pure,*
> *That fraud and deception are banished*
> *And confidence wholly secure. ...*

> *Think not. When you gather to Zion,*
> *The Saints here have nothing to do*
> *But to look to your personal welfare,*
> *And always be comforting you.*[181]

In the current LDS hymnal, ten hymns have lyrics composed by Snow, proving the continuing aptness of her title as Zion's poetess. One of the frequently sung hymns, "O My Father," asks the question: "In the heav'ns are parents single?" and then gives an answer, "No, the thought makes reason stare; / Truth is reason—truth eternal / Tells me I've a mother there." The final stanza expresses a hope of rejoining heavenly parents:

> *When I leave this frail existence—*
> *When I lay this mortal by,*
> *Father, mother, may I meet you*
> *In your royal court on high?*
> *Then at length, when I've completed*
> *All you sent me forth to do,*
> *With your mutual approbation*
> *Let me come and dwell with you.*[182]

Eliza's introduction to the idea of a Heavenly Mother possibly can be traced to her close friendship with Zina Diantha Huntington, who was comforted by Joseph Smith with this teaching when her mother died in 1839.[183] Eliza's writing went beyond hymnody to include published volumes of poetry as well.

She received the title *high priestess* because of her involvement in the religious ceremonies of the Nauvoo Temple as well as in the Endowment House in pioneer Salt Lake City. She was active in blessing the sick and washing and anointing women about to be confined for childbirth.

In assessing her title of *prophetess*, Maureen Beecher writes that "about half the prophesies uttered by Eliza were fulfilled, about half were not," calling this tallying "likely an unfair gage." She notes that "Heber J. Grant testified to his childhood memory of the prophecy uttered in tongues by Eliza and translated by Zina Huntington, that he would become an apostle. He did. And Mary Ann Chadwick Hall, having buried two children in two years, was promised by Eliza that she would have a daughter (she was pregnant at the time) who would grow to womanhood. The child, born healthy, was indeed a girl, and lived to age twenty."[184] Maureen says that Eliza had "other prophetic gifts not so easily judged [and] ... understanding and aware-

nesses that are a more important expression of prophecy than are any number of predictions. ... [T]he favorite example is the concept of a Heavenly Mother."[185]

Certainly Eliza's participation in blessing meetings with other women had prophetic elements. Patty Sessions wrote in her diary for May 1, 1847: *Silvia and I went to a meeting to Sister Leonard's. None but females there. We had a good meeting. I presided. It was got up by E. R. Snow. They spoke in tongues. I interpreted. Some prophesied. It was a feast.*[186] These meetings brought women into close spiritual sisterhood and were a positive emotional support as the women went through difficult times, leaving established homes and following pioneer trails seeking new places of refuge.

Eliza earned the title *presidentess* because of her ability to preside, to utilize her organizational ability as a catalyst for implementation of ideas initiated by others. About 1855, Brigham Young asked her to facilitate the reorganization of the Relief Society in some of the Salt Lake wards. She had already served as secretary of the Nauvoo Female Relief Society, organized in March of 1842 with Emma Smith as president, and had watched the society grow from twenty-eight members to over 1,300 a year later.[187] This experience gave her a sense of what the organization could accomplish. In 1867, when Relief Society was re-instituted among the various church units in Utah under Eliza's direction, "additional activities beyond the traditional roles assigned to women were rapidly introduced. The sisters increased their roles in economic, political, and commercial activities. They built and owned Relief Society halls, ran cooperatives; raised silk; bought, stored, and sold grain; and collectively supported the medical education of women as doctors and nurses, eventually establishing their own Deseret Hospital in Salt Lake City."[188] Eliza served as the general Relief Society president for twenty years.

She also organized Retrenchment Societies, which later became the Young Ladies' Mutual Improvement Association. Building on suggestions from Aurelia Rogers about offering religious training for children, which came to be called the Primary Association: "In one remarkable jaunt to southern Utah in 1880-81 the seventy-six-year-old woman [Snow] rode nearly two thousand miles by train and wagon to establish some thirty-five Primaries among the Saints there."[189]

Did Eliza ever marvel at the turns of her life, feeling with her contemporary and friend, Emmeline B. Wells, "What a remarkable destiny"? Beecher, editor of Eliza's diaries, writes: "By 1867 Eliza of the trail—passive observer and quiet chronicler—had become Sister Snow, dynamic organizer and daring activist."[190]

As we entered Salt Lake City, I asked Neal to drive downtown past the Lion House where Eliza had lived with Brigham Young's other wives until her death in 1887. I stretched back in time and envisioned her leaving from and returning to this communal home to attend to her various duties, making her distinct imprint in so many areas of endeavor. I wonder if she ever compared her situation in the elegant Lion House to the fourteen-by-sixteen-foot cabin in the fort she initially shared with Clarissa in 1847. Did she wonder at a past that shaped a present that became a future?

Young women today may not be able to guess their futures, but they can know their options because of Eliza and other women of the past. My daughters and daughters-in-law have college educations. If they choose to work, they may; but the option to be stay-at-home mothers is open to them as well. Because they have a choice, they can better enjoy their roles and the people they touch. I'm grateful for the many choices they have, enhanced by woman after woman who went before, opening passages once closed, broadening paths once narrow, and mapping territory once obscure. As I view my young granddaughters, six of them, I wonder what they will find in their futures, what will be the factors influencing their choosing, and if they will fully realize their debt to the past.

Will one of them become the Eliza R. Snow of the twenty-first century? Perhaps not, but the promise is that because of Eliza and women like her, my grand-daughters can be individuals in ways many women in the past found difficult.

21.

"Little Denmark"

Leaving Salt Lake, we drove down old Highway 89 toward Manti, passing through Pleasant Grove, Thistle, Fairview, Mt. Pleasant, and Spring City. Most of the place names connote a sense of hope—except for Thistle, which seems to be more realistic, considering pioneer efforts to tame this desert land. In Sanpete County, aptly dubbed "Little Denmark," I felt at home. My great-grandmother, Elizabeth Domgaard, was the first girl born to Danish parents in the county. Her parents, Niels Peter Domgaard and Else Kirstine Nielsen, left Denmark in December of 1852 and arrived in Manti a year later. Their daughter Elizabeth was born on July 13, 1854. Some of what I know about Elizabeth was told to me by my mother:

My grandmother had long white hair [and] ... always wore it wound into a bun at the back of her neck. She was always neat about her person and about her home. In her bedroom on her high bed, she had a mattress and a feather tick and pillows. She had a beautiful white bedspread, and she would never let us sit on the bed. That's why I always turn the bedspread back when I sit on a bed today. I remember when my grandfather died how the grandkids took turns staying with Grandma, sleeping in her big high bed with her.

She had a small upstairs and the steps were steep, and we kids loved to go up there. I don't even remember what was there, but we loved to go up. In the par-

Elizabeth Domgaard (shown here with her husband, Andrew Christian Andersen, and seven of their nine children, ca. 1896) was born in 1854 in Manti, Utah. In her autobiography, she said: "When I was a couple of days old, there was a big rain storm. My father had to hold some covering up to keep mother from getting too wet. She didn't have much to eat at that time. ... She told me the best meal she had, while in bed, was two saleratus biscuits and a pint cup of buttermilk." *Family photograph in possession of the author*

147

lor she had a beautiful organ, but I don't remember if she played. A great big gold-framed mirror hung on one wall. My grandparents didn't have an indoor toilet, just an outhouse. Grandma had an old rooster who wouldn't let anyone go in there, it would try to peck you. The rooster wouldn't behave until Grandma came and talked to it and got it away.

I used to have warts sometimes, they said because I played with the pollywogs down in the creek, and Grandma could always take [the warts] off with a potato or a red string. I would close my eyes and she'd rub the wart with a cut potato and then throw it over her shoulder so I couldn't see where it went. Or she'd put the red string around the wart and tie some sort of a knot and hold it there for a minute, mumbling something under her breath. In a couple days the wart would be gone.

I remember loving to go to Grandmother's home, which was about one block from our house, because we could go down in the orchard and pick apples. She told us grandchildren we could have what we could carry in our hands, but I always wanted a few more, so I would stuff some in my bloomer legs; I'm sure she knew what I was doing, but she never let on. She would let us have anything in the garden but the raspberries because she wanted to bottle those for the winter. When I pick raspberries and make jam, I always think of my grandmother's garden. We loved to sleigh ride down the hill located just above the orchard. Our grandfather would pour water down it in the winter to make

a slippery sledding hill. There was a storage shed next to the house where they kept all of their potatoes and carrots stored for the winter, old furniture, Grandma's cream separator, and probably a lot of other things that I don't remember. I wonder what happened to all the old things.[191]

I learned more about my great-grandmother through the brief autobiography she wrote in 1929 when she was seventy-five years old. She tells of the circumstances surrounding her birth:

> I was born in Manti, July 13, 1854. My father being a blacksmith, I was born in the shop as the house was not finished. The partition between the anvil and mother's bed was the fireplace and bellows. The shop had a dirt roof. When I was a couple of days old, there was a big rainstorm. My father had to hold some covering up to keep mother from getting too wet. She didn't have much to eat at that time. Father had plenty of work but couldn't get much pay. They couldn't get food. Mother told me the best meal she had, while in bed, was two saleratus biscuits and a pint cup of buttermilk. Some women brought it to her. She said it seemed it was the best meal she had ever had.

Because of his work experience in Denmark, Elizabeth's father was able to improve his family's situation fairly quickly:

> After the first year, father and mother had plenty. They had a good home. He made the first threshing machine in

Manti. He had turning lathes, to turn iron for the mills. At one time father was one of the most well-to-do men in Manti. He worked in the shop most of the time. I helped turn the wheel when he turned the iron. The first I can remember about the shop was when mother would tell me to tell father to come to supper; and when he went out to work, I went with him, sometimes, and I would sit by the fireplace and see the sparks go up. I thought sparks made the stars.

Elizabeth gives hair-raising examples of mishaps in her accident-prone youth:

When I was eight years old, I fell in the Big Creek. I crossed it to pick berries. The water was the highest in June. I went half a block. In the turn of the creek, the water must have pushed me to the edge and I got hold of some willows. My sister, Elsie, five years old, and Rency Andersen, seven years old, got to the edge and helped me out. Mother couldn't see how I ever got out.

Another time, in the winter, I got in[to] a water hole [up] to my waist. There was a fence across the creek, and I got hold of it but couldn't get my feet on the bottom, so I hung there for some time. I called and cried for someone. No one heard me. Then Anna Marker came after a bucket of water and got me out. I was about to give up. It was New Year's night and it was dark and cold.

Another time, when I was about thirteen years old, I was in the field helping father water. The horse was staked down [and] … to save father from walking so far, I went down and pulled the stake. When the horse found he was

loose and the reins were down, he wanted to go home. I tried to hold him, but I couldn't. He got the rope around my legs. I had shoes on, but not stockings, so the rope sawed my one leg pretty bad. The horse ran up a ten-acre and across another ten-acre before I got loose. Father thought I was killed. I had another accident, but lived through them all.

Like most pioneer girls, Elizabeth played an important role in helping the family farm, her responsibilities not limited to domestic chores:

When I got older, I would help weed the black seed out of the wheat. We weeded many days. I helped drive grasshoppers in places to kill them to save our wheat. I have seen the time when grasshoppers were so thick that when they started to fly, we couldn't see the sun in the middle of the day.

I helped to rake and bind the grain. It was cut with the cradle. There wasn't any machine. I remember when flour was twenty dollars a hundred and wheat was six dollars a bushel. Father had a lot of wheat and flour at times. He hauled them to Salt Lake City. I helped pick up potatoes and milked cows and made butter that was sent to Salt Lake City. Father not having any boys, I had to do all I could to help him. I helped make nails, also molasses. I helped to wash sheep. Father and other men made a platform and four flumes so we could let the water run on the sheep to clean them before the wool was off. The water was from the Warm Springs. We kids were as wet as the sheep. We had woolen dresses on, so we didn't feel the cold. We *quite enjoyed it. I guess they washed the sheep to keep their skins clean, free from scab.*

I helped my mother dip candles in a keg of tallow. That was the light we had at that time. I could card and spin yarn. I have a pillow that I spun yarn for when I was nine years old. We scrubbed our board floors with saleratus and wheat straw, used in place of brushes. I helped my mother make soap. We used lime and saleratus. We didn't have lye. I helped color yarn all colors. We had it woven into cloth for our clothes. There weren't any stores then in Manti.

She remembers the beginning of the Black Hawk War and the impact on the settlement:

I remember the afternoon when John Lowry pulled the Indian off the horse. The next day the Indians killed Peter Lowry. That started the Black Hawk War. The Indians took a lot of cattle with them that day. Father lost ten head. My brother-in-law, Fritz Nelsen, was wounded and four or five men were killed that day. The Indians went up Salina Canyon. The people in the South were in danger so they came to Sanpete. We lived in fear of the Indians. For some time they would steal and kill all they could when they got a chance. One day they killed five men and two women in Ephraim and took all the cattle they could.

Elizabeth explains how limited her education was:

My first teacher was Mary Lowry. The school children got the itch [lice] so we couldn't go any more. Then I went

to Mary Billing's school in the house where she lived. She had two children. We had to help tend them when she had class. We studied the best we could. That lasted six weeks. I went to John Reid's school. The school term was three months of the year. I went to John Bench's two months. That was my school days.

When she was sixteen, she left to work in the city:

In 1870, I went to Salt Lake to work. I lived with [the] Wilford Woodruff [family] about six months. ... I stayed part of the summer [and] ... came home with an ox-team with Deanie Hansen, her brother, and her brother-in-law, and two other men. It was a slow ride, but we felt fine. When we got in Salt Creek Canyon, it started to rain, thunder, and lightning. It just poured down. We had to sit up all night. We just had cover on one wagon. It took us five days to Manti.

First of October, Christena Madsen and I [returned] to ... work in the Salt Lake Laundry. We came home with Bishop Moffit and three other men. It was in January 1872. It was cold and snowing. The men had goods from the stores, so we had to keep going. When we got a chance, we camped in the canyon and the snow was so deep on the Divide that they had to put two span of horses on the wagon, go a little way, then change again. It took them all day to Fountain Green. We were about half frozen. We got in a house and had supper. Next day we got to Manti.

After her return to Manti, Elizabeth began preparing for her marriage:

I stayed home that summer and spun for my folks and made my trousseau. I had six quilts and five pairs of pillow-cases, sheets, and a bed, and everything that goes with it. It was all my own work[. I made] a straw tick. We didn't have a spring and mattress. I bought my bed.[192]

The autobiography ends there, with "I bought my bed." Perhaps she felt the family photograph with her husband and seven of their nine children told the rest of the story. Forming images of Elizabeth from her brief account and from my mother's memories gives me some sense of who she was. Certainly, I knew her better than my other great-grandmother, Barbara Schell, who is sadly only a name and date on a census sheet.

I am so grateful that Elizabeth's daughter Grace wrote her mother's history as an addition to the auto-biography.[193] My great-aunt's words tie me to this woman I never knew, letting me see more clearly her character and feel gratitude for one of the persons who passed to me, not only a heritage of genes, but also a heritage of values. Aunt Grace's words create pictures of Elizabeth's life, giving me a personal insight into the themes I have spent years studying: pioneer romance, childbirth, sickness and death, religious devotion, homemaking practices, work, and education. As I read my great-grandmother's history, I detected, in my own life, echoes of hers sounding down a corridor of time.

From Aunt Grace, I learn details that explain Elizabeth's romance and marriage to my great-grand-father, Andrew Christian Andersen:

Wearing a purple printed calico dress with mutton-leg sleeves, an infant waist, and a full skirt, Elizabeth had attended a party at the home of Christena Miller. "It was on a Sunday night, I [Elizabeth] was fourteen years old. Andrew's folks were visiting at the Miller home. They had brought with them from Ephraim their two sons, Niels and Andrew. Another boy, John Petersen, was there. We played the game of Smut. I was the loser so had to have black soot from the stove lid put on my nose as a penalty. Niels was very anxious to do the deed, but Andrew protected me and wouldn't let him. Of course that pleased me very much because I felt he liked me a little, and I thought he was very good looking.

"I met Andrew again at [church] conferences and also one time when I was hunting cattle. Christena was in love with Andrew, but I was so happy when Andrew asked to take me home for the first time. I was sixteen years old then.

"My father and mother approved of him. I, of course, had other boy friends through the years, Fred Alder, Hans Larson, and Jens Michaelsen. Stena [future sister-in-law] told me, after taking me home that first night he made this remark, 'Elizabeth is going to be my wife some day.' Stena answered him by saying, 'It's early for you to be thinking of a wife.'"

I identify with Elizabeth's adolescent longing for someone who would be kind, considerate of her feelings. I share my great-grandmother's excitement at a chance meeting when her heart must have raced as mine did in similar circumstances, her pride at being chosen over some other girl. Like Elizabeth, I had "other boyfriends through the years," but the joy when I saw "the one" walking across a crowded floor to ask me, not some other girl, to dance!

At the age of eighteen Elizabeth and Andrew started to go steady and in two years they made plans for their marriage. Accompanied by Elizabeth's parents and Andrew's younger sister Stena and her fiancé George, they made a four-day trip to Salt Lake, where they were married in the Endowment House, July 6, 1874. Elizabeth wore a dress of white mull, dotted, with a full skirt, full sleeves, and a lace collar. Apostle Wilford Woodruff performed the ceremony. This was particularly meaningful as Elizabeth had worked in his home, and she often mentioned how kind and good he and his wife were to her. She remembered whenever Sister Woodruff was blue and downhearted, she would sit in her rocking chair and while rocking, sing "Count Your Many Blessings." One day Apostle Woodruff had opened a box and showed Elizabeth the red handkerchief that the Prophet Joseph Smith had used in Nauvoo when he administered to the sick. Elizabeth felt as if she were looking at something sacred and holy.

I recall my marriage in the Manti temple, three great-aunts, my Aunt Grace among them, bustling around me like fairy-godmothers, making sure the experience was perfect. Like Cinderella in her ball gown, I felt transformed in my white silk organza wedding dress, and after the temple ceremony I felt transformed in a spiritual way. My new husband and I had vowed our commitment across an altar and then viewed ourselves in two facing mirrors. Our shared, reflected image forever stretching backward was a kind of connection to all who had gone before and all who would come after.

Elizabeth and Andrew came back to Ephraim, and when they had been married ten months, their first child, a baby boy with light curly hair and clear blue eyes, was born. Elizabeth's mother, Else, lived in Manti, a distance of seven miles. Elizabeth explains her unexpected arrival: "Two days had passed since our baby had arrived. I was wishing my mother was nearer so she could see me and her new grandson. Almost immediately my wish came true. There she stood in the doorway. Naturally we both cried, but they were tears of happiness and love. I asked mother who brought her over. She tried to change the subject, but after much questioning she admitted she had walked the entire distance. She said she just couldn't wait for anyone to bring her. She stayed with me for a few days. I was very happy to have her with me."

A second curly haired son named Niels Peter Arthur, who became my grandfather, was born two years later. I hope Elizabeth's mother came again to help. How much I loved my own mother's presence after the birth of each of my children. I was particularly grateful for her presence after the birth of my fifth child as, for a few days, I didn't want to attend to the needs of the rest of the family. I just wanted to immerse myself in emotion with my new infant, enjoying our little island of perfect compatibility. We fit together exactly, he at my breast, his small body curled across my stomach, my arms encircling him. We seemed not two but one, just as we had been one for nine months, but now he was my visible other part and open to new joys.

I would touch his silky black hair and, with my fingers, softly trace the circled crown. I would stroke his glass-smooth cheek until it dimpled in pleasure, then wedge my finger in the tiny fist and spread the slender fingers, awed by such perfection. At all this tender touching, my baby's bright eyes would open, gaze about in wonder, and softly close to peaceful sleep once more.

I wanted to shut the door to the world and have just him and me. I wanted to listen to the sounds he made, hear the barely audible breathing interrupted by occasional high-pitched squeals of who knows what emotion. I was so grateful for a mother who came to keep my outer world of household, husband, and other children functioning so I could have my quiet inner world for a time. Elizabeth might have felt the same way.

When my grandparents' second son was learning to walk and toddling after his older brother,

Elizabeth and Andrew went to spend Christmas with Stena in Mayfield, leaving their home in Ephraim. There Andrew told his wife that he had been talking with the men and they had almost persuaded him to stay in Mayfield, buy land, and make it their home. Elizabeth refused to listen and put up some sound arguments against it, but in the end she was over-ruled and arrangements were made for them to move. A storm came up and because of the bad weather, she didn't go back with Andrew to get their furniture, and she never saw their Ephraim home again.

In Mayfield, they moved into a one-room log cabin with a dirt floor. The rats were so numerous that they had the two children sleep with [their parents] for fear they would be bitten. In time they got rid of the rodents by scattering poison wheat around. Days, weeks, and months passed. Many times at night Elizabeth dreamed she was back in Ephraim, happy in her little home. When she would awaken and realize where she was, she'd be overcome with grief.

In the spring, Andrew purchased a lot and with the help of friends built a log house that was finished by fall, just one room in the beginning. Elizabeth placed pink and blue cambric shams on her red four-poster bed, which was strung with rope. This rope held up a straw-tick with a feather bed on it, then blankets or sheets and quilts on top. She covered her pillows with cases that showed her crochet work. At the windows, she hung curtains that were handmade. Homemade rugs were scattered on the floor, which she scrubbed with salerastas. She had a trundle bed for her two children, five chairs, a rocking chair, a table and a cupboard.

After she had been in the home two years, she had enough rags to have a carpet woven. Under the carpet they put clean, fresh straw every fall, then tacked the carpet close to the wall against the baseboards. Three more babies, all daughters, were born while they lived in the log house, a lean-to added in 1879 providing a little more space.

I remember the home that Neal and I purchased in California two years after we were married and time spent painting walls while our baby rested nearby. Neil spent after-work hours patching up an old ice drop, replacing faded linoleum, and refinishing second-hand furniture to make our home attractive on a very small budget. I made curtains for my home, just as Elizabeth had, and felt personal satisfaction when I hung them at the windows. How close to her I feel as I remember my pride in my first home.

A diphtheria epidemic erupted in Mayfield in 1880. Andrew, five years old and Arthur, two and one half years old, contracted the disease in a very severe form. There was no vaccine at that time. Andrew practically choked to death. In order to relieve him, the doctor did the only thing he knew to do. He scraped the white growth in his throat off with a silver spoon. Poison set in and on February 29, 1880, Andrew passed away. Elizabeth grieved, but explained, "One must go on and live whether you want to or not and besides I had to think of Arthur and my husband, who, also, was in sorrow. And then, too, I was expecting a new baby in August."

But little Arthur didn't let Elizabeth forget about Andrew. As he was sleeping when the men came at night and carried the casket away, Arthur was worried about what had happened to his brother. He had called the casket a box and believed that Andrew was asleep in it. All during the summer, he hunted for Andrew in the boxes that he would find and was continually asking about him.

I remember my four-year-old daughter's reaction to the death of her little brother when he was one and a half. In winter, after the first Utah snowfall, she wanted to make a blanket to put on his grave in Elsinore "to keep him warm."

In 1888 Andrew built a four-room adobe house, and the log house was pulled over to the north and used as a granary, till someone bought it to use for a home. Four children, three daughters and a son, were born in the adobe house.

These additional children must have been a comfort to Andrew and Elizabeth after the death of their oldest son, just as the birth of four more children after our son's death in some way lessened the hurt for Neal and me. An additional support for Elizabeth was her religious activity; turning outward to help others lessened the preoccupation with her own difficulties.

Elizabeth was first counselor in the Primary Association from 1884-90, adding concern for other people's children to her concern for her own large family. She began serving as a Relief Society teacher when she was sixteen years old and continued as one until she was eighty years old. After that, she was put on the Sunshine Committee, a group that visited the women who were homebound and ill.

She was the "head teacher" for many years. Each fall, she and her teacher partner would drive a team of horses on a wagon, call at the home of each family and get from one half to one bushel of wheat to be placed in the church granary for the welfare of those in need. When planting time came in the spring, farmers could borrow this wheat for planting, then in the fall, pay it back with a ten percent interest in wheat.

This way Mayfield had a goodly amount of wheat when the church called it into the General Welfare, during World War I. As in all wards, they received interest on their wheat to be used for welfare in the ward. Later each ward was privileged to use it for general purposes. It was hard work gathering that wheat, but it helped many families who needed assistance.

In the early years of Mayfield, women wanted to have a place to worship in the town, so they decided to give their "Sunday eggs." Each Monday every family would bring the eggs their chickens had laid on Sunday to Elizabeth's house. By Monday night a washtub and two or three buckets of eggs were sitting on the floor. She would take them to the store and get cash for them. In this way the women paid for the erection of their Relief Society building. This building was initially the only church building in Mayfield. It was the chapel, the recreation hall, the theatre, and was used as the meeting place for anything of importance.

Like Elizabeth ninety years before me, I worked in Relief Society when I was in my twenties. Preparing lessons during the months my baby had leukemia, I found comfort in my attempt to inspire others. I taught from a literature series called *Out of the Best Books* that was compiled thematically for Relief Society use by two BYU professors. Certainly, the selections that centered around "The Place of Suffering in Life" were as important to me as the teacher as to those I taught.

Those volumes still occupy a prominent place on my bookshelves as a resource of inspiration. Regularly I visit a neighbor, a former English teacher afflicted with macular degeneration, and think of a selection in one of the volumes by the great English poet John Milton. When Milton was going blind and trying to cope with the resulting sense of uselessness, he wrote a sonnet that includes an affirmative ending line, his discovery that "they also serve who only stand and wait." I want my neighbor to know how true that is.

As I visit with the elderly women in our area, I always return home with a better appreciation of aging and ideas for how I can live my future with dignity. Because my English students have recorded and transcribed over four hundred oral histories of local residents, I know something about many of their earlier lives as well and talk with them about their youth, careers, service in the military, and other topics. Each person represents a whole life to me, not just the later years of living.

Like many other pioneer women, Elizabeth had a miraculous story involving a visit from a needy stranger:

> In 1884 Elizabeth and a woman named Gusta Andersen were visiting Gusta's mother. A strange man stopped at the door and asked for something to eat. Dinnertime was past and all the bread Gusta's mother had left was two biscuits, but she invited the stranger in and set the table with a clean tablecloth. The food consisted of the two biscuits, green onions, and the little food that was left from the dinner. The man bowed his head as if he were blessing the food. He ate the lunch and as he stood to leave he said, "Thank you. I promise you that your table will be spread with plenty of food to supply your family." He disappeared quickly. Elizabeth, Gusta, and her mother went outside to see where he had gone but to their amazement they were unable to see him.

I have never had an experience with a needy stranger who disappeared suddenly. All the needy people I help seem to stay around for a long time. We don't hear stories like Elizabeth's any more. Are our perceptions different living in a world where we trust science to explain the unexpected? Would we fear derision if we suspected a supernatural encounter?

Spiritual premonitions are often reported by the pioneers. One such experience of my great-grandmother when she was at Funks Lake, now called Palisade Park, on June 22, 1878, was retold in story form by her daughter Grace:

> People from Ephraim and Manti had planned a big celebration at the lake, to be followed that night by a

dance in Mayfield. Wagons and buggies, full of people, could be seen along the roads. Andrew and Elizabeth, with their two young sons, were among them.

Arriving at the lake, they met their friends and exchanged greetings, enjoying a day of news-gathering. A program, prepared by individuals from each town, was given in the forenoon meeting. At noontime each group opened baskets and cooked over the open fire, the aroma of food filling the air. Many joined in the games, others just sat around in the shade and told stories. Some of the young boys went for a swim.

Daniel Funk owned and operated a small steamboat. He charged each passenger ten cents a ride to cross the lake and back. Everyone was anxious to participate in this special entertainment. Between the couple, the decision was made that Andrew and his three-year-old son should go with the first group. Elizabeth and Arthur, one year old, should accompany the ones on the second trip. The water was calm and very blue. The group waved their hands to those standing on the shore and soon could be heard their happy voices over the water.

After a pleasant time on the water, the first group returned. It was time now for the second group of people to get into the boat. Elizabeth took her baby and was going toward the boat when Andrew asked her not to go. She wanted to know why, but again he asked her not to go. Her reaction to this was, "Now that you have enjoyed a ride, why deprive me of the same pleasure?" So she gave a little shrug and got into the boat.

She sat down and looked back at Andrew, startled to see a deep expression of anxiety on his face. A still small voice seemed to say, "Get off the boat." Before realizing anything, she stepped out of the boat on to the shore. The boat steamed away with thirteen happy carefree people. Elizabeth stood on the shore a little hurt and disappointed.

The boat crossed the lake. When it started on its return trip, a light wind began to blow. Quickly heavy black clouds appeared, the wind gained in velocity, the high waves dashed against the boat causing it to dance and sway upon the water. The passengers became panicky and in trying to get adjusted, too many rushed to one side and the boat capsized. In a few moments thirteen people were floundering in the water, thirteen voices calling for help.

When relatives and friends on the shore realized what had happened, they became hysterical, screaming and crying. Pandemonium broke out. Only two men made it to shore. Eleven people who could not swim drowned. Hours throughout the night and the next day were spent in recovering the bodies. Throughout her life Elizabeth counseled her children to listen to "the still small voice."

One wonders, in the case of Elizabeth, why thirteen people would not apprehend danger the way she did. Philosophical writers have struggled with similar complexities in human events. Thorton Wilder, in his Pulitzer Prize winning novel, *The Bridge of San Luis*

Rey, explored questions surrounding why some people survived the collapse of a Peruvian bridge. I am not specifically aware of a time when I have felt uneasy about something and was spared accident, but I have sometimes felt a sense of imminent disaster. Months before my breast cancer was diagnosed, I had a sense of time fleeting. The words from a Renaissance poem, "But at my back I always hear Time's wing'd chariot hurrying near,"[194] came frequently to my mind. I wonder if my body knew something that my mind could not consciously understand. I wonder how many other whisperings I have missed because I wasn't attuned to them.

Elizabeth's spiritual life was important to her, but she also took pride in the temporal, always serving her food on a clean tablecloth with bright, shining dishes. She believed that food served that way was more appetizing and had the appearance of a more elaborate meal. I feel the same way. I always set the table with place mats, matched dishes, and napkins, though the meal may be simple. Sometimes my husband complains about the excess of dishes, but I have yet to change. Is it in my genes; if so, how could I?

> Elizabeth managed the household affairs, and it was her desire that her children should have an education, even with the tightness of their budget. To put over a point to her children, Elizabeth would quote lines from different poets. Also she quoted from the Bible to impress them of their duties to God and mankind. One thing she asked her children to refrain from saying was, never call anyone a fool or a liar. Biblical injunctions like Matthew 5:22, "Whosoever shall say, Thou fool, shall be in danger of hell fire," and Revelations 21:8, "and all liars, shall have their part in the lake which burneth with fire and brimstone: which is the second death," were not just words on a page; they were precepts to be lived.

Like Elizabeth, I have spent a lifetime teaching my children not to judge other people and to be honest. I have tried to teach by scripture and literature and example, including in this reservoir of advice the wisdom of our ancestors. Though I have read other pioneer women's experiences similar to those of Elizabeth, I take hers more into my being because she is my progenitor, really part of who I am. Even before I ever knew Elizabeth's story, her experiences were at work shaping the future I would inherit.

On Sunday, August 20, 1939, Elizabeth attended Sunday school and had planned to go to sacrament meeting at night, but in the afternoon of that day she suffered a stroke. She didn't respond to the doctor's treatment, and on Wednesday morning, August 23, she passed away at eighty-five years of age. The final song at her funeral in Mayfield was "The End of a Perfect Day." Some might find that choice sentimental, but what do we really know, living in an age of discontent, about a "perfect day"? A note from Heber Larsen, who was the same age as Elizabeth's oldest daughter, Ella, dated December 16, 1923, postmarked Los Angeles, California, captured the sense of longing for the perfect past.

> Dear Sister Anderson,
>
> When Christmas comes, we all go home, in mind at least, and we see the faces, and hear again the voices of those whom we have loved and friends whom we have appreciated, just as I see you now sitting alone, and I see Andrew and Pa and Ma. I see the old street and the ditches and footboards. I'm back again in the days of boyhood serenading. Aunt Stena and you and Aunt Sena have all given us cakes and cookies and sent us on our way with a cheer and full pockets. Ah! Those never-to-be-forgotten days and always-to-be-remembered faces. Sister Anderson, they are not being replaced in this world of change. They are gone, that kind is passing away just as the old Christmas is passing away—only a show remains.[195]

After her death, among Elizabeth's keepsakes were two pictures and a poem. Her daughter Grace explained that the elderly Elizabeth was invited one day to an afternoon social at Maria Dyreng's home, but that Elizabeth was unable to attend. Her friends sent her the poem and pictures instead, including a photograph of themselves at Manti's Warm Springs, taken many years before when they were all still girls. The poem was composed by Elizabeth Munk, one of the women who attended the Dyreng social.

THE WARM SPRINGS OF MANTI

I wonder Warm Springs if you miss us,
That bunch of old-fashioned girls,
Who would seek your bright sparkling waters
To bathe on a hot summer day?
With our coarse home-made shoes and sun-bonnets,
We would walk every step of the way.

Do you remember the thick homemade linsey,
Our mothers fashioned with care,
Served well, I am sure, for a bathing suit,
Grown soft with washing and wear?

We were gay with chatter and laughter
As we'd sport in your sparkling swirl.
Speak up Warm Spring and tell us
Is the flapper that now sports your water
As happy as the old-fashioned girl?

I wonder Warm Springs if you'd know us,
That bunch of old-fashioned girls,
As we sit around in a circle
And vistas of life are opened
And glimpses of heaven unfurl.

Deep lines envelope our features,
And silvered with gray is our hair.
Our forms are bent with the toiling,
And illness and fretting and care.

Dear Warm Springs we have learned what life is.
We have tasted the bitter—the sweet.
We are now going down on the home stretch,
God willing, our loved ones to meet.

Reading this poem, I picture the group of lively young women from Little Denmark, probably laughing as they splash in the water. Their joyful reality softens my image of pioneer women and the lives they lived. I can see myself young again—and my daughters, as well—doing the very same thing, enjoying our connection to other women. And I like the connection to Elizabeth, knowing that we share common joys as well as common sorrows and that I am more than just her genetic heir.

22.

Mayfield

We left Manti going south on Highway 89 and took the turnoff to Mayfield and the cemetery overlooking the valley. The graves of both my Andersen grandparents and great-grandparents are here. I think this would be a nice place to be buried, particularly if you had lived much of your life in such a scenic valley. The cemetery surveys the pastoral appearing town stretched out below the hill. Like the deceased in *Our Town*, the Mayfield dead can view their place of life and perhaps, like Emily, long to return for a day.

We walked to the graves of Elizabeth and Andrew, lying side by side in death as they had in life. What day would they choose for a returning, their wedding day with all the anticipation ahead or their fiftieth anniversary with all the memories behind?

In 1924 Elizabeth and Andrew celebrated their fiftieth anniversary. A photo captures their faces emerging from a dark background, her high cheek bones accentuated by carefully combed-back hair and his still handsome face enhanced by a neatly trimmed moustache. How does one quantify the difference between the understanding of love they had when they first married and what love must have meant to them after sharing fifty years of life? He had been her support when their children were born; she had been his when his arm was almost torn off in a threshing accident and his leg was amputated due to diabetes.

The familiar public image of love is found in romantic novels and bride magazines, but the private image is much more obscure. As my children have courted, I have enjoyed their idealism and spontaneity. I have loved watching them contemplate marriage.

In the process of watching them, I have relived my own discovery of love, and I have thought about the contrast between young and old love.

Young love is decorating someone's room on Valentine's Day with hearts that say, "I love you." Old love is going to work, getting up at night with fussy children, fixing a flat tire, and being there when things are tough. Young love tries to figure out what pleases another person, old love is knowing and doing it even if it requires giving up what pleases you.

When I became engaged, I was majoring in English at Brigham Young University. I was taking a class in Renaissance literature, taught impressively and emotionally by Clinton Larsen. Inspired by the Renaissance love sonnets we studied, I wrote a poem for Neal called "Solace," in which I expressed my eagerness for a comforting closeness: "... when people say something / that hurts and no one understands or shares / the feeling that I have ... / ... all I want is you to put your arms around / me close and say that they were wrong and wall / away all thoughts of bad far from my sound. / Your loving heart to me you freely give / and this, thy care, enables me to live." I thought I really knew something about worlds falling apart and someone being there for support, but of course, I didn't. I had yet to experience what it means to share a life with a husband, both giving and receiving sustenance. I had not yet faced the realities of a child dying, a struggle with cancer, the loss of a father, and the minor crises which surface every week in any family.

Years later I wrote another poem for Neal about the comfort of having someone close each night when going to bed. We never bought a king-sized or even queen-sized bed. I like the old double bed we've had since our early days of marriage. I like my husband close enough that I can hear his breathing and feel his body warmth and sense when he's left. When my mother-in-law became a widow, I realized the sense of loss that comes when a bed is not shared anymore. I used to send a grandchild over to fill, in some measure, the emptiness by spending the night.

But love is shared in ways beyond sleeping in the same bed. Old love does not have to be spoken or expressed with gifts. It is the quiet dedication of being there through the good times and bad, the quiet trust that knows, even if someone is not there for a day or night or even for a week, he will be back.

In 1924 Andrew and Elizabeth Andersen celebrated their fiftieth wedding anniversary. Notice her carefully combed-back hair, his neatly trimmed moustache, and the twinkle in their eyes. How does one quantify the love shared over fifty years of living on the edge of civilization? *Family photograph in possession of the author*

Old love is something that can be expressed any place or any time. When we had been married a few years, I wrote this for Neal:

One time
We were at a meeting
And you took off your glasses
And sort of rubbed the
Bridge of your nose
Where your glasses had been
And turned your head a little
And the light fell on your face
And on your hair
I saw your eyes and
Loved you a little more.
At that moment
I wanted to get up
And touch you,
But I couldn't
Across the room,
So I loved you
With my eyes
Did you feel it?

After more than forty years of marriage, I still "love" my husband across a room. Carol Lynn Pear-son's "Double Wedding" illustrates two kinds of love as *eros* and *agape*—*eros* being passionate, romantic love and *agape* being love that is caring and giving.

Let's have a double wedding,
You and me
And eros and agape.

Let us post
Interchangeable notes
On bedroom wall
And refrigerator:
"Love thy lover"
And "Love thy neighbor."

Let us hold hands
In movies
And in the hospital.

Let us kiss
Shoulders and eyelids
And the cut fingers
Of small children.

Let us serve one another
Apple blossoms in vases
And quartered fruit
On trays.

Let us write poems
And wills to each other.
Let us have nights
As friendly lovers
And days as loving friends.

And let the four of us,
You and me
And eros and agape,
Stand in line together,
At the grocery store
And at a golden
Anniversary.[196]

This poem makes me think about Andrew and Elizabeth at their golden anniversary and how their life together might have contrasted with Mormons living in polygamy during the same time period. Andrew's choice to be monogamous certainly had something to do with his reaction when his father, Niels Peter Andersen, married a second wife in 1869. Perhaps his distaste at seeing another woman occupy his mother's position made him cherish his one and only wife even more.

As soon as Niels Peter had accumulated enough land in Sanpete County for a farm in 1862, he started to build a new house for his "Little Anna" and their

children, and the following year, Erastus was born— their last child. Anna went about establishing the same type of home they had had in Denmark with the same high standards of cleanliness and the same warmth of home and friendly companionship. Their family life was happy. It is said that they walked to church arm in arm and that he talked to his "Little Anna" in their native language. This peaceful companionship ended when Niels Peter followed the advice of church leaders and took a second wife into his home. His son Andrew's reaction is told in a history written by Andrew's daughter Grace.

In the year of 1869 Grandfather [Niels Peter] accepted the commandment of God, the Law of Polygamy, and married Mary Ann Christensen [aka Mariane Madsen]. As in many homes, this caused feelings. ... Father [Andrew] loved his mother dearly and couldn't stand another woman stepping in to share his father's love. Words between him and his father caused his father in an angry moment to tell him to take his blanket and leave home, for there wasn't room enough in the house when he felt as he did. Of course we know the bitterness that comes to one's mind under circumstances such as these. Father was seventeen years old at the time.

My father left home and for three days traveled on foot and without food. When he reached Salt Lake City, he went to the tithing office thinking someone would offer him food, but he failed to get any. He finally went back to Sandy and there he came upon two workingmen who were eating their lunch. They noticed his pallor and weakness and gave him some food. When Father told this story he said, "They were, to me, good Samaritans."

A few days later he reached [the mining town of] Bingham and secured work. Just when things were looking a bit brighter and a few dollars were in his pocket, he contracted a bad case of erysipelas. His eyes swelled shut; he was unable to crawl to the water barrel for a drink. His friends went to work every morning expecting to find him dead when they returned at night. They asked him one morning, "Just in case you die, where shall we send word and to whom?" He answered, "Just drag me out in the brush." In his heart he knew that his mother was waiting for him to come home and he knew that home was a haven of rest. He decided to return home and make things right with his father. He was in a daze when the boss paid him for the days he had worked. He walked for some time and then found his legs would carry him no farther, so he lay down and went to sleep. The rays of the sun woke him up and he found that he had slept for many hours. And he also learned by counting his money that his boss had never [actually] paid him.

On his way home he passed a wagon loaded with wheat. This was to be taken to Salt Lake City and exchanged for other goods, such as clothing. Riding in the wagon were two girls, Elizabeth Domgaard and Christena Madsen. They were going to the city to work. Father managed to stay as far as possible from the wagon because of his unkempt clothing and sickly pallor. Little did he realize that Elizabeth would later become his wife.

The welcome he received at home was never to be forgotten; his father, no less than his mother, greeted him with open arms. Life became a joy and satisfaction because he worked side by side with his father, bringing logs from the mountains to make furniture for both families.[197]

Despite this reconciliation with their son, Anna and Niels Peter were unable to reconcile their own differences over the additional wife. Niels Peter built his second wife a home across the street from Anna, but it wasn't long before the happy relationship they had always known ceased to exist, and he separated from her and went to live with his second wife and raise a young family. Anna died on May 23, 1884, at the age of sixty-six with her family all at her bedside to receive her blessing. Just seven months later, Niels Peter passed away, and it is said that he had grieved for her companionship, but that she could not accept him as long as he had another wife. His first love was his last love, according to family tradition. He was laid to rest next to his "Little Anna" in the Ephraim cemetery.[198]

Perhaps Anna should have used the persuasive technique of another Scandinavian when her husband, Hans Zobell, approached her about practicing polygamy. "When Hans once broached the subject to her, he found at dinner time one day only two potted geraniums on the table, one young and full of swelling buds, the other a plant nearly bloomed out which had been about the house a long time. 'Which of these will you keep?' she wanted to know. 'Study them, take your time, and then tell me what you decide.' Hans understood and no second wife ever crossed the threshold."[199] I wonder if Niels Peter Andersen would have "understood" the metaphor as well as Hans Zobell did.

23.

Twelve Mile Canyon

The fertile valley where Mayfield lies is located at the mouth of Twelve Mile Canyon. Nine Mile and Six Mile are other nearby canyon names, so designated by their distance from the temple in Manti. My mother recalls Easter holidays in her childhood when she and her friends would climb the hills above Mayfield laden with boiled eggs. Reaching the hilltops, they would roll their eggs down the slopes to crack the shells, then follow, often wearing out a pair of shoes in their quick descent. A reward was eating eggs with their Easter lunch and laughing with friends.

Niels Peter Domgaard with his first wife, Else. At the same time this photograph was taken, Niels Peter sat for a family portrait with his younger wife, Mette, and three of their children. What were the thoughts of Else as she watched the photographer arrange the family group with Mette Sophie Hansen, twenty-three years her junior? *Family photograph in possession of the author*

Utah canyons were sometimes places of desperate rather than joyful activity in the 1870s and 1880s as federal marshals searched for Mormon men practicing polygamy who might find the remote locations convenient for hiding. One canyon in Capitol Reef National Park is today still called Cohab Canyon as its craggy terrain offered hiding places for "cohabitants" on the run. Children were instructed to conceal, not only their fathers' whereabouts, but also their identities. A father in prison often meant economic disaster for a family as well as personal trials.

The Edmunds Bill was passed by Congress in March 1882, amending the less stringent anti-bigamy statute of 1862. The new bill provided legal justification to arrest men practicing polygamy and send them to the penitentiary, to place women in prison for refusing to testify against their husbands, and to deny voting rights to polygamists and even former polygamists. In addition, "The law further declared all registration and election offices vacant in the territory and provided for Federal appointees in their place."[200] The Edmunds-Tucker Act passed by Congress in March 1887 further tried to suppress polygamy by disincorporating the LDS church and appropriating much of its property. A United States marshal took charge of the real and personal property of the church and, in order to retain use of its buildings, they were charged high rental fees by the government.[201]

It was in 1864, at age fifty-one, that my great-great-grandfather Niels Peter Domgaard took an eighteen-year-old second wife. His first wife, Else, was forty-one. According to federal law, he could have been prosecuted under the Congressional anti-bigamy bill "signed by President Lincoln, July 8, 1862, [that] made the contracting of a plural marriage punishable by a fine of $500 or imprisonment for a term of five years, or both. ... Out of friendship for the Mormons, with whom he had become acquainted in Illinois, President Lincoln neglected to appoint officers to enforce the anti-bigamy law."[202] Perhaps this leniency made Niels Peter less fearful of punishment, or perhaps he would have proceeded regardless of legal threats. The reasons for his decision to practice polygamy would

be interesting to know, as the majority of his Scandinavian countrymen in Sanpete County were monogamous.[203]

Perhaps Niels Peter entered polygamy at the request of a church authority whom he respected, as was common at that time. Perhaps he was pressured by local leaders, being considered "well-off" by Manti standards and able to support a second family. Perhaps because Else had borne him only daughters since their arrival in America, he longed in some measure to replace the baby son who had died on a ship in Liverpool harbor during the Domgaards' emigrant journey after their conversion to Mormonism in Denmark. Else had borne her sixth and last child in 1861, three years prior to the new marriage. Niels Peter fathered nine children by Mette, the last when he was sixty-eight years old. Of the nine children, seven were sons.

I do not really know the reasoning of any of the three parties in their decision to enter polygamy. Niels Peter, Else, Mette—what were their feelings both before and after the marriage? I have a faded photograph of Niels Peter with his wife Else and another with Mette and their three children. From Niels Peter's appearance, the pictures seem to have been taken at the same time. What were the thoughts of Else, my great-great-grandmother, as she watched the photographer arrange the family group with Mette Sophie Hansen, twenty-three years her junior, as the wife?

I do not know if Niels Peter went into hiding or concealed his second wife and her children as hunts for polygamists intensified under the Edmunds Bill and the Edmunds-Tucker Act. Lacking diaries or memoirs from this period, I do not know the feelings of Niels Peter, Else, Mette, and their children about the persecution and prosecution surrounding them.

It is difficult to understand Mormon polygamy without knowing something about its background, which can be traced partially to a desire to restore a biblical practice but also in concert with a revelation Joseph Smith received in the 1830s, recorded in 1843 and later added to the church's Doctrine and Covenants. During a period of Bible study, Joseph felt he had received God's approbation for polygamy, sanctified by a religious joining of a couple.[204]

After the Saints settled in Nauvoo, Illinois, in 1839, Joseph Smith explained the doctrine of plural marriage to some of his closest associates and the Church leadership. Many of these Church leaders found polygamy difficult to accept. Brigham Young, for example, later reported, "Some of the brethren know what my feelings were at the time Joseph revealed the doctrine; I was not desirous of shrinking

from any duty, nor of failing in the lack to do as I was commanded, but it was the first time in my life that I desired the grave, and I could hardly get over it for a long time." John Taylor explained, "I had always entertained strict ideas of virtue, and I felt as a married man that this was to me ... an appalling thing to do." Yet despite their misgivings, Brigham Young, John Taylor, Joseph Smith's brother Hyrum, and many of the other leaders eventually married additional wives.[205]

Plural marriage ceremonies were performed secretly. When rumors of plural marriages began to circulate, public reaction resulted:

By the fall of 1843 the subject of plurality was on every tongue in the city. Charlotte Haven [a woman visiting Nauvoo] wrote a letter to her family alluding to "wonderful revelations not yet made public" and discussing the case of Elder George Adams, who had returned from England with a second wife. "I am told that his first wife is reconciled to this at first unwelcome guest in her home," wrote Haven, "for her husband and some others have reasoned with her that plurality of wives is taught in the Bible. Abraham, Jacob, Solomon, David and indeed all the old prophets and good men, had several wives, and if it is all right for them, it is all right for the Latter Day Saints."[206]

Emma, the wife of Joseph Smith, "allegedly burned

the revelation on plural marriage first recorded by Smith's scribe, William Clayton."[207] One of the reasons for the demise of the Nauvoo Female Relief Society, of which Emma was president, was her "personal opposition to plural marriage and her use of the Relief Society in combating the spread of this doctrine among Church sisters." Relief Society meetings waned in number after this time, and meetings were held in private homes.[208] Emma chose to remain in Nauvoo after her husband's martyrdom in 1844 and not to go west with the rest of the Saints. The Relief Society organization was not formally revived until 1867 in Utah.

Public perception of polygamy was frequently at odds with the private attitudes of those who practiced it:

> Although the national press portrayed plural marriage as a monstrous dehumanization of women, Mormons, including many leading women, spoke out in its defense. For them it was a practical, honorable means of providing marriage and motherhood for thousands of deserving women who would otherwise be condemned to a life of spinsterhood; it was an alternative to a variety of social evils; and it was commanded by God as a means of raising up a righteous generation. That its primary justification—and the primary motivation of its practitioners—was religious obligation,

no one who has examined the diaries and the letters of the time can deny.[209]

Reading diaries, letters, and memoirs, as well as historical studies, reveals many different reactions to "the principle," as it was called. Eliza Snow was married to Joseph Smith in secret, and she does not openly discuss it in her diary, but her entry for that day may hint at the event:

> *City of Nauvoo, June 29th 1842*
>
> *This is a day of much interest to my feelings. Reflecting on past occurrences, a variety of thoughts have presented themselves to my mind with regard to events which have chas'd each other in rapid succession in the scenery of human life. ...*

Historian Maureen Beecher writes: "The event itself could not be mentioned. In proposing marriage to the thirty-eight-year-old spinster, Joseph Smith had placed her in an emotional, spiritual, intellectual, and social bind. ... Eliza had to bend to the breaking point her sense of moral accountability, her convictions about the social order, her adherence to biblical injunction, her family values, and her judgment of herself as a righteous, God-loving Christian."[210]

Beecher further analyzes the obscurity of meaning in the diary entry:

No language, especially that which must conceal its content, could convey the intensity of the deliberations that had brought her to this point. "Though I rejoice in the blessing of the society of the saints," she wrote, "and the approbation of God; a lonely feeling will steal over me before I am aware while I am contemplating the present state of society—the pow'rs of darkness, and the prejudices of the human mind, which stand array'd like an impregnable barrier against the work of God."[211]

As Beecher interprets it: "To whom could she vouchsafe her secret? ... Not until the 1880s could she acknowledge publicly her feeling for this first husband, ... 'the choice of my heart and the crown of my life.'" Two years later when Joseph was martyred in June 1844, Eliza was forced to mourn publicly, not as a widow, but as a devoted follower.[212]

After the death of Joseph Smith, Eliza accepted a marriage proposal from Brigham Young. They were married for time in October of 1844, but Eliza did not use Young as her surname. She remained Eliza R. Snow, though she lived in the Lion House with Brigham's other wives until her death. With her fine intelligence, organizational abilities, writing skills, and her faith and vision, she was an asset to him in many ways.

In her writings, Eliza always refers to her husband formally as President Young, and their relationship through the years was one of mutual respect. Thirty years after her first polygamous marriage, she reflected, "As I increased in knowledge concerning the principle and design of Plural Marriage, I grew in love with it."[213] She maintained throughout her life that Utah women had more "rights than any women in the world."[214]

Other women were similarly convinced of divine sanction for plural marriage, several of whom are chronicled in Carol Madsen's *In Their Own Words: Women and the Story of Nauvoo*. Bathsheba Wilson Bigler Smith shared her feelings in a reminiscence:

> ... I believed firmly in Joseph Smith as a Prophet of the Most High. ... I became thoroughly convinced, as well as my husband, that the doctrine of "plurality of wives" as taught by Joseph the Prophet, in our hearing, was a revelation from God; and having a fixed determination to obtain to Celestial Glory, I felt to embrace every principle. ... I had in the last year, like Sarah of old, given to my husband five wives—good virtuous honorable women who had gathered to Zion without their families. Four of these women were considerably older than I and two of them older than my husband. They were all deeply religious. I was young, only twenty-three years old and Mr. Smith but twenty-eight, though I believe we were mature for our years on account of experiences gained amid the perilous times through which we had already passed.[215]

Patty Sessions found plural marriage a trial when her husband David took a second wife. The other woman, Rosilla Cowans, was

> sealed (in essence, married) to David ... for time and all eternity by Brigham Young in Nauvoo on October 3, 1845. Rosilla did not accompany David and Patty when they left Nauvoo, but joined them on June 22, 1846, four months later. At that point Patty's lifelong trials with the Mormon institution of polygamy began. Patty's marriage to David was severely tested by the strain that was imposed by another wife. After Rosilla's arrival and David's subsequent disappearance from Patty's bed, Patty recorded her sadness of July 11, 1847: *I eat my breakfast but I am so full of grief that there is no room for food and I soon threw it up. I can only say I feel bad.* Patty and David became further estranged later in July, after which a severe illness confined Patty to her bed for a month. She emerged from her illness to her old problems, and wrote of her disappointment on September 8, 1847:

> > *I feel bad again. He has been and talked to Rosilla and she fild his ears full and when he came to my bed I was quite chled [chilled,] he was gone so long and I was so cold I had been crying. He began to talk hard to me before he got into bed and threatens me very hard of leaving me.*[216]

Part of the problem was that Rosilla would not help with the housework as Patty thought she should:

The two wives refused to speak to each other. Patty was especially fearful about the prospects of David's leaving her. Rosilla was *trying to have him take her to Nauvoo and then to Maine and leave me for good. ... I go to bed know[ing] not what to do.* Patty's desperation and loneliness severely tried her patience, but she was able to ride out the storm. After another month of altercations and misunderstanding, Rosilla left for Nauvoo. This unfortunate experience with polygamy made it difficult for Patty to cope with similar trials later in her life.[217]

In 1849, David courted another woman, Harriet Teeples, and asked Brigham Young's permission to marry her. This was especially frustrating to Patty because David had not followed the protocol of asking her permission first. In her diary for December 30, 1849, Patty wrote: *I wish to do right but I fear I shall fail through sorrow. Oh Lord give me thy spirit to guide me safe in the right way.*[218] David married Harriet on January 13, 1850, and a month later Patty allowed her to move into their home. David died in August and Harriet moved. However, Patty, with the help of her son Perrigrine, continued to support her and even delivered Harriet's child a few months after David's death.[219]

Bathsheba Smith's experience with polygamy began in Nauvoo. She "helped her husband [George

A. Smith] select five wives within one year—Lucy Meserve; Zilpha Stark; Sarah Ann Libby; Sarah's sister, Hannah Maria Libby; and Nancy Clement." She noted:

> *They all had their home with us, being proud of my husband and loving him very much, knowing him to be a man of God and believing he would not love them less, because he loves me more. I had joy in having a testimony that what I had done was acceptable to my Father in Heaven.*[220]

In contrast to Patty Sessions's trials, Bathsheba was able to function well in the role of first wife in the household.

> Bathsheba accepted her husband's other wives as sisters. She felt compassion for their sorrows and trials and shared with them the material things that she had, feeling responsible for their welfare in his absence. When discord arose among the wives while George was absent, it was Bathsheba, as the first wife, who was called upon as a mediator to establish harmony.[221]

Perhaps the sister wives were a comfort to her through her husband's extensive mission service for the church, the situation of numerous other Mormon wives as well:

> Loneliness, a constant problem on the frontier when the husband was frequently absent on church assignments and working in the fields or canyon, could be alleviated with an adult female companion. True, she would be a plural wife, but for many hours of the day she would be working alongside or nearby the first wife. When sisters were married simultaneously, or when the first wife asked her husband to take her unmarried sister as plural wife, the arrangement seemed to be a way of perpetuating an existing congenial relationship.[222]

Perhaps Bathsheba's mediation with her sister wives gave her experience for settling organizational and personality issues when she became a member of the general Relief Society presidency in 1888 and president in 1891.

One advantage for sister wives was having someone to assist with child care. For Ellis Shipp in Utah in 1875, polygamy allowed her to leave her children while she became educated as a doctor. She was later able to use her profession and income to help the rest of the family. It must have eased the burden of polygamy somewhat when the secret practice became openly acknowledged in Utah and thereby took away some of the stigma that had been associated with it:

> From a clandestine arrangement, limited to the Prophet and two or three dozen leading men and the wives who were party to the practice, Mormon polygamy slowly expanded after the Prophet's death in

1844, especially during ceremonies in the newly completed Nauvoo Temple at the end of 1845 and beginning of 1846. After the Mormons arrived in the Great Basin, plural marriages continued to be performed. Finally in 1852, the practice was openly acknowledged at a general church conference, at which Apostle Orson Pratt gave a lengthy defense of polygamy.[223]

Some polygamous marriages involved cohabitation and some did not; some were only for eternity, meaning after this earth life, and some for time, meaning on this earth and not honored in the afterlife. Some marriages were for both time and eternity. Some people may wonder at marriages to older women, beyond what was considered marriageable age:

> Plural marriage meant a respectable means of family and support. ... "Was this worse than the alternatives of leaving them to live alone as wards of the church or state?" argued the rhetoric of the system's proponents. With their new families, when it worked out well, they had chores to contribute to the operation of the household, children to call them aunt or grandma, food to eat, a place to sleep—in short a hearth and a home.[224]

As the practice of plural marriage continued, many daughters were expected to marry in the same manner as their mothers:

> They were already persuaded of the religious basis of the system, having seen it in their parental family; they were not surprised or insulted when they were asked to be plural wives, or, if they were first wives, when they were requested to allow the husband to take other women. Indeed, a few women were so full of zeal that the initiative came from them, for they insisted that the husband fulfill his responsibility.[225]

Annie Clark Tanner was reared in a family where polygamy was practiced in harmony. Her father was a supportive husband to his wives, and Annie expected the same type of relationship when she married. Chronicled in her autobiography, *A Mormon Mother,* published by her tenth and last child, Obert Tanner, her life personified the public image/private attitude dualism evident in many polygamous marriages.

Annie chose to become a plural wife late in 1883, a time when there was increasing government pressure against polygamy under the federal Edmunds-Tucker Act. Attending Brigham Young Academy in 1882-83, she became enamored of a gifted professor, Joseph Marion Tanner: "As a teacher he seemed perfect. There seemed to be no limit to his knowledge. He gave lectures on various subjects all winter. He took me or asked me to come and see his first wife. ... I felt favored above all the other girls in the school."[226]

At the end of the school year, Annie went home and Mr. Tanner, as Annie refers to him throughout her book, began to write to her, requesting that their "correspondence should be through Mrs. Tanner, his first wife." Annie comments, "Consequently, there were no letters."[227] Mr. Tanner and his wife Jennie then visited Annie, Mrs. Tanner explaining privately: "I have no children although I have been married for five years. I can't deprive Marion of a family, and of all the girls I know, you are my choice." Mr. Tanner visited Annie a few times that fall. Being only nineteen, Annie felt hesitant about marrying so young, but Mr. Tanner "insisted that a long courtship in cases of polygamy was entirely improper."[228]

On December 27, 1883, Annie journeyed to Salt Lake, was taken to the Endowment House by Mrs. Tanner, and there was married to Mr. Tanner. "After the ceremony, Mr. Tanner and Aunt Jennie, as we familiarly called the first wife, and I took the northbound train. I got off at Farmington and they went on to Ogden."

Annie's brother Wilford met her at the train and took her home. Mr. Tanner had promised to meet her in a couple weeks, which he did not. A few days later she received a letter of apology giving various church and business demands as an excuse. Annie writes: "When he treated so lightly his appointment to come to see me two weeks after our marriage, is there any wonder that I was brokenhearted. A week later he came, but my enthusiasm was gone."[229] She adds: "I was never sure he would keep his appointments after that first disappointment. ... In time I learned to steel myself against disappointment of his failure to come. However, I learned to dearly love my husband, and I wondered later if anyone was a more ardent lover than myself."[230] Mr. Tanner's failure to keep appointments was a harbinger of their future life as man and wife. Though Mr. Tanner fathered ten children, it was Annie who largely supported them, both emotionally and financially.

Marion Tanner's public image was one of success, just as Annie says of him: "I was very proud of his ability as a public speaker. Thousands of young people listened to his inspirational sermons and they inwardly resolved to reach higher levels. Hundreds of young men owe their success to the impressions and inspiration received from Mr. Tanner."[231] But in contrast to the service given publicly, Marion neglected his private life as a husband to Annie and as a father to their children. In 1912 he told Annie that he would not be coming to Farmington anymore and that she should look to her brothers for financial help. He moved to Canada with another plural wife.

Annie's youngest son, Obert, became a professor of

philosophy at the University of Utah and a prominent businessman. He concluded his introduction to his mother's autobiography with this paragraph:

> Though her zest for life was chastened with personal reservations about her deepest convictions, and though tragic disappointments were her companions of the way, she walked to the end with the quiet dignity of one who lived and taught her children, over and over again, the words of Shakespeare: "To thine own self be true."[232]

Annie was only one of the thousands of women who experienced polygamy firsthand. It is estimated that "12 percent of Mormon married women were involved in the principle."[233] Perhaps being true to oneself was a quality needed by many of those women, women who triumphed over the difficulties this lifestyle could engender.

The fact that so many prominent Mormon women stood up in defense of polygamy remains puzzling to critics of the practice. It is ironic that opponents perceived women in polygamy as slaves, while many of the women in it perceived themselves as liberated. An editorial in the *Woman's Exponent* stated: "We have left the petted slave in the Greek household, to go onward and forward. We have left the idle toy and the painted doll. ... God lead us to find the true Woman in the free American home."[234] Many found "true Woman" by working for women's rights. "One of the interesting anomalies of nineteenth-century women's history is the fact that one of its most vocal feminist groups comprised the Mormon women of Utah defending their territorial right to vote and their religious practice of polygyny, called 'plural' or 'patriarchal' marriage. Utah was the second territory in the United States to grant female suffrage. ... Utah women were the first to vote in the country."[235]

As governmental pressure against polygamy advanced, "Mormons presented a united front against the attacks on their marriage practice. During the 1870s and 1880s, with the national legislative-judicial campaign increasing in intensity, women met in indignation meetings where they gave speeches and signed petitions. Some of these are eloquent statements, but there were concessions that the principle was a 'trial,' although God certainly expected his [chosen] people to be 'tried.'"[236] One example of eloquence are the words of Artimesia Beman Snow, who began her remarks with "Sisters, I am a sincere believer in plural marriage. In 1844 my husband first asked my consent to take to himself other wives. I freely gave it, believing such an order of marriage to be a pure and holy principle, revealed from the heavens ... and knowing also my husband to be a virtuous man. ... I have lived in the order of Celestial marriage thirty-five years. I have no wish—I have no desire—to have it changed or abolished."[237]

But it was indeed abolished in September 1890 by the Manifesto issued by church president Wilford Woodruff, in which he stated, "I publicly declare that my advice to the Latter-day Saints is to refrain from contracting any marriages forbidden by the law of the land." His journal entry the previous day stated, "I have arrived at a point in the history of the Church of Jesus Christ of Latter-day Saints where I am under the necessity of acting for the temporal salvation of the Church."[238]

I am personally grateful for Wilford Woodruff's Manifesto. The way I see it, it saved me from having to be "tried" through the "trial" of polygamy in order to be true to my faith. Over my life, seeing good Mormon women who longed to marry and have children but could not find good Mormon men, I have on occasion, momentarily—only momentarily—thought about what a gift it must have been to share one's husband. But how would it be to look across a room to trace a husband's profile only to find him seated next to another wife? How would it be to long for solace in a husband's arms and know they were entwined around another? How would it be to lie alone in a bed and listen to the sounds of love-making in an adjacent bedroom when a second wife did not have a separate home? How would it be to rear children as a single mother while your husband was "away"? And how would it be to hide your children's paternity to save your husband from imprisonment? How would it be? I like having sisters in the gospel, but not sister wives. I'm glad I live in the present of mainstream Mormonism and not in its past.

24.

Caineville

As we left Mayfield, I was caught between two opposing desires: to get home and to continue traveling. I looked at Neal and then said hesitantly, "What if we don't go straight home?"

"What do you mean?"

"Could we take a detour to Caineville, just for a few hours? I've been thinking about this quilt that

Granny Pectol pieced together and that it would be nice to end our pioneer journey where she lived."

"Okay, I'm just your driver."

"What do you remember most about your grandma?"

Neal thought for a moment, laughed, and then said, "One thing is the way she'd rush around and say, 'Ye gods and little fishes.' She was always bustling around. She ran the store in Torrey much of the time while Grandpa was busy serving in the state legislature, being bishop of the Torrey ward, displaying his relic collection, and promoting Wayne Wonderland."

"That's what he wanted to call Capitol Reef National Park, right?"

"Yes, without his help, it might never have been protected, just ended up a place to graze a few cattle.

Dorothy Delilah and husband, Ephraim Portman Pectol, ca. 1907, their daughter Florence between them, with daughters Elenor, Leona, and Fontella left to right (inserts of later additions to the family: daughters Devona and Golda and an adopted son, Ephraim). Fontella wrote: "My mother was independent and efficient all her life. If she wanted a piano moved, she moved it; if she needed wood to keep the house warm, she chopped it; if she needed a ditch dug to water her garden, she dug it. She could take down a wall in the house, or build a new one." *Family photograph in possession of Gloria Kuhn*

He also had help from Granny's brother Joe Hickman, who was in the state legislature in 1925 when the area was designated a state park."

"I remember you telling me that and seeing the pictures of Port Pectol and Joe Hickman at the park visitors center. Maybe there ought to be a plaque honoring your grandma, too."

"I think so. 'Dedicated to the little lady who made it all possible.'" Neal smiled as he said this, then continued: "A few years back, Aunt Fontella said that there was no limit to her mother's energy and ability. She said if Granny hadn't been at the helm of the Pectol Raft, it would have capsized more times than once. She also said that if Granny wanted the piano moved, she moved it; if she needed wood to keep the house warm, she chopped it; if she needed a ditch dug to water her garden, she dug it."

"She must have been some woman! What do you remember about the Chuck Wagon general store in Torrey when your grandparents owned it? Didn't they call it the Wayne Umpire?"

"Yes, and I've wondered about the name. You'd think it would be *empire,* wouldn't you? Maybe it was because Granny settled so many disputes there, I don't know."

"What else do you remember about the store?"

"One of my most vivid memories was sitting on Grandpa's desk chair. In the wintertime I would place it right over the heater vent, which was the warmest place in Torrey in the winter. I think there was only that one heater vent for the whole store, coming up from the coal furnace in the basement. I also remember the hand-operated gas pump and how much fun it was to pump gas to the top of the dispenser, measure out five gallons, and drain it into the car. But I think my strongest memory besides Grandpa and Granny being in the store was the building itself, made of Torrey red rock. When our car reached town and I could see the store and their home next to it, how excited I'd get!"

"Do you remember your grandmother in the store?"

"I think she did a lot more before I was born. But in the early forties, before Aunt Florence bought the store, I remember Granny waiting on customers and straightening shelves—that kind of thing. But she was usually busy in the house cooking meals when we were there. I think Grandpa did the billing. I know they extended a lot of credit during the Depression. I've seen boxes filled with unpaid bills. If Grandma had been doing the ledgers, she would have gone after people with a rolling pin if they didn't pay their bills."

"Where did she learn how to run the store?"

"Oh, I think she just learned by doing. When Grandpa was away, she learned to be independent."

"Your grandfather went on his mission to New Zealand around 1907, didn't he?"

"Yes. He went to teach Maori children."

"It's hard to believe they would send a man away to New Zealand when he had a wife and four children at home. The girls were little, weren't they?"

"Well, let's see. Florence would have been about seven and Leona four. That would make Elenor about three and Fontella just past one. Mom and Devona weren't born yet, and Eph wasn't part of the family yet."

"How could your grandpa leave so many small children behind?"

"I know it wasn't easy. Did you know he wrote a poem for each child?"

"Yes, I've read them. They're kind of flowery like poems were in that era, but you can tell how much he loved his children."

"Before he left, he had to finish his contract as superintendent of schools and as a teacher in Caineville. I know they rode in a wagon to the train depot in Richfield and it took them three days. They visited different relatives along the way. Let's see, he would

have been thirty-two and she was about twenty-seven."

"That seems so young. Think how we were when we were that age."

"I like what he wrote in his diary as the train left Richfield—about his baby's kisses and how the other children had clung to him. I've been reading Granny's diary, too. She didn't start her diary for about three months. In it, she keeps saying how much she longs to see him, how lonely she is. 'Have been blue today, almost to despair,' she says. It seems like Sundays were the worst for her. I think she felt better when she was busy and had to concentrate on other things. She sang in the ward choir on Sundays, but during the week she managed the farm and had to hire workers and sell crops, in addition to being the Caineville postmistress. She raised bees for honey. At Christmas she did the Sears catalogue business. She worried about finances and told Grandpa she lacked confidence, but he wrote back and told her she was doing fine and not to worry."

"So, you're reading their letters?"

"Yes, his took about two months to arrive. They came by ship across the ocean, then by train, and I guess by wagon to Caineville. People there lived like pioneers did fifty years earlier in other places."

"I can't imagine a time lag of two months. I wonder what they wrote about."

"Oh, he told her about the trip over on the boat, about the Maori children he was teaching, about other missionaries. In one letter, he asks her for 'receits,' their word for recipes. He wanted her recipes for pea soup, custard pies, for making jerky and drying fish."

"He had to learn how to cook and she had to be the breadwinner. They switched roles."

"That's right, isn't it? I think the separation brought them closer together, too, in that it helped them understand and appreciate each other the rest of their lives. I can remember how he used to peck her on the cheek, and there's one photo where they're in their sixties and he's standing behind her with his arms about her waist like he might be reaching to kiss her, and she's smiling, kind of laughing."

"I've seen that photo. I wish I had known them, both when they were young and when they were older. What else was in their letters?"

"When she wrote to him, she'd ask what to do with the farm and bees and so on. She told him about a measles epidemic. She had gone to visit her family in Grover for Christmas, and that's where the children were exposed to it. She felt terrible about this and frantic without him there to help her. Fortunately,

her brothers and parents helped. Elenor nearly died one night, her breath was so shallow. Granny's father came in, and she ran for the consecrated oil so he could give the child a blessing. The children all recovered after weeks of sickness. Oh, you know something else? They developed a secret code to communicate their feelings for one another. That way, when the letters were passed among family to read, their personal feelings remained private."

"If you were far away, would you write romantic things to me in secret code?"

"Of course I would."

"I'd do the same for you."

"Would you? Sometimes you seem so caught up in other things, it's like you don't need anything besides your books and your computer."

"Does it seem like that? I guess I become obsessive, don't I? But I do need you."

"I had this funny dream a while back. We bought an extra burial plot in Elsinore."

"Why would we do that?"

"For you in one plot, me in another, and the computer between us." Neal couldn't hide his smile as he said, "Okay, I am kidding, but you know that glass-encased picture of my parents on their gravestone, well, I thought we could have one like it on ours only your face would be replaced by a computer screen."

I gave him my here-we-go-again look. "Do you really resent the time I spend on other things?"

"That's not the right word for it. I don't *resent* it. You just seem so busy all the time. If it's not with books, you're with the kids or doing church work. I really liked this last couple weeks, just the two of us together every day."

"I liked it, too. Remember that night in Grand Island when the wind was blowing so hard and I wouldn't let you go get something to eat unless you took me with you?"

"Yes, it seemed so unlike you. You're so darned independent."

"I don't know that I am. Okay, I have strong opinions and lots of interests, but they wouldn't mean very much without you. Remember when I told you about Emmeline Wells' relationship with her husband, Daniel? She said something like, 'He cannot know the cravings of my nature.' You're kind of like her husband. I don't think you really know what my needs are."

"And just what are those, Ms. Independent?"

"It's mostly for you to be affectionate and to love me for the person I really am—to let me have my own space in the midst of you and the children, to be able to share my interests with you and them and not feel

threatened because you might feel resentful. It's nice to be able to share like we have these last two weeks, where you're interested in what I'm doing, supporting me, and vice versa. I guess I want to be strong like Granny Pectol was and to be able to handle things on my own when I have to, and yet I want you to know that if you were gone, I'd be like her in that I'd be depressed, 'almost to despair.' That's what she said, wasn't it?"

"Yes, 'almost to despair.'"

"Maybe that's her gift to me."

"What?"

"To show me how much I really love you, Neal." I giggled as I added, "almost as much as the computer."

Neal gritted his teeth, trying to hide his familiar smile and said, "Why do you always have to make a joke?"

"What would I do without you to tease?" I moved closer. "Without you to love?"

"I don't know what I'd do without you either, although sometimes I don't know what to do *with* you. Anyway, I am glad we made the trip together."

"*Trip* doesn't quite fit it; it was a real journey, wasn't it?"

"It *was* a journey."

We reached Caineville and turned off Highway 24

onto a dirt road and parked our van near the abandoned schoolhouse that had served as the church meeting house and social hall. The crumbling porches and weathered brown boards were reminders of how harsh the climate can be there. It ages the wood as well as the people. The old school bell in the tower over the front foyer had long since disappeared. The bare hills across the road from the schoolhouse looked like models from pictures sent by satellite from some distant planet. Could any place in the world contrast more with the lush greenery of New Zealand?

We skirted around dry sagebrush and broken glass to reach the back door of the schoolhouse, which was ajar. We could see the decaying walls and floor, illuminated by light pouring in through open windows on the other side, our view becoming a sort of passage to the past. We entered and fell silent. Having been a teacher, I could easily imagine the learning that had occurred in this room almost a century ago. I could visualize the dances held here, couples having to take numbers for turns to dance on the crowded floor of the small room. In that harsh environment, in that isolation, they still managed to have fun.

"They tried to connect through the stars," Neal said.

"What do you mean?"

"In one of Grandpa's letters from New Zealand, he wrote that he couldn't even see the North Star where he was; then he asked her to try to find the constellations he could see. He drew a little diagram, showing how they looked in the Southern Hemisphere, noting how one looked like a pair of scissors. He wanted her to draw the stars as she saw them."

"I think that's romantic. I can imagine her standing outside in her nightgown on a summer night and wondering if he were seeing the same stars. It must have connected them in some way."

"I guess we all need to be connected, don't we? When I'm in Wayne County, I feel connected in ways I never do in Sevier County; but speaking of which, we'd better head home and connect with the family."

"Yes, they'll be wondering why we're not home yet. Thanks for the detour. I needed it."

"I did, too."

25.

Richfield

After traveling on Highway 24 past the Fish Lake turnoff, we wound down the Glenwood Dugway to Richfield and turned onto Fourth North, driving west toward the Red Hills. The craggy profile of Bull's Head was still visible, silhouetted against the evening autumn sky. We eased into the familiar driveway and noticed that Jeremy had mowed and weeded, so that everything looked pretty much the same as when we had left two weeks earlier. But Neal and I felt different, as if we had been changed by the country we'd seen, the people we'd met, and the ideas we'd shared with each other. I entered the house with a combination of anticipation and reluctance. Children rushed up the steps from the family room and asked about our "adventure." We shared a few memories as they helped unload the van. I was grateful to dump dirty clothes and bedding into a washer rather than to do laundry in a creek or tub as my progenitors had. A modern home did have distinct advantages.

Tired, I told the children we'd tell them more about our trip in the morning. Neal and I climbed into the four-poster bed we'd shared since our early married days. I had laid Granny Pectol's quilt over the heirloom rocker that occupied one corner of our bedroom. Feeling a need for the quilt to cover us as it had the past weeks, I retrieved it, placed it on the bed, smoothed it over Neal, and climbed back in beside him, moving close.

"Doesn't it feel good to be in our own bed again?"

Neal responded with a groggy, "I've got to be back in the store tomorrow."

Granny Pectol, in her diary, always used to say,

"Goodnight, my dear husband," so I placed my head in the crook of Neal's arm and murmured: "Goodnight, my dear husband."

In the quiet of the following morning after Neal had left for work and the children had left for school, I finished unpacking. I carried Granny Pectol's quilt to the attic storage trunk. As I refolded it to proper dimensions, I caught sight of three pieced tops, still unquilted, which were stacked one on another in the bottom of the trunk, tops pieced by my grandmother. I removed them and traced their varied patterns with the tips of my fingers ... and the memories began.

My grandfather's house, high on the avenues in Salt Lake City, was the home to come home to during my peripatetic childhood years. I say *grandfather's* because my grandmother died when I was six years old. For most of my childhood, Papa, as we affection-

A quilting bee in Pendroy, North Dakota, ca. 1888. Piecing together women's history from scant sources is like piecing a quilt. We arrange scraps of memory into blocks of a life, fleshing out designs with our lips and hands. We wonder at the blue denim: Did it come from some man's overalls? The black and white gingham: Was it once a kitchen apron? The pink stripe: Did some young girl wear it to church on a spring morning? What circumstances dictated the pattern of the blocks? Might some other woman's pattern fit our lives? And so we connect across the miles and years. *Courtesy of State Historical Society of North Dakota, BO338*

ately called him, was the central figure of the home, whether seated in a green velour chair playing solitaire or, fedora perched on his head, stabbing at some recalcitrant garden weed in the back yard. To me, Grandmother was a hazy figure, only visible in a few dim memories; in one, opening the door to greet a little girl happily garbed in Grandma's patent shoes and veiled pillbox hat, playing grown-up-lady-come-to-visit; in another, folding her arms across her breast and breathing one long sigh as I, hushed by something as immense as death, stood transfixed near the bedside, pressed between my mother and Uncle LaMar.

These memories become a metaphor in my mind for a journey into feelings about womanhood. Just as my grandfather was the prominent figure in my childhood family memories, so men were prominent in my childhood societal memories. Women waved while George Washington led the American historical parade, closely followed by Abraham Lincoln and a contingent of notable males marching behind in even rank and file. Their female counterparts had slipped away from me even more easily than my grandmother had; in fact, I had not even been aware of their deaths. I had to grow up to understand the immensity of my loss in the aggregate demise of historical women. I never had an opportunity to play come-to-visit with any of them because I didn't know they existed. I was able to play dress-up by clicking my heels only on familiar porches and knocking at safe doors. After all, it was taboo to talk to strangers.

The tall, balconied, frame house was the place where as an adult I discovered a trunk of quilt tops in a dusty corner of the old attic. They must have lain there for forty years or more. Certainly, I had never seen them in my lifetime. Of course, I could never have found them in my childhood because then the attic was a place which produced ambivalent feelings, a place I both wanted to know and didn't want to know. We cousins used to open the low door, which conveniently creaked, and peer into the inky blackness. One voice would say, "I dare you to go in." Another would respond, "I double dare you." I was always afraid that if I entered, my boy cousins would slam the door and leave me a garret prisoner. I recall entering the attic only two or three steps ever, one hand still clinging to the doorframe.

I had to wait decades—after college, marriage, children, and a career—until I was courageous enough to leave the well-lighted second floor landing and brave crawling into the darkness, cobwebs brushing my face and narrow rafters cutting into my knees, my desire to know what was really at the back of the attic out-

weighing any fear of what might be there. I think my experience is not so different from that of many other women, except I may have crawled farther than some, and through scarring my knees, found I could have taken an easier route if someone had warned me of the rough places. I might have even stood up if I had known the attic was taller than I imagined.

The retrieval of the quilt tops, the edging into the unknown, became another metaphor for my "journey" into redefining my womanhood, a trip that was difficult to begin since I was so strongly attached to life on the well-lighted second floor of a male-built house. I had been programmed for that kind of life. In the 1940s at age eight, I knew that to be a woman meant imitating Betty Grable, hair upswept crowning her carefully made up face, peering coquettishly over a bare shoulder which balanced beautifully with her shapely exposed legs. At ten, role playing meant dressing up with my best friend and strolling through Liberty Park in our mothers' high heels, our mouths smeared with red lipstick, our undershirts stuffed with Kleenex, pushing our Betsy-Wetsy dolls in buggies, convinced that passersby thought us young mothers.

In high school, the 1950s style of womanhood meant knowing that attractive dates were more important than attractive grades. At Brigham Young

University, I identified with the true woman who hoped never to become a senior girl who went on a church mission because no one wanted to marry her. When I stepped out of the typical BYU mold and went to the Soviet Union as an exchange student, I found blonde Ukrainian men, bowing low, vying to dance with me, and dark-haired Georgian men, eyes flashing, vying to carry my suitcase, much more affirming than the plodding Communist Party men who wanted to discuss Marxist philosophy with me. When I returned to BYU in my junior year, I met my future husband who, one year later, saved me from senior panic by giving me a Christmas diamond.

Venturing into the attic had to wait until after college graduation, marriage, and the birth of my first child. It was 1963 when I eased my grip on the doorframe of *Fascinating Womanhood* enough to take three steps into the attic of *The Feminine Mystique*. I was caught, as in childhood, by ambivalence, wanting to know and not wanting to know what lay beyond the safety of the second floor. I stood suspended between the familiar landing and the inviting attic for some time, balancing. My "fascinating" self could wear ruffled nightgowns and be prolific in baby production and even tremble at heavy traffic or quail at moving anything heavier than twenty pounds when the situation demanded it. My feminist self could return to school, complete a French minor, and earn a teaching degree, medical insurance against contracting "the problem that has no name."[239]

In 1964 a problem that had a name was evident to me as a social worker in the Aid to Dependent Children program in California. As I made a quarterly check-up visit, one of my clients was cradling two small children in her ample arms, while three other children, a little older, hung on the worn arms of a green upholstered chair. When she looked defiantly at me, I tried, across a social, cultural, intellectual, and ethnic gulf, to really look at her, to see in her a victim of poor judgment and repeated alliances with men who had deserted her. How might an experience with feminist consciousness-raising ten years earlier have altered her life?

A quarterly women's newspaper, *Exponent II*, was a source of information for me. It was begun in the 1970s by a group of Mormon women in Boston after they discovered, in the Widener Library at Harvard University, copies of the original *Woman's Exponent*, published in Utah from 1872 to 1914. It seemed appropriate to call the newspaper *Exponent II* as its purpose was "to provide a forum for Mormon women to share their life experiences in an atmosphere of trust and acceptance." Each issue guided me farther along the attic's narrow rafters. Sometimes articles plunged me into darkness even though I had never personally known the despair created by an abusive husband, a drug-addicted child, or an inability to bear children. Sometimes I found garret windows letting in the bright light of women who were changing their individual worlds or sharing their philosophies in essays and poetry, women like Helen Candland Stark, Mary Bradford, and Emma Lou Thayne.

In 1975 I served on the committee for the Utah observation of International Women's Year. At the Convention Center in Salt Lake City, I watched, appalled, as some women came to hiss and boo feminists whose perspectives were inaccessible to them. Sheltered by living in traditional family structures with a network of support around them, they could not understand the "other." Conveniently forgetting their own historical legacy of persecution, they became the persecutors.

In 1981 I went deeper into the attic through an alternative route, a three-week-long Women's Studies Institute course in Tucson, Arizona. Leaving home a husband and five children ranging in age from three to seventeen, I immersed myself in women's literature and history. I was a social conservative encountering

social moderates, first curious about and then impressed by their logic. I was also a social conservative encountering feminist radicals and militants, wondering where their ideas might lead, questioning the power of their anger. I came home with my consciousness raised and my vision altered.

Reading was a vehicle for exploration. Works such as *Sister Saints* and *Women's Voices* had a way of lighting my way into some forgotten corners of Mormon history. I met women who were doctors, farmers, entrepreneurs, educators, administrators, novelists, lawyers, editors, politicians and journalists, women who were polygamous, monogamous, and single.

In 1983, I first read Betty Friedan's *The Second Stage* and realized that leaving the landing for the attic had its risks. Friedan told of women, biological clocks ticking, yearning for husbands and families to replace the isolation of corporate success. Their searching for the American dream had created a new problem, equally as vexing as the problem that had no name. I could see other problems reflected in the eyes of alienated husbands and resentful children of some of my more militant feminist married friends. All of this was a warning about plunging too quickly and enthusiastically into unexplored places.

I had a whole year to explore the attic of pioneer

women's lives. I retraced the Oregon and Mormon trails, stopping to listen to the voices women recorded in their diaries, letters, and memoirs. I was making important discoveries that allowed me to move back and forth between "the landing" and "the attic" with an ease my pioneer sisters might have found amazing. The fact that the attic, as well as the landing, had become illuminated by feminist thought assured the confidence and safety of my movement. I realized the advantages and limitations of standing in each place and I liked my acquired mobility. I could take three minutes in the morning to put ingredients into a bread maker before I started on a day of writing and serve hot bread to my family at dinner without evidence of my truancy. I could leave for several days of research or classes and return to find a home, though certainly not spotless, at least intact, and children frequently relieved by my short absences so they could leave rooms messy, watch videos late, and eat ordered-in pizza. An important fringe benefit for the children was having a mother content with her own life so she didn't need to live theirs.

I had retrieved not only quilts from my family attic, but quilts from other attics as well, although I was still ignorant of many of the patterns. Classes at Brigham Young University in theoretical discourse and women's texts helped me discern designs as I looked at women's writings guided by feminist theory. Quilt tops became my metaphors as I sought to compare the small and large bits of material collected and patterned over my lifetime with past women's materials collected over theirs and folded into diaries and letters and memoirs. How could I understand it all? I asked the same questions that historian Maureen Beecher had asked in her Alice Louise Reynolds lecture at BYU: "What principles can guide our reading? How do they reach us, these private pieces?"[240] She found a partial answer in the quilting metaphor: "Each recorded moment, each diary entry, is a piece saved from the fabric of a woman's day. Ragged, incomplete, misshapen— only its color and its pattern left to show how it fits with its mates. A diary or a journal is a jumble of unconnected pieces, tossed together into a box and pushed under the bed."[241] Women seeking meaning had to "make the small pieces into larger blocks" or even "arrange them into a full quilt top."[242]

In my research I had found pieces, sometimes blocks, and sometimes whole quilt tops. The scraps, or pieces, were bits from women's lives: Eliza R. Snow seated in a cart, letting a cup down by a string to dip water from a river as the Saints moved from Nauvoo toward Winter Quarters.[243] The wife of Sir George Grant, an English nobleman, "pioneering" with tea and crumpets, bone china, and sterling flatware in Victoria, Kansas.[244] Maggie Brown delivering her sixth baby in New Mexico, her only baby to survive childhood.[245]

The blocks of fabric, in a metaphorical sense, were groups of women who fit together in some sort of unifying pattern: literary creations like Willa Cather's Ántonia Shimerda, an earth mother who produced children, and her model, Annie Sadilek Pavelka. Or Cather's Alexandra Bergson, an earth mother who produced crops, and her real life models. The numerous female homesteaders like Eudora Ammons Kohl, who felt that women had more independence in the West than in any other part of the world, formed their own patterns.[246] Mormon women who had been tested in the crucible of their faith or who had shaped the future for women who followed them formed additional blocks. The individual blocks of similar women were joined to others in various ways, for example by geography, ethnicity, or chronology, thereby creating quilts of history.

The quilt tops I retrieved from the attic and the metaphorical blocks I have discovered are better understood now, but they are not yet quilted. Women of the here and now will have to stitch them. We will have to join around a quilting frame and stretch first a new and sturdy backing, tacking it down well. We will lay upon it a dacron batt, so much lightened in comparison to the heavy cotton our grandmothers pulled across their frames. And we will stretch the batt until it fits, our multiple hands smoothing in unison. We will lovingly lay the old quilt top on our new foundation; and as women do, we will talk as we quilt, fleshing out designs with our lips as well as our hands. We will wonder at the blue denim. Did it come from some man's overalls? The black and white gingham, was it a kitchen apron once? The pink stripe, did some young girl wear it to church on a spring morning? What circumstances dictated the pattern of the blocks? Might some other woman's pattern fit our lives? And so we will connect across the miles and years.

And when the quilt is removed from the frame and we are beyond "working" on it, the quilting experience itself will echo in our heads, and we will think on our individual threads sewn in and around and over some other woman's stitches which held her life together and recall the pieces of conversation, fitted in and around and over other women's voices.

I replaced my grandmother's unquilted tops in the trunk and then lifted Granny Pectol's quilt onto them.

Her quilt had comforted my husband and me for two weeks on our pioneer journey. We had traveled over freeways six lanes wide, going both east and west. These highways followed in many places the dusty, rutted trails pioneer women had crossed. In some places wheel marks from pioneer wagons were still visible, carved ten feet deep into the soft sandstone. A wagon, the women in it, and men as well, were forced to follow the ruts of those who had gone before. Maybe they chose to follow what they considered to be, not ruts, but a marked path. I thought about those who still willingly follow and those who risk and leave the patterned path. I felt my connection to all those whose journeys I had shared and would share.

I realized that the process of pioneering had not ended with the coming of the railroad or rural electrification. I smoothed the brightness of Granny Pectol's quilt blocks with my hands, tracing Golda Pectol Busk's strong and even stitches with my fingers. Pioneering was a continuing journey for women guided by their individual and collective pasts, pushing at the frontiers of their individual and collective futures.

Before closing the lid, I dug deep into the trunk for one more look at my grandmother's patterned quilt squares. Some pleased my eye in their soft harmony and orderly arrangement; others aggravated me by their garish brightness and too-busy prints. I thought about women I had met in history and in real life who equated with those quilt pieces. I thought about a society tolerant enough and diverse enough to accommodate them all.

I visualized narrow trails expanded to multi-lane highways with frequent side roads and lanes that lead to browse sections. I thought about the need for both off-ramps and on-ramps. I realized that my journey was enriched by a thousand and more women, even more enriched by sharing it with my husband, and wondered if my journey could be the impetus for a thousand and more journeys for me and others. I closed the trunk, knowing I could open it again at any time.

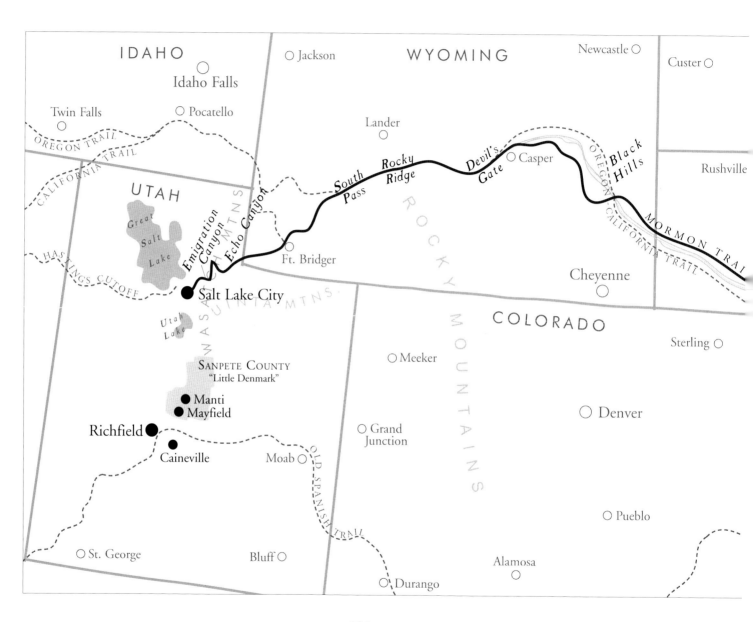

IDAHO

○ Jackson

WYOMING

Newcastle ○

Custer ○

Idaho Falls ○

Twin Falls
○

○ Pocatello

Lander
○

Rushville

OREGON TRAIL

CALIFORNIA TRAIL

UTAH

*Great
Salt
Lake*

*Emigration
Canyon*

Echo Canyon

*South
Pass*

*Rocky
Ridge*

*Devil's
Gate*

○ Casper

*Black
Hills*

OREGON-CALIFORNIA TRAIL

MORMON TRAIL

○ Ft. Bridger

HASTING'S CUTOFF

*Utah
Lake*

WASATCH MTNS.

UINTA MTNS.

● Salt Lake City

Cheyenne ○

COLORADO

ROCKY MOUNTAINS

SANPETE COUNTY
"Little Denmark"

● Manti
● Mayfield

Richfield ●

● Caineville

Moab ○

○ Grand
Junction

Sterling ○

○ Denver

OLD SPANISH TRAIL

○ St. George

Bluff ○

Alamosa
○

○ Pueblo

○ Durango

SOUTH DAKOTA

Rosebud

NEBRASKA

Sioux Falls

MINNESOTA

WISCONSIN

IOWA

Sioux City

So. Sioux City

Winter Quarters

Omaha

Council Bluffs

Grand Island
(Stuhr Museum)

Platte River

Des Moines

Iowa City

Mt. Pisgah

Nauvoo

ILLINOIS

Lone Tree

Ogallala

MISSOURI

Red Cloud

Oberlin

KANSAS

St. Joseph

Ft. Leavenworth

Independence

Kansas City

St. Louis

Goodland

SANTA FE TRAIL

OREGON-CALIFORNIA TRAIL

Missouri River

Mississippi River

The Mormon and Pioneer Trails

sources: *Mormon Pioneer Trail*, map, National Park Service;
William E. Hill, *Mormon Trail: Yesterday and Today*.

Progenitors of Judy Ray Shell

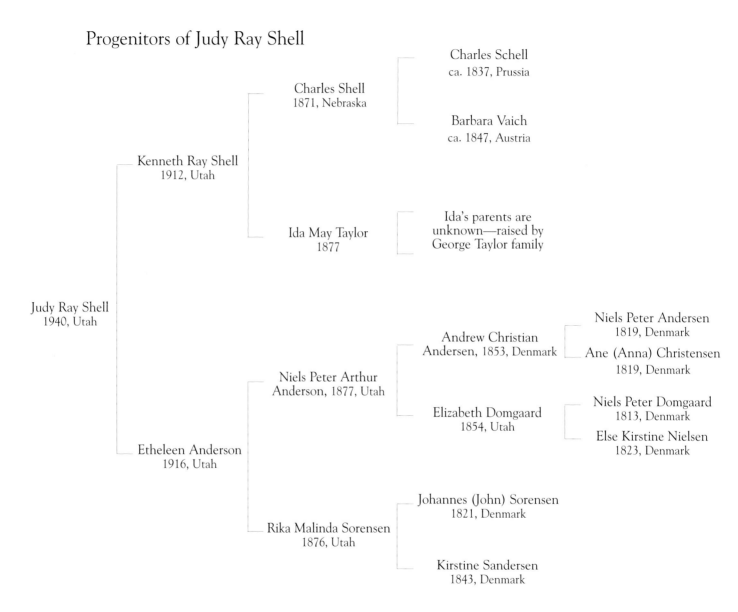

Judy Ray Shell
1940, Utah

Kenneth Ray Shell
1912, Utah

Charles Shell
1871, Nebraska

Charles Schell
ca. 1837, Prussia

Barbara Vaich
ca. 1847, Austria

Ida May Taylor
1877

Ida's parents are
unknown—raised by
George Taylor family

Etheleen Anderson
1916, Utah

Niels Peter Arthur
Anderson, 1877, Utah

Andrew Christian
Andersen, 1853, Denmark

Niels Peter Andersen
1819, Denmark

Ane (Anna) Christensen
1819, Denmark

Elizabeth Domgaard
1854, Utah

Niels Peter Domgaard
1813, Denmark

Else Kirstine Nielsen
1823, Denmark

Rika Malinda Sorensen
1876, Utah

Johannes (John) Sorensen
1821, Denmark

Kirstine Sandersen
1843, Denmark

Progenitors of Neal Portman Busk

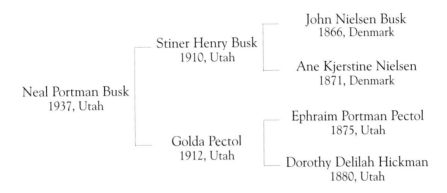

Neal Portman Busk
1937, Utah

Stiner Henry Busk
1910, Utah

John Nielsen Busk
1866, Denmark

Ane Kjerstine Nielsen
1871, Denmark

Golda Pectol
1912, Utah

Ephraim Portman Pectol
1875, Utah

Dorothy Delilah Hickman
1880, Utah

Children of Neal Portman Busk and Judy Ray Shell: Kerri Nicole, 1963, California; Michael Neal, 1966, California; Ane Kirsten, 1968, California; Neal Christian, 1974, Utah; Jeremy Ephraim Kenneth, 1976, Utah; Belinda Noelle, 1978, Utah.

Endnotes

1. Kenneth M. Godfrey, Audrey M. Godfrey, and Jill Mulvay Derr, *Women's Voices: An Untold History of the Latter Day Saints, 1830-1900* (Salt Lake City: Deseret Book, 1982), 157.

2. Lillian Schlissel, Byrd Gibbens, and Elizabeth Hampsten, *Far from Home: Families of the Westward Journey* (New York: Schocken Books, 1989), 123.

3. Godfrey et al., *Women's Voices*, 222-42.

4. Willa Cather, *O Pioneers!* (New York: Signet, 1989), 50.

5. Wallace Stegner, *Where the Bluebird Sings to the Lemonade Springs* (New York: Random House, 1992), 201-02.

6. Annie Dillard "To Fashion a Text," in *Inventing the Truth*, ed. William Zinsser (Boston: Houghton Mifflin, 1987) p. 70.

7. Margaret, Duchess of Newcastle, "A True Relation of My Birth, Breeding, and Life," in *The Lives of William Cavendish, Duke of Newcastle, and of His Wife, Margaret Duchess of Newcastle*, ed. Mark Antony Lover [Lower] (London: John Russell, 1892), 309-10; qtd. in Domna C. Stanton, *The Female Autograph* (Chicago: University of Chicago Press, 1984), 14.

8. Maureen Ursenbach Beecher, "'Tryed and Purified as Gold': Mormon Women's 'Lives,'" typescript, Alice Louise Reynolds Lecture, Harold B. Lee Libraries, 17 March 1994, 5.

9. Telephone interview with Bradley L. Edgington, psychologist, 20 January 2003.

10. Laurel Thatcher Ulrich, *A Midwife's Tale: The Life of Martha Ballard Based on Her Diary, 1785-1812* (New York: Vintage/Random House, 1990/1991).

11. Maureen Ursenbach Beecher, lecture, Women's Texts class, Brigham Young University.

12. William E. Hill, *Mormon Trail* (Logan: Utah State University Press, 1996), 53.

13. Lillian Schlissel, *Women's Diaries of the Westward Journey* (New York: Schocken Books, 1982), 111.

14. Sandra L. Myres, *Westering Women and the Frontier Experience, 1800-1915* (Albuquerque: University of New Mexico, 1982), 2-3.

15. Ibid., 8.

16. Ibid., 2.

17. Ibid., 8.

18. Ibid., 4.

19. Ibid., 10.

20. Ibid., 11.

21. The Doctrine and Covenants of The Church of Jesus Christ of Latter-day Saints, Section 116.

22. Godfrey et al., *Women's Voices,* 24.

23. Ibid., 83.

24. Ibid., 108.

25. Ibid., 117.

26. Ibid., 124.

27. Leonard J. Arrington and Davis Bitton, *The Mormon Experience: A History of the Latter-day Saints* (Urbana: University of Illinois Press, 1992), 68.

28. Ibid., 69.

29. S. George Ellsworth, ed., *The History of Louisa Barnes Pratt: The Autobiography of a Mormon Missionary Widow and Pioneer* (Logan, Utah State University Press, 1998), 65-66.

30. Ibid., 108-09.

31. "Autobiography of Niels Peter Domgaard, 1860," recorded by John Bench, scribe, 27 April 1860; trans. Peter C. Hansen; typescript in possession of the author.

32. Andrew Jenson, *History of the Scandinavian Mission* (New York: Arno Press, 1979), 70-71.

33. William Mulder, *Homeward to Zion: The Mormon Migration from Scandinavia* (Minneapolis: University of Minnesota Press, 1956), 159.

34. Grace Madsen, "Additional Information about Niels Peter Domgaard," typescript in possession of the author; journal entries, typescript, in possession of the author.

35. Ibid.

36. Mulder, *Homeward to Zion,* 163.

37. Godfrey et al., *Women's Voices,* 366.

38. Ibid., 367.

39. Ibid., 369.

40. Ibid.

41. Ibid., 367.

42. Ibid., 370

43. Ibid., 371

44. Vicki Burgess-Olson, *Sister Saints* (Provo: Brigham Young University Press, 1978), viii.

45. Godfrey et al., *Women's Voices,* 125.

46. Ibid.

47. Ibid., 126.

48. Godfrey et al, *Women's Voices,* 130.

49. Ibid.

50. William Edwin Berrett, *The Restored Church,* 10th ed. (Salt Lake: Deseret Book, 1961), 171.

51. Ibid., 131.

52. Ibid., 120.

53. Elizabeth Hampsten, *Read This Only to Yourself: The Private Writings of Midwestern Women, 1880-1910* (Bloomington: Indiana University, 1982), 102-10.

54. Schlissel, et al., *Far from Home*, 204-05.

55. Hampsten, *Read This Only to Yourself,* 108.

56. Ibid., 47.

57. Wallace Stegner, *The Gathering of Zion* (Salt Lake City, Utah: Westwater Press, 1963, 1981), 50.

58. Schlissel, *Women's Diaries*, 123.

59. Ibid., 120.

60. Ibid., 123.

61. Norma Sorensen Taylor, "History of Kirstine Sandersen Sorensen," typescript in possession of the author; used by permission.

62. Hill, *Mormon Trail*, 98.

63. Deut. 34:1.

64. Wallace Stegner, *Mormon Country* (Lincoln: University of Nebraska Press, 1942), rpt. 1970, 60.

65. R. Don Oscarson and Stanley B. Kimball, *The Travelers' Guide to Historic Mormon America* (Salt Lake City: Bookcraft,1965), 73.

66. Schlissel, *Far from Home*, 111.

67. Ibid., 153.

68. Ibid., 159.

69. Ibid., 164.

70. Ibid., 165.

71. Schlissel, *Far from Home*, 141.

72. Maureen Ursenbach Beecher, *Eliza and Her Sisters* (Salt Lake: Aspen Books, 1991), 90.

73. William Slaughter and Michael Landon, *Trail of Hope: The Story of the Mormon Trail* (Salt Lake City: Shadow Mountain, 1997), 46-47.

74. Ibid., 45-46.

75. Ibid., 46.

76. Ibid.

77. Ibid.

78. Mulder, *Homeward to Zion*, 163.

79. Stegner, *Gathering of Zion*, 248

80. Ibid., 256.

81. Joanna L. Stratton, *Pioneer Women: Voices from the Kansas Frontier* (New York: Simon and Schuster, 1981), 54.

82. John Carter, *Solomon Butcher: Photographing the American Dream* (Lincoln: University of Nebraska Press, 1985), 23.

83. Ibid., 15.

84. Ibid., 2.

85. Ibid., 55

86. Ibid., 53.

87. Ibid., 43.

88. William E. Hill, *The Mormon Trail Yesterday and Today* (Logan: Utah State University, 1996), 86.

89. "Pawnee Earth Lodge," *A Living History Experience! Stuhr Museum of the Prarie Pioneer,* online at http://www.stuhrmuseum.org/tourlodge.htm.

90. "Pawnee," *EMuseum@Minnesota State University, Mankato,* online at http://www.mnsu.edu/emuseum/cultural/northamerica/pawnee.html.

91. Ibid.

92. Helen Sekaquaptewa, *Me and Mine: The Life Story of Helen Sekaquaptewa as Told to Louise Udall* (Tucson: University of Arizona Press, 1969). © The Arizona Board of Regents. Reprinted by permission of the University of Arizona Press.

93. "The Sacrifice," typescript in possession of the author.

94. Nelda Dugi, "Other Than Grinding Corn," *Soundings* (Richfield High School literary magazine), 1986, 100-02.

95. Willa Cather, *My Ántonia* (Boston: Houghton Mifflin, 1918), 156.

96. Dillard, "To Fashion a Text," 76.

97. Interview with Marilyn Arnold, St. George, Utah, 13 October 1993.

98. Ibid.

99. Glenda Riley, *The Female Frontier: A Comparative View of Women on the Prairie and the Plains* (Lawrence: University Press of Kansas, 1988), 20.

100. Ibid.

101. Ibid., 137-38.

102. Ibid., 138.

103. Cather, *My Ántonia,* 218.

104. Ibid., 236-37.

105. Cather, *O Pioneers!* 87.

106. Ibid.

107. Ibid., 218.

108. Ibid., 87.

109. Cather, *My Ántonia,* 212.

110. Ibid., 213.

111. Ibid., 217-18.

112. Barry Turner, *Simply My Ántonia* (McCook, NE: B. Turner, 1997), 41.

113. Ibid., 42.

114. Wallace Stegner, "Ordeal by Handcart," in *Out of the Best Books,* vol. 4, eds. Bruce B. Clark and Robert K. Thomas (Salt Lake City, Utah: Deseret Book, 1968), 62.

115. Ibid.

116. O. E. Rölvaag, *Giants in the Earth: A Saga of the Prairie* (New York: Harper & Brothers, 1927), 3.

117. Ibid., 43.

118. Riley, *Female Frontier,* 1.

119. Myres, *Westering Women,* 108.

120. Hill, *Mormon Trail,* 72, quoting Piercy's diary.

121. Cather, *My Ántonia,* 7.

122. Ibid, 21.

123. Carter, *Solomon Butcher,* 29.

124. Hill, *Mormon Trail,* 131.

125. Henry J. Wolfinger, "Jane Manning James: A Test of Faith," in *Worth Their Salt: Notable but Often Unnoted Women of Utah,* ed. Colleen Whitley (Logan, Utah State University Press, 1996), 261n13.

126. Margaret Blair Young and Darius Aidan Gray, *One More River to Cross* (Salt Lake City: Bookcraft, 2000), 157.

127. Ibid., 233.

128. Wolfinger, "Jane Manning James," 20.

129. Ibid., 22.

130. Kate B. Carter, *The Story of the Negro Pioneer* (Salt Lake City: Daughters of the Utah P...), 11.

Traveling, and Surviving on the Trail (Kearney, NE: Morris Publishing, 1993), 173-193.

143. Schlissel, *Women's Diaries,* 60.

144. Matthew Cowley, "The Faith of a Child," address delivered in the Salt Lake Tabernacle, April 5, 1953, in *Matthew Cowley Speaks* (Salt Lake: Deseret Book, 1971), 68-69.

...cred Loneliness: The Plural ...e City: Signature Books,

...*One Day in the Life of* ...am, 1963).

...n-Gadsby and Judith ...lanche Woodward ..." in *Sister Saints* by ...am Young University

...Mormon Woman in ...artment of History,

...Emmeline Blanche

...78, quoting ...Carolyn Chouinard, 24 Aug.

154. Ibid., 78.

155. Ibid., 34.

156. Ibid., 37, 48.

157. Ibid., 50.

158. Janet Peterson and LaRene Gaunt, "Emmeline B. Wells," in *Elect Ladies* (Salt Lake City: Deseret Book, 1990), 83, quoting *Woman's Exponent*, 1 June 1888, 1-2.

159. Madsen, "A Mormon Woman," 62.

160. Ibid., 59.

161. Ibid.

162. Ibid., 54.

163. Peterson and Gaunt, "Emmeline B. Wells," 86, citing Phyllis C. Southwick, "Emmeline B. Wells—If She Were Here Today," paper delivered at the "Perspectives on Women" conference, Salt Lake City, 16 Oct. 1974.

164. Richard Neitzel Holzapfel and Jeni Broberg Holzapfel, *Women of Nauvoo* (Salt Lake City: Bookcraft, 1992), 181.

165. Madsen, "Mormon Woman," 237-8.

166. Easton-Gadsby and Dushku, "Emmeline Blanche Woodward Wells," 473.

167. Ibid., 94.

168. Madsen, "Mormon Woman," 90.

169. Godfrey et al., *Women's Voices*, 152.

170. Ibid., 154.

171. Ibid., 156-57.

172. Ibid., 157.

173. Ibid., 158.

174. Ibid., 158-59.

175. Ibid., 160-61.

176. Ibid., 162-63.

177. Ibid., 163-64.

178. Maureen Ursenbach Beecher, "The Eliza Enigma: The Life and Legend of Eliza R. Snow," in *Sister Saints* by Vicki Burgess-Olson (Provo: Brigham Young University Press, 1978), 3.

179. Ibid., 9.

180. Maureen Ursenbach Beecher, ed., *The Personal Writings of Eliza Roxcy Snow* (Salt Lake City: University of Utah Press, 1995), 116.

181. Mulder, *Homeward to Zion*, 90.

182. Holzapfel and Holzapfel, *Women of Nauvoo*, 93.

183. Beecher, "Eliza Enigma," 10-11.

184. Ibid., 10.

185. Ibid.

186. Ibid.

187. Holzapfel and Holzapfel, *Women of Nauvoo*, 110.

188. Ibid., 181.

189. Beecher, "Eliza Enigma," 14.

190. Beecher, *Personal Writings of Eliza Roxcy Snow*, 175.

191. Interview with Etheleen Anderson Shell Bowler, St. George, Utah, Mar. 2003.

192. "Autobiography of Elizabeth Domgaard Andersen," typescript in possession of author.

193. Grace Madsen, "History of Elizabeth Domgaard Andersen," typescript in possession of author, with *Eliza-*

beth substituted for *mother* and *Andrew* for *father* throughout.

194. Andrew Marvell, "To His Coy Mistress," in *Renaissance England: Poetry and Prose from the Reformation to the Restoration*, eds. Roy Lamson and Hallett Smith (New York: W.W. Norton, 1956), 293.

195. Ibid.

196. Carol Lynn Pearson, "Double Wedding," in *I Can't Stop Smiling* (Salt Lake: Parliament Publishers, 1984), 54-55; used by permission.

197. Grace Madsen, "History of Andrew Christian Andersen," typescript in possession of author, with *Andrew* substituted for *father* and *Elizabeth* for *mother* throughout.

198. From "Biography of Niels Peter Andersen," transcribed by Mrs. Earl O. Anderson, typescript in possession of author.

199. Mulder, *Homeward to Zion*, 239.

200. Berrett, *The Restored Church*, 318.

201. Ibid.

202. Ibid, 316.

203. Mulder, *Homeward to Zion*, 241.

204. Jessie L. Embry, *Mormon Polygamous Families: Life in the Principle* (Salt Lake City: University of Utah Press, 1987), 6.

205. Ibid., 7.

206. Arrington and Bitton, *Mormon Experience*, 69-70.

207. Ibid., 223.

208. Holzapfel and Holzapfel, *Women of Nauvoo*, 10.

209. Arrington and Bitton, *Mormon Experience*, 199.

210. Beecher, ed., *Personal Writings of Eliza Roxcy Snow*, 50.

211. Ibid.

212. Ibid., 50-51.

213. Ibid., 51.

214. Ibid.

215. Carol Cornwall Madsen, *In Their Own Words: Women and the Story of Nauvoo* (Salt Lake City: Deseret Book, 1994), 212.

216. Susan Sessions Rugh, "Patty B. Sessions," in *Sister Saints* by Vicki Burgess-Olson (Provo: Brigham Young University Press, 1978), 311; italics added.

217. Ibid., 311.

218. Ibid., 316.

219. Ibid., 316.

220. Holzapfel and Holzapfel, *Women of Nauvoo*, 101.

221. Barbara Fluckiger Watt, "Bathsheba B. Smith," in *Sister Saints* by Vicki Burgess-Olson (Provo: Brigham Young University Press, 1978), 207.

222. Arrington and Bitton, *Mormon Experience*, 200.

223. Ibid., 199.

224. Ibid., 200-201.

225. Ibid., 200.

226. Annie Clark Tanner, *A Mormon Mother: An Autobiography*, 3rd ed. (Salt Lake City: Tanner Trust Fund, University of Utah Marriott Library, 1991), 50.

227. Ibid., 63.

228. Ibid, 64.

229. Ibid., 68.

230. Ibid., 69.

231. Ibid., 159.

232. Ibid., xxxiii.

233. Arrington and Bitton, *Mormon Experience,* 199. This is an admittedly conservative estimate, other studies determining that about a third of all marriageable LDS women (25 percent of LDS adults) were involved in polygamous relationships. See Danel Bachman and Ronald K. Esplin, "Plural Marriage," in *Encyclopedia of Mormonism,* ed. Daniel H. Ludlow (New York: Macmillan, 1992), 3:1095.

234. Holzapfel and Holzapfel, *Women of Nauvoo,* 182.

235. Ibid., 181.

236. Arrington and Bitton, *Mormon Experience,* 201.

237. Ibid., 201.

238. Embry, *Mormon Polygamous Families,* 12.

239. Betty Freidan, *The Feminine Mystique* (New York: Dell, 1963), 11.

240. Beecher, "Tryed and Purified," 10.

241. Ibid., 11.

242. Ibid., 12.

243. Godfrey, *Women's Voices,* 157.

244. Stratton, *Pioneer Women,* 223-30.

245. Schlissel, *Far from Home,* 165.

246. Riley, *Female Frontier,* 137.

Questions for Discussion

The author suggests the following questions for book club and/or class use.
Questions are keyed to particular chapters or photos.

Frontispiece

The photograph opposite the title page shows four types of pioneer women in typical poses: the stern, full-breasted lady in the Mother Hubbard dress, frying pan in hand; the innocent child in the white blouse and black skirt; the unsmiling woman in the loose-fitting jacket, seated and looking bored; and the slender, graceful woman in white, her attitude dreamy and pensive. Behind the poses, what do you think the reality is of these women's lives?

Introduction

In *Charting the Course*, the author describes her book as a "gift" for her daughters. What information would you like to pass on to your daughters about pioneer women? About significant things in your life? About lessons from your own mother that have been important in charting your life course?

Chapter One

The stereotypes of pioneer women range from silently suffering, "submissive but sturdy" women in "sunbonnet[s], baby at breast, rifle at the ready, ... dedicated to ... restoring civilization as rapidly as possible" and the soiled doves like the Belle Starr and the Calamity Jane who "drank, smoked, and cursed and was handy with a poker deck, a six-gun, and a horse." What do you make of these characterizations and how have they influenced the perceptions of modern Western women?

Chapter Two

Many immigrants to America came for religious reasons. What impact has this religious heritage had on your life and that of your community? Did religious conviction make it easier or more difficult for the immigrants to face the hardships and challenges of the New World?

Chapter Three

Artists sometimes idealize their subjects to emphasize their heroic qualities. In real life, heroines such as Dr. Ellis Shipp may not have had the thin waist and striking profile of the statues in the Women's Garden, nor were their families models of harmony. In your own lives, what dilemmas do you face in reconciling the real with the ideal?

Chapter Four

Discuss some of the domestic endeavors you may have attempted and were less than successful in achieving. Where do you see the fulcrum resting in the balance between domestic chores and endeavors such as intellectual and cultural pursuits?

Chapter Five

Discuss the bearing (or not bearing) of children and the impact it has had on your life. If you were among those faced with, as Wallace Stegner characterized it, "the opportunity to drop their young like animals in any crude shelter," would you, as Stegner suggested, "covet" the opportunity to do so or choose to remain behind until your child was born? Is Stegner's viewpoint a valid one or not?

Chapter Six

Discuss how you received or gave care during an illness and also the relative inconvenience of being sick on the road. How would you have cared for someone while traveling along the Oregon and Mormon Trails in a covered wagon?

Chapter Seven

Any death produces trauma for family members, but the death of a child is said to be the most strenuous and lasting, emotionally and physiologically. Discuss whether the happy memories of a child's life ever replace the heartache in remembering a child's death.

Chapter Eight

What do material possessions represent in a positive and negative sense? Some visitors to log cabins say, "How did they keep house with so little?" to which I want to respond, "How do we keep house with so much"? When you escape to the peace and quiet of the outdoors, what effect does that have on you—and how would you respond if a nature-surrounded existence were imposed on you with no access to city life?

Chapter Nine

Discuss bearded vs. clean-shaven or other grooming choices that might affect male-female relations, as well as the general issue of hygiene (drinking from a common cup during the eucharist, for instance).

Chapter Ten

Discuss the impact of the westward movement on Native Americans from various perspectives, including your own if you are Native American.

Chapter Eleven

Think of female literary characters with which you are familiar (or specifically Willa Cather's earth mothers: Ántonia who raises children and Alexandra the professional woman who raises crops) and what they represent. Discuss their impact on both female and male readers.

Chapter Twelve

Have you ever been afflicted with "Better Homes and Gardens syndrome"? What were the symptoms, the prognosis for recovery, and the cures?

Chapter Thirteen

Discuss W. H. D. Koerner's *Madonna of the Prairie* and Harvey Dunn's painting, *The Homesteader's Wife,* and how such art images shape definition.

Chapter Fourteen

Discuss the practice of frugality in the lives of your parents and grandparents, your own life, and the lives of your children.

Chapter Fifteen

Discuss your experiences with African Americans or, as an African American, with people of other races. How have your associations changed over the years?

Chapter Sixteen

If you or someone you know has been depressed, how was the depression overcome? Have you helped an older woman—a mother, mother-in-law, grandmother, or friend —through depression or sickness? If so, what impact did that experience have on you?

Chapter Seventeen

Discuss medical cures and home remedies for ailments and the role of spiritual comfort when ill.

Chapter Eighteen

It may be that breast cancer was overlooked in earlier times because people died younger of other disorders. Discuss this and other health problems confronting women and how they were dealt with on the frontier and how they are dealt with now.

Chapter Nineteen

Susan B. Anthony and Emmeline Wells, among others, were pathfinders for women in terms of suffrage and other rights, but they also paid the price in that Anthony never married and Wells barely knew her husband, Daniel, when they married and saw him infrequently thereafter. How can a couple preserve individuality and independence but preserve closeness?

Chapter Twenty

What did you think of the life of Eliza R. Snow, married to Brigham Young but retaining her name and identity separate from his and not bearing him children, even addressing him formally as "President Young"? What did you think about her various roles in the leadership of Mormon women? Was her position as a wife of President Young a help or a hindrance in this leadership? Why do you think so? Was her leadership of Mormon women a help or a hindrance to Brigham Young in governing the church? Explain your reasoning.

Chapter Twenty-one

As recounted in her autobiography and history, Elizabeth Domgaard had experiences of significance. Pick one or more of her experiences and explore the parallels in your own life, discussing their significance to you.

Chapter Twenty-two

How would *you* describe the contrast between young love and old love? Consider the complication in the case of Niels Peter Andersen taking a second wife and the reaction of his son, Andrew. What would be a comparable modern situation?

Chapter Twenty-three

What further insights about the early Mormon practice of polygamy did you gain from this chapter—fifty-one-year-old Niels Peter Domgaard marrying an eighteen-year-old when his first wife was forty-one; Bathsheba Smith acting as a mentor to her husband's younger wives; Annie Tanner finding herself, as a younger wife, neglected by her husband; and so on?

Chapter Twenty-four

What do you think of women like Granny Pectol who, "if she needed the piano moved, she moved it; if she needed wood to keep the house warm, she chopped it; if she needed a ditch dug to water her garden, she dug it"? Although her independence was forced on her, it didn't dampen her ardor for her husband while he was away in New Zealand. How does she manage to be strong, yet convey a sense of dependence on her husband? How is she practical, yet romantic? Are there lessons for contemporary women in her example?

Chapter Twenty-five

Discuss some of the significant experiences in your journey from childhood to womanhood, as well as what other factors may have contributed to the sum of *your* past. From your perspective, what would characterize a better world for women?

Index

"*The Sum of Our Past* combines intriguing and intimate knowledge of pioneer women with a personal memoir that is thoughtful and humorous, one which explores the inevitable relationship we all have to the courageous, remarkable women Busk discovers through their diaries. These are not just stories of sunbonneted Saints traveling to their promised land or a frivolous travelogue on Busk's part as she and her husband explore the trails, sod houses, Indian earth lodges, and geographical sites along the trails. Rather, one senses authenticity in these enriching stories, real honesty in Busk's hearty sense of humor, and her significant research into public and private lives of pioneer women.

"As a librarian, I enthusiastically recommend this book for libraries large and small. As a traveler and a former geographer, I appreciated the treatment of physical places across the country which gave a balanced perspective of the land. I also valued hearing the voices of real women who lived in these places, women who helped shape the world we live in today."

LINDA FIELDS
Richfield City Librarian

About the Author

Judy Busk (M.A., Brigham Young University) has been a popular columnist for Southern Utah's *Daily Spectrum* and a distinguished English and journalism teacher in Richfield, Utah—the recipient of a National Endowment for the Humanities/*Reader's Digest* Teacher Scholar Award. She created and oversaw the successful Sevier County Oral History Project (excerpted on the *Columbia University New Deal Network* website) with grants from the Utah Humanities Council and Utah State Historical Society. Earlier, she was an exchange student to the Soviet Union, and she and her family have lived in Germany and Japan. More recently, she has enjoyed her new status as a "mature" graduate student and her responsibility to other women in her community as an LDS Relief Society president. She serves on the Utah Humanities Council board of directors, among other civic positions.